The Immigrant

ANTHONY CHRIST

All the main characters and happenings in this book are real. Some of the names of minor characters and some of the dialogue were fictionalized, but all of the events are true.

ISBN 978-0-578-68579-3

Dedicated to my wife, Lee Ann,
and to our children,
Brian, Katelyn, and Ashley

Table of Contents

Preface

IT IS WITH PRIDE, pleasure, a feeling of responsibility, as well as a surge of emotion from my past—a different era—that I have agreed to write this preface on the life and times of Chrysostomos Chrisostomides, known in America as Chris Christ, who, in our younger years, I affectionately dubbed *Breadcrumb* because of his small size, blue eyes, fair hair, and infectious smile. His tale is, in many respects, the tale of an extraordinary man who prided himself in living an ordinary life. It is my hope that the generations of today will be mindful of the crisis period from which we both emerged, for the best protection against future crisis is to learn from the mistakes of the past.

Although I have not spoken publicly during my life as Archbishop of the Orthodox Church in America of the atrocities that surrounded us as children, I now feel it is important they be brought to the fore—not for retribution but as a clarion call for present generations to be vigilant and take care. The childhood experiences Chris and I shared began quite peacefully on our tiny island of Imbroz—a Greek island off the coast of Turkey that had changed little since the dawn of antiquity. We were a simple people with a simple faith in God, family, and country. Yet soon the Young Turks unleashed aggression and persecution that spread to our island.

Such persecution was not new in the eyes of history, and dated back to antiquity, but the magnitude and ferocity during the twentieth century was unparalleled. Indeed, through four centuries of invasion, repression, and persecution at the hands of the Ottoman Empire, the ways of Christians on our island never wavered. We enjoyed freedom. This time, however, the perpetrators took control of our tiny island home in 1923 and freedom was lost.

When the Ottomans came in 1453, under King Osman, who declared a warrior, or *ghazi*, state, bound to *jihad*, or holy war, against Christians, the Ottomans began inflicting some of the harshest methods of oppression the world had ever seen. They promised that those who died in battle against a nonbeliever were guaranteed passage to heaven. This ensured for us a greater hell on earth.

Nonetheless, from 1453 to 1908, we survived under the yoke of the Ottomans. However, the mistreatment that occurred during that time pales in comparison to the systematic genocidal elimination of Christians that occurred from 1908 through 1923, a Christian holocaust, and the ongoing extreme prejudice endured by the Christians who survived the holocaust is unconscionable. The Christian holocaust was pure evil. It was the first of a series of genocidal manias by governments that indelibly scarred the twentieth century.

After the turn of the twentieth century, under the guise of a falsely coined "democratic constitution" the Committee of Union and Progress, or CUP, took control of Turkey in 1908. Abruptly in 1909 our hopes for a constitution and rights for the Christian minorities were dashed. What followed was purely diabolical—an unrelenting genocide of millions of Christians, including Armenians, Assyrians, and Greeks. During this period up to 4,000,000 poor, unarmed Christian souls perished. Families were exterminated and those who remained were uprooted, their properties stolen. Businesses collapsed from extortion and outright theft. Unadulterated evil reigned as the Christian population in Turkey was erased. Those that survived suffered at the edge of poverty and starvation.

Consistent with the 1948 United Nations definition of genocide, the Christian holocaust began in earnest in 1909 in Adana with the slaughter of Armenian Christians, then Assyrian Christians, and ended with the massacres of the Greek Christians in Smyrna in September of 1922, where, in the span of only ten days, over three hundred thousand unarmed Christians were ruthlessly slaughtered. The venerable Archbishop of Smyrna, refusing to leave his people, was beheaded, dismembered, and dragged through the streets. Subsequent genocides occurred throughout the century.

Surely, we thought the world would notice, but, in 1923, the world was distracted by the Treaty of Lausanne, which ceded our small island home to the Turkish barbarians. The world seemed to ignore the genocides that preceded the Treaty as well as the ongoing extreme persecution that followed. This tragic genocide erased the Byzantine culture from Anatolia that had thrived and prospered for millennia. On our tiny island of Imbroz, the number of Christians dwindled from twelve thousand to one thousand and eventually to only two hundred.

We believed now the world would see, but soon the Depression came, then World War II. Meanwhile the world suffered other genocides. In Stalin's Holodomor genocide of mass starvation from 1932 to 1933, over 7,000,000 perished in the region around Ukraine, followed by up to 1,200,000 executions during the Great Terror of 1937 to 1938. Then came Hitler's Holocaust in Germany from 1941 through 1945 when nearly 6,000,000 Jews perished. The civilized world was immersed in crisis after crisis, and we became a tragic footnote in history.

After World War II things began to improve. Never again, vowed the world, would such atrocities occur. The survivors, who learned firsthand the price of peace and the responsibility of privilege, made their brave vows for a better tomorrow. They believed it was possible to guard our precious freedoms and protect our children so such unconscionable atrocities could never occur again. We would be vigilant. We would not become distracted. Never again.

For a time we were vigilant. A generation passed with beloved peace and prosperity. We have had marvelous medical progress and technological gains—yet we seem more distracted than ever. Have we lost our focus? Have we lost the spirit exemplified by the life of my friend, Breadcrumb?

Ask yourself this as you read about his life's journey. His was a journey that led him to America and freedom, while never forgetting his humble roots or the people whom he loved along the way. He was a man who devoted his life to God and his family, who weathered difficult times with an infectious smile and a positive attitude.

Today, at a time of uncertainty and lost identity, the story of Breadcrumb's immigration is a story for all ages, for all times. His were simple beliefs that seem all too lacking today. I admonish you to learn from this man. Please remember you are all guardians of your beliefs and your human rights. God bless you all and God bless America. Go in peace with God forever.

—Archbishop Iakovos of America (Jimmy), 1911–2005

1923

N
IMVROS
KASTRO
AGIOI THEODOROI
PANAGIA
SHOINOYDI
AEGEAN SEA

CONSTANTINOPLE
(INSTABUL)

Part I: Old World

SAMOTHRACE
IMBROZ

CHAPTER 1

Visions

I look for aged pots
of prehistoric days,
and then I measure them
in lots and lots of different ways.
And then (like you) I start to write.
My words are twice as long as yours,
and far more erudite.
—AGATHA CHRISTIE, 1944

THE LATE WINTER OF 1994 had been unseasonably harsh for metropolitan Washington, D.C. Sheets of ice had covered roads and toppled power lines for weeks. The thaw finally came by mid-March, and now, on this particular Sunday, just days later, the appearance of my little friends had banished winter's drear, and the pageantry of spring had begun.

As a general surveying his troops, I walked with hands crossed behind my back, though my face reflected the pleasure and simple pride of beholding one of God's most captivating sights: my azaleas beginning to bloom. Bright colors—corals, pinks, reds, and violets—adorned my half-acre of paradise. Over the years I had planted azaleas everywhere until azaleas spilled over on top of azaleas. Late March often sees their showy blooms, joined a little later by the like-colored blossoms of my towering rhododendrons.

It was my habit to awaken as early as five in the morning so I could walk outside among the blossoms. As no other time of day, the morning's soft dawn light made my little backyard a fairyland full of God's wonder. So began my Sunday. Soon I would be sipping coffee with Helen, my wife of forty-six years. From there the day's pace would accelerate to a peaceful bustle as we would dress for church, allowing enough time to pick up Christina Regas, our friend of many years.

It was the usual church service, and afterwards I enjoyed the short social hour with parishioners, many of whom I had only recently gotten familiar with in my retirement years. Today's big news was the death of two Greek Orthodox priests killed tragically in a car accident in New York. Being kinsmen, the news struck the congregation deeply, though many had never met them.

Brunch at the Key Bridge Marriott after church was a special treat that we enjoyed only a handful of times throughout the year. The difference today was a new presence: a cool spring breeze and a final farewell to a lengthy winter's chill. The change had infected everyone. It might have been a routine Sunday morning, but that day I had no appetite. As soon as we returned home, I resumed my vigilant backyard review.

Lifting my voice and peering through the cracked back door, I called out to Helen, "Honey, you see the azaleas?"

I began picking up fallen branches and straightening up around the bushes, not even bothering to change out of my Sunday clothes. I felt unusually tired, yet I pored over my azaleas intently, my eyes refusing to leave the first buds of spring.

In a distant echo I heard Helen. "Yes, dear," she replied dutifully. She didn't share the excitement over my garden.

"Remember, we have to go to the children's house to help them move," she said, walking toward the door.

As I entered the kitchen, I saw Helen putting away dishes. "I'm going to the den to rest a bit," I told her.

"Wake me a little before three, please."

"Okay, Chris," she smiled, and continued her work in the kitchen.

Walking to the window I opened the blinds to take one final glance at my azaleas and then sat in the corner of the sofa, directly exposed to shafts of warm sunlight. Though recent years had labeled sunlight a danger, and my wife often worried about overexposure,

I ignored the risk. Old men often ignore new risks in pursuit of the comfort of old habits.

Yawning, I placed my hands behind my neck with fingers interlaced. As the muted shafts of light burrowed through my closed eyelids, I felt the friendly warmth of the sunlight on my shoulders and arms lulling me to doze. Such were my naps in the sun.

I seemed to have no energy. I had experienced unusual fatigue like this several times over the last couple of months, but had not wanted to worry Helen or the children. This time the sensation was very heavy. My body succumbed to sleep while my mind remained restless and awake, my thoughts winding through old memories.

My life over three quarters of a century had been blessed, I thought. I arrived in America in March of 1945, shortly before the returning GI's. Since then I worked long hours every day, year in and year out, with an occasional half-day off on Sunday to go to church. The ability to work and provide for my family was a source of unending joy for me. I thank God for the leisure I could enjoy, but it had not always been that way.

Out of habit my hand went to the collar of my t-shirt and found the relic coin fastened there by a safety pin, as it always had been since Papa gave it to me as a child. It was a timeless symbol of connection with the past. If a holy coin and my indomitable faith allowed me to survive the Christian holocaust in Turkey, then could anyone fault me for a little appreciation of God's favor?

My fatigue deepened as I reclined on the sofa. My life had always been meticulously organized, methodical, and focused, but now my thoughts resembled a series of unconnected images passing on a screen. I felt as though I was moving in slow motion, but my mind was racing. A parade of people flashed before me at an alarming rate. They were moving in a different world and I could not pass through to it except for brief snatches of time when I felt for a moment I was back with them.

Darkness came over me for a brief moment, then I heard her voice. "Chrysostomos?" It was very distant and muted at first, then much louder.

"Mama?" I mumbled, faintly realizing it was a dream.

"Chrysostomos." Alarmingly, her voice seemed to fade again.

"Mama, is it really you?" I mumbled, then I saw her with Papa, but they couldn't hear me.

I could see Papa's store, its windows boarded up. It was in disrepair, in need of paint and maintenance. Losing myself in memory, I felt the presence of the Turks, that sharpening of the senses, that unceasing alertness that had caused us to constantly check over our shoulders, or drop our voices to a whisper whenever Greek was spoken outside the relative safety of our home. It became second nature. It was how we lived.

"Mama, don't worry," I could hear my young self saying. "I'll work and send you money." I remember hoping the words sounded more confident than I felt.

"Big words for such a little man," she said.

Mama was crying, though trying her best to smile through her tears. Papa patted me on the back trying to offer the assurance we both did not feel.

"Take care of yourself," Papa forced a smile, a tremble in his voice.

The images were so vivid.

My lips moved again. "Mama, Papa, I love you," I whispered in an empty room.

For a moment I realized I was no longer a boy but an old man in the twilight of his life, daydreaming.

These things I had not thought of for more than half a century, yet the vivid memories now caused an ache from deep within. I moved restlessly on the sofa, aching to see Mama and Papa again, but my kaleidoscopic mind conjured images of my older sister, Katina, instead, large as life and standing right in front of me.

"Chrysostomos, we are all so proud of you," she said smiling before fading away.

"Katina, don't go," I whispered, but her image left me as quickly as the others had, another soon taking its place.

At first I couldn't make it out, but a moment later I was a young teenager standing with Mama and Papa in front of our small house.

"Chrysostomos," Mama said, "take care of yourself. Your father and I love you very much." Mama handed me the silk suit she had woven for me so long ago when I left for Constantinople.

"Goodbye, Chrysostomos. God be with you, my son." That silk suit still hangs in my closet today, over sixty years later.

"Mama, Papa, I miss you so," I whispered.

As the image of Papa, Mama, Katina, and my sunny island home disappeared, I saw myself as a young man in the midst of a severe blizzard. The wind was howling and the snow was blowing almost horizontally, the temperature below zero.

My eyelashes had ice on them and I remember it hurt just to blink. Although it was long past sunrise, the storm was so intense that the day seemed dark as night. The year was 1941 and I stood at attention by a gate near the Russian border, barely discernible through the swirling white powder. I wore a heavy military-issued coat, and I had strips of cloth wrapped around my hands, neck, and face for protection from the frigid wind. To the right a hundred yards off was a pup tent. Suddenly I was at the tent.

"Gregory," my young self-called out, pushing open the tent flap. "You'll freeze if you stay here. You need to come with me now!" I was uncharacteristically firm.

"Please, Gregory," I pleaded one more time.

"In a minute," Gregory said. "You go ahead, I'll be right behind you." Gregory's image vanished as suddenly as the cold chill of the night air.

As I dozed off, my thoughts continued to page through my life, spontaneously and unapologetically. I felt myself giving way to my past again as I meandered through long forgotten memories of when I was a boy before the Turks came.

Instantly, as if peering from the bow of a fast-approaching ship, I saw her from a distance—Imbroz, my tiny island home—just as beautiful as she was over three-quarters of a century ago. Groves of olive trees graced her landscape and sheep grazed on her rocky hillsides as they had for untold centuries.

Papa's image came back into focus and we peered into the Aegean Sea together from our porch. Papa was telling stories about the ancient philosophers and gods. How I used to love to hear Papa's stories.

"The stables of the winged horses of Poseidon are said to lie there," he said, pointing to the water. I stared in wonder at the vast sea as the waves gently receded and crashed into the shoreline.

"Really, Papa, it's not true?"

"Of course, it is—so it was written about in Homer's *Iliad* eight centuries before Christ."

I have carried my island home with me to America, and I will carry it with me for eternity. Neither the Turks nor death itself will separate me from my roots and my traditions. Imbroz was and is my way of life. I know no other.

CHAPTER 2

Imbroz

There is a broad cavern in the depths
half way between Tenedos and rocky Imbros.
There the Earth-Shaker halted, loosed his horses,
and fed them their ambrosial fodder.
He hobbled their legs with unbreakable gold restraints,
so they would stay till his return…

—HOMER, 750 B.C.

IT WAS NEAR MIDNIGHT and slowly, one by one, all the oil lanterns were extinguished. Bishop Iakavos started lighting the candles. Each member of the congregation lit his neighbor's candle, one after the other, until the flickers became bright lights that illuminated the darkened church with a new eternal light.

The parishioners began chanting, "*Christos anesti*," Christ is risen.

"*Alathos anesti*," truly He is risen. Papa recited the response in unison with the others, and then turned to smile at me.

I proudly sat next to Papa at the end of the second pew to the left side, an inquiring five-year-old boy in his finest Easter clothes.

Not a tall man, Papa was a little stout around the middle. His handlebar mustache stretched from ear-to-ear and curled upwards at both ends. His most distinct features were his piercing blue eyes and sandy hair, a rarity on our island that I inherited.

Everyone began filing outside the church as the *phenos*, or new light, cast shadows along the outside walls. After about ten minutes the candles were extinguished. The service went on after midnight for two more hours back inside the little stone church, but we planned to head home early.

"Papa," I asked as we stood outside, "are Yiayia and Papou Dracoulas coming with us?" Yiayia and Papou Dracoulas were my maternal grandparents.

"Yes, son, they are," Papa said.

Although my grandparents spent time with us, they lived mostly with Uncle Russo and Aunt Cleo on Samothraki Island. They had travelled that evening to attend the Easter service with us, but due to the crowd we had yet to find them, and the darkness was making it more difficult.

"There is Yiayia!" I cried suddenly. Grabbing my father's hand, I started pulling him through the church crowd.

"Ioanni, is that you?" someone called out to Papa.

"Mr. Chrisostomides," another friend cried out, "Christ has risen!"

"Truly he has risen," Papa replied again.

This happened everywhere we went. Everyone knew Papa. He was on the town council, kept the village records, and saw practically everyone at his small convenience store. He also served as the town dentist when someone needed a tooth removed. More importantly, he always had words of wisdom for all who crossed his path, and particularly for me.

"Hi, Yiayia!" I greeted my grandmother. Yiayia Sultana was a small woman who always had hugs and kisses for me.

"Hello, my precious. Come here, let me see you."

Although she seemed old to me, I was told that her mother, Great Yiayia Theopisti, was almost 100 years old. Since Great Yiayia lived on Samothraki with Uncle Russo and Aunt Cleo, I had yet to meet her.

"Yiayia," I asked, "what do you have in the sack?"

"I have cheese, Easter eggs, and *tsoreki,*" or sweet bread.

I saw my mother approach us. "Hello, Mama," my mother greeted Yiayia. "How was your trip?"

"Not bad," Yiayia responded.

Although Yiayia and Papou Dracoulas were getting old, they were able to walk all the way from Castro where the boat docked. Papou and Yiayia Chrisostomides, Papa's parents, were older and lived in a village on the other side of the island. They would join us for Easter dinner tomorrow.

Our house was a fifteen-minute walk from the church and the center of town. Mama walked alongside the donkey with Costa and Sultana—my younger brother and sister—placed on top while Katina and I followed behind. As we headed home, I saw my aunt and uncle, Thea Kirata and Theo Dimitris. Theo Dimitris was my father's older brother and my favorite uncle. He and Thea Kirata would attend Easter dinner tomorrow, too.

"Hello, Blue Eyes," Theo Dimitris said, making me laugh. "How are you today?"

Although I had not seen my uncle in church, I had seen Jimmy Coucouzes, who was now walking up to join us.

"Hello, Mr. and Mrs. Chrisostomides," Jimmy greeted my parents. "Christ has risen!"

"Truly he has risen!" Papa responded.

Jimmy and his family lived in the Agios Theodora, but Jimmy's aunt was Maria Karazou, who lived next door to us. He was six years older than I was and a good deal taller. Even as adults many years later he would tower over me.

"Hi, Christo," he said, falling into step with me. "I liked the service tonight, didn't you?"

"Yes," I agreed, tilting my head to look up at him.

"When are you going to grow taller, my little friend?" Jimmy asked, and when I laughed, he laughed with me.

"Did you take Communion tonight?" he went on.

"No." Eyes cast down, I shook my head.

"I did," Jimmy told me matter-of-factly.

"Do you know you should take Communion at least six times a year as well as all major holidays, or you might be damned for all eternity?" Jimmy was very interested in the church.

"No," I replied, wide-eyed. I would be sure to tell Mama and Papa what Jimmy said.

"Hey, maybe we can play ball tomorrow?" he suggested.

"Sure, Jimmy." I nodded happily. My one toy growing up was a partly deflated leather sack about the size of a soccer ball, and Jimmy and I would often kick it around when we played.

Despite our age difference, Jimmy and I always had a special bond. Our paths would cross several times during the course of our different, yet parallel, lives, and through trials and tribulations we would remain friends.

When we reached our house, Mama and Papa continued their preparations for tomorrow's Easter dinner. Yiayia and Thea Kirata helped Mama tend to various dishes on the stove—a heavy steel cylinder with a firebox that burned either wood or coal, and which was our only source of heat on cold nights. It had a flat top for cooking and its chimney vented through the roof.

Papa shooed the women away so he could stoke the stove and lay additional logs on the fire. The seasoned lamb, a treat that we enjoyed only on holidays, was stuffed into a pan, covered completely and ready for the oven the next morning. Many people had already placed their lambs in large outdoor baking ovens earlier on Saturday, but Papa always insisted it would be tastier if cooked early Easter Day. My favorite of Papa's, though, was his *avgolemono* soup, a traditional chicken and rice broth whipped with lemon and egg. Famished from the deprivation of Lent, we gulped the soup down before going to bed that night. In less than a moment, I fell into a deep sleep.

Before he married Mama, Papa had purchased our land and built our house himself on a small lot along the road to Panayia facing the mountains. He had worked years to do this. Our home was no more than 800 square feet with an attic upstairs where the children slept. Papa's small convenience store stood attached to its right. Papou Chrisostomides, my paternal grandfather, once had a small store of his own and he helped Papa to build his. Our farming fields were across the road from our house except for one, which was almost a mile away. Behind our house and over a hill lay the Aegean Sea.

• • •

On Easter Day in 1923 there would be no work. Papa's store would be closed, unless someone really needed something. It was a day to be spent in the company of family and close friends, a time for reverence and joy, and a time to thank God for our blessings. It was also a time for dressing up in our finest clothes, cracking painted eggs, and eating *tsoreki.*

The next morning I awoke to the aroma of our traditional leg of lamb roasting in the oven. Mama was making rice pilaf, and Yiayia's *spanakopita*, or spinach pie, was heating on the stove. Yiayia and Papou Chrisostomides arrived during our preparation. When dinner was finally ready, the adults ate around our small kitchen table. For the children, who were usually fed first, Papa brought a second table over from the store along with four chairs. Even little Costa had his own chair.

Before we began to eat, Papa said a prayer. We all bowed our heads and closed our eyes, but just as we began to pray our door burst open and there was Bishop Iakovos, wearing his traditional black headdress from service the night before. Although not very tall, he was still a little taller than Papa. He was also a few years younger than Papa, but he already had acquired a long white beard which, along with his long staff, gave him the cherubic appearance of being a wise man. His protruding stomach boasted of excess.

Bishop Iakovos was senior to the four priests who ministered the seven villages of our ancient island. He was a very intelligent man and spoke a number of languages. Though Papa was not educated beyond high school on the island, he was self-taught and well read. Papa was Bishop Iakovos's friend and mentor.

When the Bishop appeared, everyone quickly stood up. Mama went to his side to greet him at once. As was tradition, Mama bowed, kissing his hand. "Hello, Your Grace," she said.

"Welcome, we were not expecting you," greeted Papa by her side.

Bishop Iakovos acknowledged them both and sat down, glancing around the table.

"How would you like your lamb?" Papa asked, gesturing to the roast.

"From the top, please." The Bishop's eyes roamed over the various foods that we had prepared specially for Easter.

"What would you like with your lamb? Rice pilaf? Spinach pie? Olives? Sweetbread? Of course, Greek salad and some wine?" Mama offered, jumping in to serve him.

Iakovos acknowledged each with a small though eager nod.

He had eaten with us before and he loved everything my parents made. My father and mother were excellent cooks, and the Bishop always ate a very full meal when he had dinner at our home. My family continued on with the meal, yet they sensed from the Bishop's demeanor that something was not right.

His eyes fell suddenly on the tapestry that hung on the wall next to our front door for as long as I could remember. Mama had embroidered the tapestry, which had six rows and six columns with thirty-six squares forming a large diamond shape. Each square contained a phrase or word that Papa wrote in *Koine* Greek, the biblical language, imparting simple guidance of how to live your life. No doubt the Bishop was reflecting on the importance of these simple truths.

After the meal, the adults sat and talked, and Katina and I were allowed to go outside and play with Jimmy, who had come over as promised from his aunt's house next door. It was a beautiful Easter Sunday; flowers were in bloom everywhere and we began a game of kick ball. Even though Jimmy was older and taller, I was quicker and could almost hold my own. Katina wasn't bad herself.

When Mama finally called us in, we overheard Papa talking with the Bishop and Theo Dimitris about the Turks. I later learned that they were discussing the massacre at Smyrna, which had occurred seven months earlier in September of 1922.

"The port city of Smyrna, Homer's home, was an old and beautiful Greek city that had been founded in 3000 B.C., pre-dating Christianity. It had stood as an important and prosperous economic center for forty-nine centuries—but in only ten days' time, an undetermined number, believed to be at least 300,000 innocent Christians, were slaughtered there, including the revered Archbishop of Smyrna, Chrysostom. The city burned nearly to the ground—except for the Turkish section—all under the control of Mustafa Kemal Atatürk's army." He would be elected President of Turkey in five months. The Bishop's anxiety elevated as he spoke.

This slaughter was the culmination of nearly a decade of Christian genocide that had paralyzed our small community. The horrors at Smyrna all but erased the remnants of the old Byzantine Empire and Orthodox Christians from Turkey. That our tiny island of Imbroz had remained unscathed so far was a miracle.

"Archbishop Chrysostom went to the French consulate," Bishop Iakovos told Papa.

"At the risk of his own safety he went to plead for the inhabitants of Smyrna. The consulate there urged him to stay and take refuge, but he refused, saying it was his duty to stay with his flock. That was the last time this venerable and eloquent man was seen alive."

Mama glanced over at me listening intently and quickly shooed me outside, but I hid by the crack in the front door and called for Jimmy to come join me.

"Shortly thereafter the Turkish military took him to Nureddin Pasha, the Turkish commander under Mustafa Kemal, who turned the Archbishop over to a mob in front of the military headquarters of the Kemalist forces. They stabbed him, tore his beard out by the roots, and dragged his limp body about the streets before he was finally beheaded and dismembered. His severed head was paraded around the city to make an example to all Christians."

"With his disciplined army, Atatürk could have easily prevented this brutality if he chose," the Bishop continued, choking with emotion. "He did not. What the Ottomans could not accomplish in four hundred years, Atatürk and his Young Turks have done in a decade. The complete and irretrievable extermination of Christianity in Asia Minor is upon us."

A silence fell over the group.

There was not a gathering of Greeks on our island that did not discuss the massacre of Christians in Smyrna, but we had never viewed the tragedy with the Bishop's perspective before.

"Meanwhile, his militia, aided by the general citizenry, are raping, plundering, and slaughtering our people while the Committee on Union and Progress, or CUP, that govern the Young Turks are taking our property and self-enriching themselves," Uncle Dimitris finally added, visibly disturbed by the conversation.

"The plan was to give the city up for a few days to carnage," Iakovos continued, "to make it appear as if the attack was mob related, but it wasn't. The people being slaughtered in Smyrna were unarmed citizens."

"Surely our allies must respond," Papa interjected, his optimism on full display. "Certainly, the civilized world is horrified by this latest slaughter. Your Grace?"

Bishop Iakovos shook his head doubtfully.

"In the year 156 A.D., Polycarp, the Bishop and eventual patron saint of Smyrna, was beheaded, dismembered, and burned in the ancient stadium, the contours of which are still plainly visible," he reminded the men.

"Now, nearly eighteen centuries later, a similar scene has played out before our eyes, but this time the entire Christian population was executed alongside their leader. Pure evil."

"Yes," Theo Dimitris agreed.

"Since 1908," the Bishop continued, "the genocidal campaign to eliminate the Christians from Turkey has intensified and grown viciously. The exterminations carried out by the Young Turks have indeed brought an irreversible end to our cultural heritage."

"These barbarians stole all our wealth and made our Christian women concubines throughout Turkey," Uncle Dimitris emotionally proclaimed. "So far Imbroz has been spared."

"At least for now," the Bishop said as a sober hush fell over the group.

"Papa, what is a concubine?" I asked.

The men turned around in surprise to see that Jimmy and I had been listening. "Never mind that, Christo, you should not be listening." Papa shooed us away.

"There is talk of a "peace agreement" with the Turks that would uproot the few surviving Christians from Asia Minor." The Bishop paused and glanced around more intently. "There is even discussion to cede Imbroz to Turkey," he added.

"But the world won't tolerate this, right?" Papou interjected.

"I don't know. I'm afraid turning Imbroz over seems to be a small price to pay for peace," Uncle Dimitris replied.

"I fear there may be no consequences for the perpetrators in the earthly realm," Iakovos lamented.

Papa was aghast. "You mean giving up a Greek island with a population that dates itself back to antiquity is a *small price*?"

"I'm afraid so, Ioanni," the Bishop answered. "Since Greek independence in 1821, the Mohammedan Turks have craved the Greek border islands and have consistently sought means to conquer them. Don't underestimate Turkish greed."

"In a sense," my Papou, who had been quietly listening across the room, mused, "the islands serve as an imaginary demarcation line between Christianity to the west and the Mohammedans, who have overrun Byzantium and the Roman Empire, to the east. The Turks want to redraw the map."

"And strategically," Papa added as sober realization sank in, "since Imbroz sits at the mouth of the Dardanelles Straits, we are coveted by these Young Turks all the more."

"Now you understand, Ioanni," Iakovos nodded.

On that note, I backed away from the door a little, but I was still close enough to hear Papa respond.

"We seem to be no more than a pawn in a game of chess." Papa sat down, weary from the discussion.

"Ioanni," the Bishop went on quietly, "one day soon I would like you to meet Nicholas Vasil. His family survived the genocide in Smyrna."

The air was heavy with emotion as the dinner party stared blankly at one another.

"Of course, Your Grace," Papa responded after a brief pause.

"Stop this talk, please," Mama finally chimed in. "The children can hear."

Jimmy and I backed away from the door after hearing the distress in Mama's voice and I told Jimmy it was time for him to go home.

I'm not sure we understood much of what we heard that night, but we still realized something was wrong.

"Bye, Jimmy," I said with a smile.

"When do you think you might grow taller, Chrysostomos?" he teased. I shook my head and laughed.

Suddenly a thought struck him that made him grin.

"Your grandfather bakes bread," he told me. "Your father runs a store and he bakes bread, too. Certainly, you are no more than a crumb of bread. I will call you Breadcrumb." The nickname stuck.

Among the things I remember best from my childhood on Imbroz are the beautiful flowers of spring; Greek Easters with my family; kicking my ball with Katina and Jimmy; and my nickname, Breadcrumb.

CHAPTER 3

Breadcrumb

Women scantily clad,
carrying babies in their arms or on their backs,
marched side by side with old men
hobbling along with canes…
about 1,200,000… started on this journey…
"Pray for us… we shall not see you in the world again"…
The gendarmes… became their tormentors.
They even prodded pregnant women with bayonets…
this plan of deportation developed into one of annihilation.
—HENRY MORGENTHAU, U.S. AMBASSADOR TO TURKEY, 1919

FOR A FEW FLEETING MONTHS following the Easter celebration of 1923 our lives moved through time in the same familiar manner that was the ancient rhythm of our island. However, the unsettled borders in the aftermath of the Balkan Wars of 1912–1913, followed by World War I, had economically devastated Mother Greece, leaving the Christians of Asia Minor easy prey. Exposed and vulnerable, our island stood without an ally or an advocate, as Bishop Iakovos had warned. We became a bargaining chip of appeasement given to the Young Turks.

"Christo," Papa said one evening, "tonight we are going to Papou's house." I was excited about the excursion, but had a sense that this was not an ordinary social visit. Bishop Iakovos soon arrived to accompany us on the journey.

At Papou's house, the greetings were short and mechanical, and Papou and Yiayia did not make a fuss over me as they usually did. I quickly spotted a thin man, his wife, and their three young boys sitting quietly in the room. I was too young to understand the significance of their presence, but they all had the same despondent look, which left an impression on me.

The Bishop introduced us to the family. "Ioanni, meet Nicholas and Anastasia Vasil, and their sons Nicholas, Philip, and Thomas." I noticed Thomas was about three years older than I was.

"They are the family from Smyrna I told you about," the Bishop said. "I think you should hear what they have to say."

"It is a pleasure to meet you," Papa said earnestly.

"Mr. Chrisostomides, last fall we escaped from Smyrna on a Greek ship flying the American flag. It dropped us seventy miles northwest of here on the island of Lesbos, where we were staying in a one-story abandoned house outside the island's capital of Mytilene with three other families. So many refugees are there that the living conditions became deplorable, so we came here for a brief stay with Anastasia's second cousin before leaving for mainland Greece. We are blessed to have made it this far."

"I see," Papa said gently. "Can you tell us what happened?"

"It started in earnest two weeks before the city was burned. The Turkish military uprooted countless Christian families from inland as well as from surrounding provinces and drove them into Smyrna. The population of Smyrna almost doubled before the invasion. During this period, advance elements of the Turkish military were drifting into the city. We heard regular reports of theft, rape, and murder during those few days of increasing occupation. Realizing the mounting severity of our plight, many of us stayed indoors and prayed."

"On the eve the slaughters began," he faltered for a moment before continuing, "marking the start of a horrific, incomprehensible bloodbath that went on for ten days…" he stopped, and Papa waited quietly for him to continue.

"I had a stone and concrete factory. All was lost. My wife sewed a few gold coins into the clothes of my three sons. Luckily, I had sons and not daughters. Daughters were taken and abused, often in front of their fathers. That night, the Turks broke into my home." He lifted his hand.

"They tried to cut off my finger to get a ring" he said, showing his hand to Papa, "but I was able to remove it in time." Again, he paused.

"Poor Leonides, my friend and neighbor, suffered a terrible death. He had two young daughters, fifteen and sixteen."

At this point, Papa turned to me, "Christo, go to the other room and play with Mr. Vasil's sons, please."

I wanted to stay and hear the story, but I knew better than to argue. "Yes, Papa." I walked with the boys toward the side room but lingered at the door.

"I'm sorry, go on," Papa said.

"He was forced to watch while three or four Turkish soldiers took turns and repeatedly raped his daughters. When he tried to defend them, he was stabbed with a saber in his stomach. He sat on the floor and bled to death, unable to defend his daughters who were taken away by the Turks. His wife told me this story. God rest their souls. Later after being raped multiple times by many soldiers the girls were turned into concubines."

"God be with them," Papa shook his head as Bishop Iakovos crossed himself while mumbling a prayer.

Mr. Vasil continued recounting his story.

"We were powerless, defenseless, and unarmed. We fled our home. We roamed the streets with thousands of other Christians while our homes were looted and later burned. The Turkish military and mobs of Mohammedans slaughtered countless Christians for ten days. We watched helplessly as they were stabbed to death or shot randomly in the streets. Somehow, we survived." Mr. Vasil shook his head in wonder.

"We hid for two days in the yard of an old factory near the docks without food or water while the city burned. The sky glowed red from the city's blaze, while smoke from the smoldering ruins and the stench of the dead and dying filled the air. At first light on the third morning we emerged from hiding and, with the help of an American naval officer, we boarded a Greek ship flying an American flag. God be praised."

Papa was agitated. "Smyrna is an international port—"

In anticipation of the question, Mr. Vasil responded, "From the factory I could see crowds of people forced to the sea by the fires.

Ships were docked bearing French, British, German, and American flags. To our horror, though, only a few were accepting refugees. We watched as defenseless people were refused passage and subsequently attacked by the mobs and the military. Most perished in plain view of a harbor full of empty ships bearing international flags and almost no one cared."

"In addition to this chaos the Turkish military was firing round after round at point-blank range into the crowd of Christians as they were turned away from ships. Defenseless and trapped, families had nowhere to run, with the water at their backs and the burning city before them."

He drew a breath and sighed. Everyone was silent for what seemed a long time.

"May God let those poor souls rest in peace," Bishop Iakovos said, momentarily capturing the group's attention.

"The kind Bishop has found a place for us to stay as our cousin's home was too small. Shortly, we will be going to Greece," Nicholas continued, his voice shaking, "but I warn you, you are not safe here. You must all leave before you succumb to the same fate. No Christian is safe in these parts of the world. Not even here on Imbroz." Mr. Vasil began to tremble.

Bishop Iakovos broke in, "You will be safe here, Nicholas."

"Please don't think you're safe, they will be here soon." Mr. Vasil's caution elevated to a shrill warning.

"We must all leave," Mr. Vasil repeated in an urgent but calmer tone. Turning to Papa, Bishop Iakovos said softly, "I fear he is right. Our island home is at great risk."

They talked for a while on lighter subjects, but Papa knew they were tired, and he had to open the store early the next morning. Papa stood to shake Mr. Vasil's frail hand and said, "God be with you." Papa then kissed the Bishop's hand, called me over, and we left.

I waved goodbye to his oldest son, Thomas, whose brave wide eyes peeked around from his mother's side to return the favor.

The brief meeting with Nicholas Vasil and his family was an ominous sign of the imminent loss of our island home to the barbarians of the Smyrna genocide, Kemal Mustafa and his Young Turks. The Vasils left the island a week later.

• • •

When the Treaty of Lausanne was signed on July 24, 1923, our tiny island of Imbroz was indeed annexed by the Turks. The Treaty purportedly provided protection for the Christian population on Imbroz in Article 14, which allowed locals on Imbroz and neighboring Tenedos to govern themselves in order to protect local Greek customs and institutions. The world seemed satisfied, but the reality of occupation was that the rights of all minorities were not protected.

It was very clear to those of us living this nightmare that the Turks had no intention of abiding by the treaty. Instead, that autumn, with the ink of the treaty not yet dry, the harshness of occupation became immediately apparent. In a short time, Greek schools were transitioned to Turkish schools and Greek flags were replaced with Turkish flags—all in direct violation of Article 14. The Hellenic way of life that had survived nineteen centuries on Imbroz was being slowly extinguished in the years that followed, only to remain in the hearts and minds of its conquered people.

In his capacity as a city council member of Panayia, Papa had been responsible for maintaining all the records in city hall. Thanks to the Bishop's warning that the Turks would inevitably confiscate the city's records, he kept our family's records at home early on in the occupation. Papa also distributed records to anyone who wanted them.

Thanks to his foresight, his children and his children's children would know their proper births and identity. He would not abdicate these intangibles in the face of overbearing intimidation, coercion, and repression. To be sure, we kept our records in our hearts and in our minds.

I live in Panayia, the capital city of Imbroz island. I was born on December 15, 1917. I am named Chrysostomos Ioanni Chrisostomides for my grandfather and father, as is our custom. I am the second of four children. I have two sisters, Katerina—we called her Katina—and Sultana, and a little brother, Costa. My father's name is Ioanni Chrisostomides. His parents are Katherine and Chrysostomos, and his sisters and brothers are Zafira, Kiraha, and Dimitris. My mother's name is Theopiste Dracoulas Chrisostomides. Mama's parents are Dracos Dracoulas and Sultana Dracoulas, and her sisters and brother are Keratsa, Yramatiki, Constantinos, Basilic, Cleo, and Ioanni.

These were the things I memorized from our family records and recited to myself.

Papa was also careful to tell me how I should behave if a Turk confronted me. "Christo, when a Turk comes before you and speaks to you, look him in his eyes and smile, then bow at the waist. Like this, you see?" Papa placed his hand lightly at his waist and bowed to demonstrate. "Now, you try it."

"Yes, Papa." We practiced bowing for about five minutes. "It shows respect, my son," Papa told me.

"Always look into their eyes. That way, they won't bother you."

"I'll remember."

Papa was a stubborn man. Unlike many Greeks who fled the island after the treaty was signed, Papa refused to leave his home and the business he had worked for so long and so hard. Papa believed doing so would play right into the unspoken agenda of the Turks to drive all the Christians from their homes. He was not about to give the Turks what they wanted so easily. Somehow, Papa remained an optimist. No matter how dire the circumstances were, he held out hope that things would change. They never did.

• • •

When the Turks first arrived in the winter of 1923 our family stubbornly tried to proceed with their normal activities, but change was everywhere. Every day more Greek families left the island, abandoning their property and all possessions they could not carry. Our once self-sufficient agricultural and fishing economy grew increasingly poor. Just a few months earlier, in a past that now seemed like a dream, Papa worked happily in his store, often with Mama's help. I also helped him, and I enjoyed it so much that I once told Papa I would like to quit school and work with him, but he wouldn't let me.

Our small store was not only Papa's joy, it was his livelihood. Everyone used to come to see him, and the store was always well stocked with sugar, flour, bread, cheese, milk, olives, wine, coffee, tea, cookies, fabrics, and much more. Now, in the face of a population in exodus and a suffering economy, Papa struggled hard to keep the store open, and the inventory grew more and more sparse. Sometimes, even the essentials were hard to come by for weeks.

One summer day in 1924, as I stood next to Papa at the counter, two Turkish gendarmes, or soldiers, came to the store. They were both armed with rifles and sabers, and they towered over Papa. The larger of the two laid his saber on the counter and looked at Papa.

"Fine store you have here," he said in Turkish.

"May I help you?" Papa inquired politely.

"Yes," the gendarme told him. "What is your name?"

"Ioanni," Papa said.

"Well, Ioanni," the gendarme said, "we need supplies for the Turkish military police."

Papa didn't say a word, and a moment later the gendarme lifted a bag of flour on his shoulders and carried it out to his donkey-drawn cart. Next, the gendarmes took a bag of sugar and another of rice, until the cart was full of staples.

"Excuse me," Papa said. "You owe me 500 lira."

"Of course," the first gendarme said sarcastically. "Ismet, pay Mr. Ioanni his 500 lira."

The Turk ripped off a corner of Papa's wrapping paper from the roll he kept on the countertop to wrap food in and scribbled something on it.

"Here," he said, scribbling on a piece of paper, "an IOU."

"But there is no name on this," Papa protested. "No amount, either."

"You do not need names or amounts," the first gendarme said as he buckled his saber back on. "This is by order of Kemal Mustafa for the Turkish police. We will remember and pay you later."

In an eruption of laughter between them, the gendarmes left the store. The Turkish military police never repaid Papa the debt.

• • •

The spring of 1926 brought little relief. In fact, Turkish interlopers seemed more emboldened. Muslim settlers came from the mainland to take over Christian homes that had been abandoned. The tiny island was trying to hold its population together in the face of incredible persecution and mass exodus. I was eight years old and in fourth grade now. I was attending Turkish school full time and already spoke fluent Turkish. One morning on my way to school, as I walked along the road, I rounded the usual bend to face a small pasture and slowed to let a small band of chickens scatter before me. Their squawking interrupted my daydreams and a strange sensation that something was wrong overcame me. Then I saw him.

My heart raced and I froze, rooted among the chickens as they scattered. I saw his feet first as they swayed slightly in the breeze. One of his shoes was missing. My eyes travelled up slowly as I fought to resist, fearing what more I might see, but on they went, up to the long branch of the sturdy tree that fastened the rope from which the body hanged.

It was a Greek man I recognized from town. On him was a sign that read, *"This man caught stealing chickens."* I didn't know the man well, but I knew it was a lie. Even if it was true, the punishment hardly fit the crime. I bowed my head and hastened my pace to school. That fourth-grade class was the last year of formal schooling I would ever receive in my lifetime.

Similar events were growing more and more common all over Imbroz. People were fleeing daily, leaving behind generations of possessions for Turkish settlers to seize. As the population dwindled, the Turks became more brazen and less accountable.

Papa and the other city council members had been discharged, and the Turkish authorities who replaced them were indifferent to the grievances of local Christians. The tedious passage of Turkish time was torturous.

• • •

The year was now 1927 and I was nine years old. Even though I had stopped formal schooling, I continued to learn a lot about the world around me. My lessons were not from mathematics and arithmetic, but from the brutality I saw around me. In the five years since the massacre at Smyrna and the martyrdom of Archbishop Chrysostom, Imbroz had changed enormously.

"Christo, we must be hopeful," Papa told me. "Without hope, life would be empty."

Papa was well read, particularly on the United States, and he believed that America would come to our aid.

"They will not allow this to go on," he insisted. "The United States is just and good and they will protect our rights." Papa always had a deep respect for the United States, a respect he nurtured in me from an early age. Periodically he would get an American newspaper and he had taught himself a few words in English.

"Christo, one day you will go to America," Papa said.

"Okay Papa, I will, and you will come too," I responded.

"I will be with you in spirit always, my son, that I can promise."

From that day on, going to America was my plan and dream, a dream that would define my young life for years to come. I just wasn't sure if I could take Papa with me.

It had been a year since Papa was forced to close the store. The extra taxes levied on Christian businesses made it uneconomic to stay open and he simply had no more goods to sell. Two-thirds of our sheep had also died or were stolen.

The Turks spread an abundance of hunger and sadness across our tiny island. People were slowly wasting away, and my siblings and I started coming home from school with hunger cramps in our empty stomachs. Mama and Papa knew they had to do something. There wasn't enough food to feed four children.

Soon my sister Katina went to stay with Thea Cleo and Theo Russo on Samothraki, an island just north of Imbroz. Cleo and Russo had no children and welcomed her. There she would help them with their store and attend a Greek school.

A few months later my turn would come.

The day Mama called to me I knew immediately things were more dire than ever before.

"Chrysostomos, come here." The tears that welled up in her proud eyes were the only hint of the despair she must have felt at that moment.

"Papa and I have decided to send you to Samothraki for a while to stay with Theo Russo, Thea Cleo, and Katina," she said.

My parents were proud and would never admit defeat, but I knew then how financially strapped we were.

"They have plenty of food" Mama said, "and you can attend a Greek school."

Even so, I felt all the fear and uncertainty of a ten-year-old boy leaving home for the first time. Papa knew this and he tried to reassure me.

The night before I left Imbroz, Papa motioned to me to sit down next to him on the porch. I remember feeling the cool evening breeze off the Aegean Sea to the east.

Although at the time I was too young to understand much of what was happening, I fully realized that the events of recent years had irreversibly changed our lives. The carefree happy days of my early childhood were distant memories.

The rest of the evening Papa and I talked about the ancients. Listening to him tell stories, I felt my anxiety dissipate.

"During the Trojan War, King Agamemnon and his greatest warrior, Achilles, got into an argument over a woman and Achilles left. Enraged, Apollo punished the Greek army by sending a plague to kill their soldiers."

I listened intently.

"Then Agamemnon returned the young woman to her father and Achilles rejoined the Greek army to kill the Trojans. He travelled all the way to the city of Troy where he met Hector at the gates and slew him, too."

"Then what happened, Papa?"

"Well he was shot in the heel with an arrow and died. That is why we call this the Achilles' heel." Papa pinched the area above his heel and below his calf to show me.

At that time, I was not aware how short my time would be with Papa, yet that is how I would always remember him, on the porch with me telling me stories about ancient Greek mythology.

On the eve of my departure to Samothraki I thought of America, thousands of miles across vast oceans, that awesome land of opportunity.

With barely a cent in my pocket, the possibility of ever seeing America seemed as real to me as having afternoon tea with Plato or Socrates. Yet the thought never left my mind. Papa was convinced that this was what I must do, so I had to believe that it was possible.

Soon a figure approaching from Panayia interrupted my thoughts. Within a moment the holy apparition came into focus as we made out his familiar staff, white beard, and black robe. It was Bishop Iakovos. After greeting Papa, he turned to me.

"Chrysostomos, I understand you will be going to live with your Thea and Theo?"

"Yes, Your Grace, I am going tomorrow after church."

"I see."

"I will be helping Theo Russo in his store."

"My, my," he smiled. "A big job for such a young boy," he said, adding, "Christo, you have been noticed by many on our island. You are special. Wherever you go, whatever you do, you must not forget your home on Imbroz."

"I won't forget," I told him gratefully.

"Come here, my son."

The Bishop bowed his head and said a prayer for me. I bowed my head, too, and prayed that God would watch over and protect us all.

"Amen," Bishop Iakovos said, and I kissed his hand and bowed. He was more than our religious leader; he was a friend of Papa's and a familiar face at our house. Although an Orthodox priest, Bishop Iakovos was educated in the ancients and knew the history of our small island perfectly.

I felt he always liked me and showed me special attention, and I liked him very much. I knew he had made this special visit for me.

"God be with you my son," he said.

Within five minutes Uncle Dimitris appeared, as well, and I sensed there was something beyond my departure that he wanted to discuss.

• • •

It was dusk now and Mama started to usher me to bed with my sisters and brother. I could hear Papa and the Bishop talking with Uncle Dimitris downstairs. Although I did not understand everything, I listened intently.

"Is there any news from the mainland?" Uncle Dimitris asked. "Will the Greek government intervene? What about the recent revocation of Article 14?"

On July 26, 1927, a few months earlier, Kemal Mustapha and his Young Turks passed a so-called "civil law" revoking all rights granted by the Lausanne Treaty, including those preserved for Imbroz and Tenedos in Article 14.

"They call this revocation a "civil law?" How ironic," Papa added. "Don't worry, Dimitris, they never abided by the treaty to begin with."

Uncle Dimitris would not be denied his monologue.

"Imbroz has survived attacks since twenty-four centuries ago," the Bishop added. "From 511–512 B.C. we were invaded by a Persian General under King Darius according to the account of Herodotus, the Greek historian. Even when the Ottomans took control in 1453, we sought and were granted special council with Mehmet II. We were not taken over. Although there were hostilities we were tolerated within the Ottoman Empire."

"I always thought we would be done in by an earthquake," Uncle Dimitris stated. Everyone looked at him quizzically and he tried to explain himself. "As you know, we sit between the Aegean Sea and the Eurasian Plates, right within the fault zone."

Everyone seemed to ignore this observation.

"Now, after all these centuries of relative autonomy we are being done in by a treaty to which we weren't even a party. What about the Americans?" Papa interjected.

"They never signed the Lausanne Treaty and were opposed to it from the start. I'm sorry to say but the world doesn't care," the Bishop threw up his hands.

"It is true Ioanni, the world does not care," Uncle Dimitris offered in a low voice as if he didn't want anyone to listen to what followed. I kneeled forward where the ladder hit the attic door to hear more clearly.

"It all began during the Spanish Inquisition, following the royal edict of Spanish Queen Isabella in 1492 to expel the Sephardic Jews from Spain. During this time the Jews suffered numerous horrific tortures and deaths at the hands of Spanish Catholics. Some Jews converted to Catholicism, the so-called *conversos.* 60,000 Sephardic Jews fled to Thessaloniki, which was then called "Salonika," Greece, where they lived and prospered in relative peace with the Greek Christians and Ottoman Mohammedans from the 1490s until the turn of the twentieth century.

During the first decade of the twentieth century the Ottoman Empire in practical terms had collapsed. Splinter groups promised a new constitution, freedom, and a secular society for all minorities within. In 1908, the Young Turks gained control of the Ottoman parliament, and promised multiparty representation. These so-called Young Turks also coincided in time and had connections with the Bolshevik Communists forming to the north in Russia.

The Young Turks formed the Committee of Union and Progress, or CUP, as their ruling body. The CUP began as a liberal reform movement promising freedom and human rights for all the minorities within the declining Ottoman Empire. Initially they promised the minorities a new constitution. Early on the Christians had no idea of the Young Turks' bad intensions. Donations were collected from the same Christian groups they murdered over the decade that followed.

Many CUP members were primarily Jews from Thessaloniki, pretending to be Muslim but not relinquishing their Jewish traditions. They were called *dönmeh*, or crypto-Jews. This group of Salonika Jews was actually secular, but pretended to be religious to gain power over the Mohammedan masses who sadly carried out the genocide upon their instructions. They were a force behind the 1908 revolution when CUP won a majority of seats in the Turkish parliament.

In the Balkan Wars of 1912–1913 the *dönmeh* had fought with the Ottomans and lost control of the Balkan Peninsula to the Balkan league: Bulgaria, Montenegro, Serbia, and Greece—all Christians. During the Balkan Wars no genocide was practiced against Muslims or Jews. After the Balkan Peninsula was lost, however, the Young Turks moved their armies into Turkey and carried out a holocaust of unconscionable horrors against an unarmed Christian population in Turkey. All Christians would be murdered, including women, children, and the old. Their possessions would be taken. The perpetrators of this Christian holocaust were led by the *dönmeh*. They were cowardly—pure evil.

Similar atrocities were imposed by the *dönmeh*, or crypto-Jews, on the Christians than those that had been imposed on the *dönmeh* by the Christians four hundred years earlier during the Spanish inquisition. In 1900, the number of Christians in Turkey numbered 5,500,000. Under the cover of World War I, the extermination of Christians was ongoing and accelerated. By 1923, when the Treaty of Lausanne was signed, the population of Christians in Turkey had been reduced to almost 400,000. 1,100,000 Christians fled or were deported. 4,000,000 poor souls had perished. All their wealth and possessions were confiscated by the Young Turks. Hellenism had been erased from Asia Minor."

Uncle Dimitris's voice was all but a soft whisper and I leaned in to hear him continue.

"Mustafa Kemal Atatürk himself, the so-called "Father of Turkey," a Sephardic Jew from Salonika, oversaw the Smyrna massacre. He was educated as a *dönmeh*. At the very least, he has the blood of all the unarmed Christians who died in Smyrna on his hands."

Uncle Dimitris had travelled for many years. When he returned he married late. No one was quite sure where he went or what he did during his travels. He fashioned himself as an authority on the history of religious violence between Christians, Muslims, and Jews, particularly in the Balkans and Anatolia, which makes up the majority of modern Turkey. At a time of occupation when most people remained silent, he was not afraid to say what he believed was truth, even if it put him at risk. Everyone always listened to Uncle Dimitris when he spoke.

A quiet chill fell over the group.

"One day someone will correct the injustices we are facing," Papa insisted. "The civilized world will not close the door forever. Sometimes justice—like God—acts in strange ways."

"Yanni," the Bishop insisted, using Papa's nickname, "we have been conquered."

"I will not run from tyranny," Papa insisted. "I will not give up everything I have worked for all my life. That is what they plan on, uprooting us. Of what value is freedom if you must lose everything to pursue it? I was born on Imbroz. It is my home and one day I will die here."

"Remember," Uncle Dimitris interjected, "Metropolitan Chrysostom was offered safety but he chose to stay with his people. He tried to save his people from the Turkish slaughter and became a martyr for our faith. The Turks have stopped the murders of innocent people, but who knows when they will begin again."

At once, Papa grinned. "Even though they have yet to find a cure for the common birthday, I do not intend to be a martyr. However, there is no life for my children here. One day, they must leave." Poor Papa.

"Yanni, you can't fight the Turkish gendarmes!" My Uncle was furious.

"No, I can't," my Papa said, "but as long as I stay, our island will be alive." Yet Imbroz that had remained unchanged through millennia would never be the same.

Papa, don't worry, I thought to myself as I listened in. *I will go to America one day. I will find a way.*

CHAPTER 4

Separation

Yes, as through this world I've wandered
I've seen lots of funny men;
some will rob you with a six-gun,
and some with a fountain pen.
And as through your life you travel,
yes, as through your life you roam,
you won't never see an outlaw
drive a family from their home.

—WOODY GUTHRIE, 1939

WHEN MORNING CAME, I was up and dressed even before Mama called us to get ready for church. For breakfast we had bread and a thin piece of Greek cheese. Papa and Mama drank coffee, and I shared a glass of goat's milk with my brother and sisters. As children we were often hungry. Since the Turks came—and especially since Papa closed his store—we never seemed to have enough food.

After breakfast, Mama prepared a small sack of cheese, olives, and bread for my trip to Samothraki Island. As we left for church, I glanced back at the only home I had ever known. I paused for a minute, swallowing hard at the thought that I was leaving home. A ten-year-old's pain of separation is hard to conceal. The occupation of Imbroz that had uprooted so many others had finally uprooted me.

"Mama," I asked suddenly, "did you remember to pack my ball?"

"Don't worry," she smiled. "Your ball is in your case with your other things." The cover of the ball Jimmy and I played with was leather but never perfectly round or fully inflated.

The walk to church my last morning home was solemn and uneventful, but I did notice the people at church had a worn and haggard appearance. The number of parishioners had substantially declined as well. One stood watch at the front door, and outside the church doors two Turkish gendarmes served as a daunting reminder of the occupation.

It seemed odd that church was the only thing from our past that was allowed or tolerated by Atatürk and his soldiers, as the Turks showed little curiosity and no respect for any of our traditions.

That morning Bishop Iakovos delivered a sermon on the inner strength of Christianity and admonished the congregation to stay strong. "These are difficult times we live in," he began. "Many in our villages have left or are leaving for Greece and other destinations, abandoning everything they own. We will remember them in our prayers and ask God to bless them wherever they are."

During four years of occupation, the island's population of 12,000 had been reduced by more than half, and the economy had collapsed. Some people had disappeared mysteriously at night, never to be heard from again by family or friends.

"These are your homes. This is your island," he told us emotionally. "Do not leave them easily. You have done nothing wrong. Let us pray—in the name of the Father, the Son, and the Holy Spirit. Amen."

I was pleased to see that Jimmy was at church with his parents that morning. He usually went to the church in Agios Theodora, but occasionally he attended in Panayia to hear the Bishop and visit his aunt. As the thinning congregation filed out the church doors, Jimmy sought me out.

"Hey, Breadcrumb," he called out. "When are you going to get bigger?"

I smiled, wondering the same thing. I was ten now, and Jimmy was sixteen. Jimmy towered over me even more than he had four years ago.

"What are you doing?"

"I'm going to theological school at Halki Seminary this fall. Bishop Iakovos helped arrange it."

"I will be the Bishop of Constantinople one day, Breadcrumb." Eastern Orthodox Christians trace the lineage of this Bishop directly to Andrew the Apostle. His successors are Ecumenical Patriarchs, or Bishops of Constantinople, who are the recognized religious leaders of all Eastern Orthodox Christians in the world.

"Of course you will. Good luck, Jimmy," I said, too young to really understand what that meant at the time.

"Thanks," he smiled.

"I'm leaving today for Samothraki to work at my Uncle's store," I told him, proud that I had news of my own to share.

"But Breadcrumb," he protested, "you are too small to work."

"I've worked for Papa," I replied confidently. In those days, circumstances often forced young boys into older roles.

"Well it beats going to a Turkish school. God be with you, my little friend."

A silence fell between us. "Do you have your ball?" Jimmy asked suddenly.

I grinned and walked over to Mama's bag to unpack my ball.

"Go and play with Jimmy," Mama told me. "But just for a minute, or you will miss your boat."

"But, Sultana," Papa said to Mama, "we have to go now."

"Don't deny them a moment of children's play," Mama urged. "Jimmy is going to seminary and Christo is going to Samothraki. Who knows when they will see each other again?"

There was a small yard on the side of the church where Jimmy and I kicked the ball back and forth. For a few brief moments we were untroubled children playing an uncomplicated game in a complex and often hostile world. At the time I had no idea that these few minutes playing ball with Jimmy marked the early end of my childhood and the beginning of my circuitous and often bewildering journey to America.

"Chrysostomos, come now. We have to go," Papa finally called. "Good luck, my little friend," Jimmy said affectionately, placing a hand on my shoulder as I bent over to pick up my ball.

"Goodbye, Jimmy." I tucked the ball under my arm and waved, then ran to catch up with my family.

• • •

The walk to the village of Castro with my family seemed quick. When we reached the dock, Papa called out to a man whom I did not recognize. "Hello, Captain Koutris, I have a young passenger here for you!"

Captain Koutris had a chiseled, lean, and worn look about him. He was taller than Papa and wore a knit fisherman's cap on his head. His mustache was white and brown and formed an inverted *v* on the edges of his lips. His ears and nose seemed disproportionately large, but his large eyes were engaging and friendly. My best guess was that he was at least as old as Papa.

"I have a bottle of water for you," Captain Koutris said, "but if you have to go to the bathroom, better run to those bushes now." I looked first at him and then at the bushes and decided it was a good idea.

When I returned, Mama grasped me around the shoulders and gave me a final tearful hug. "Chrysostomos, I will miss you very much," she said, her voice thick with emotion. Suddenly my little brother and sister ran up to hug me as well. After a long moment of mutual embrace, I disengaged. Then Papa stretched his hand out to me.

"Papa," I said, trying to reassure him, "don't worry, I will be fine." The appearance of Papa's warm, gentle smile set me at ease.

A short distance away Captain Koutris stepped into his boat. "Christo," he called out, interrupting us, "please come; we must hurry to catch the tide."

"Chrysostomos, my son," Papa said, "remember what I have told you."

"I will, Papa," I promised, acting a lot older than I was.

Everyone followed me onto the dock as I got on the boat, calling out farewells.

Captain Koutris looked at me with concern.

"Are you ready, Chrysostomos?"

"Yes," I nodded, not trusting myself to speak. "Goodbye, Mama; goodbye Papa," I said silently.

As the figures of my family grew smaller in the distance it was the fear of separation and the uncertainty of my future that made me uneasy, not the tossing waves and open sea before us.

"I will go to America one day."

"I see," the captain responded, not giving any more attention to what I had just said.

Soon Mama, Papa, Sultana, and Costa were no more than silhouettes on an ever-shrinking shoreline, yet my eyes and my thoughts stayed with them. Long after they disappeared from view I felt emptiness deep inside.

It was mid-day. The trip was about fifteen miles. It would take five to six hours. The sun would be setting when we arrived. My little island home was no more than a speck on the horizon. A silence had fallen between Captain Koutris and me, each of us in our own thoughts.

"Young man," the Captain said, startling me, "I can see that you are tired. "It will be a while on the water. You should go to sleep. There is a blanket behind you in the stern."

Although I didn't want to admit it, Captain Koutris was right. I was tired, and it had been an emotional day of long goodbyes. I found the blanket and pulled it around me.

For a long time I lay awake, watching quietly as we rowed on the gentle rocking water. *One day I will be the captain of my own small boat that I will take out to sea,* I thought dreamily, falling in and out of sleep.

The time passed quickly as I was lulled to sleep by the gentle rocking Aegean Sea. Then Captain Koutris startled me. "There, Samothraki," he pointed to the approaching dock, as if surprised he had actually found it.

We docked the boat in silence and I stepped onto an empty pier. Suddenly, I saw a small group of people walking towards me—it was Aunt Cleo, Uncle Russo, and my sister Katina. I smiled in the brisk evening air at the sight of familiar faces. Suddenly, with family around me, it felt good to be on Samothraki.

"Goodbye, son," Captain Koutris said as he watched my family crowd happily and noisily around me. "God be with you, Chrysostomos."

"Wait!" I cried, breaking free of Aunt Cleo's embrace. "Uncle Russo, Aunt Cleo, I want you to meet Captain Koutris from Imbroz."

He was a little uncomfortable being the center of attention but he smiled, bowed his head, and waved. His was a solitary existence that seemed to suit him just fine, but I felt very close to the man with whom I had shared the first six hours of my new life.

"Goodbye, Captain Koutris," I said as he handed me the last of my gear. "Please tell Mama and Papa that I made it all right."

"I will, son," the Captain promised, as his sail caught the morning breeze.

As we made our way to my aunt and uncle's house, we both stared at Mount Fengari in the distance. Fengari, which means *moon*, I believe was the highest peak in the Aegean Sea. Papa told us that, according to Greek mythology, Poseidon perched at its peak to watch the Trojan War. Legend also has it that anyone who stands at the top of the mountain during the night of a full moon will see something they wish coming true. I should be so lucky.

I bit off a piece of bread Mama had packed and smiled at Katina as we walked in the shadow of the great mountain, whose peak was hidden in the clouds. Katina was older than I was by a year, but since I was the oldest son, the responsibility for her fell on me. That's the way it was in those days. It was up to me now to show that I could contribute and help my family. Although merely a child of ten, I gladly accepted this responsibility.

CHAPTER 5

Samothraki

Happy those early days!
When I shined in my angel infancy.
Before I understood this place
appointed for my second race,
or taught my soul to fancy aught
but a white, celestial thought...
—HENRY VAUGHN, 1695

UNCLE RUSSO'S HOME was about two hundred meters off the main road outside the island's capital city of Protevousa. It was twice the size of our home on Imbroz, but it lacked white walls and cheerful blue doors and shutters, and the outhouse was built of wood rather than stone. It was, in fact, the largest house I had ever been in, yet for all its impressive size it was empty, for Aunt Cleo could not have children.

Uncle Russo said nothing during the walk, but when we reached the house, he turned to me. "Welcome, Chrysostomos," he said. "Your aunt will give you something to eat. Rest today, and tomorrow you may come to the store with me." Uncle Russo was a man of few words.

"Yes, Uncle Russo," I nodded obediently. I was anxious to show Uncle Russo how good I was with chores.

"Now you'll greet your great grandmother, Yiayia Theopisti," Aunt Cleo interrupted. That evening I met the oldest lady I had ever seen. No one knew exactly how old she was, but everyone said she was 100 years old, which seemed ancient to me. She sat in a chair with a cane across her knees rolling a cigarette in her lap. "Yiayia,"

Thea Cleo said, "this is Chrysostomos, Theopisti and Ioanni's son, your great grandson."

Yiayia Theopisti's eyes sparkled as she surveyed me, then she took my hand and welcomed me with a hug. "What a beautiful, precious child," she declared. Instantly, I felt a bond with her that oddly seems to occur between very old and very young relatives. The stories about her were true and I was convinced she was every bit of 100 years old.

I was so transfixed by her that I failed to realize she was slowly approaching me hoisting a large jug of water.

"Christo, into the tub," she ordered, nodding in the direction of a small room, "and get ready to take a bath."

"But Yiayia, I had a bath before I left Imbroz," I protested.

"Cleanliness," she intoned firmly, "is next to godliness."

The large sinewy woman stood in the doorway, a trail of smoke hanging in the air from the tip of the cigarette that dangled from the corner of her wrinkled mouth. As she steered me to the tub I discovered that her hands were disproportionately large and her grip was surprisingly firm.

Half an hour later, scrubbed within an inch of my life and smelling of strong soap, I was finally allowed to eat. The meal was filling and I thought about my family at home who had so little to eat. After dinner my eyes began to grow heavy. The long trip had fatigued me, and the bath and food had made me sleepy. Aunt Cleo led me to bed and within seconds I was fast asleep.

• • •

The next morning I was up at daybreak, climbing over Katina to get out of bed. I had not seen my older sister for months.

This wasn't Katina's first time off Imbroz. When I was a baby, in 1920, Katina almost died of influenza. She was almost four years old. Mama and Papa were so worried that they took her to see a doctor on mainland Turkey. When they returned three days later, they kept her outside on the porch during the day, where the warmth of the sun and the sea breeze could help clear her breathing. The Spanish Flu struck 500,000,000 people when it was all said and done, more than a quarter of the world's population, killing up to 50,000,000. Years later, I learned the influenza was spread by mailmen.

"Chrysostomos, what are you doing up so early?"

I could see the first glimmers of daybreak and to me that meant it was time to get up. I dressed and went outside. When I returned to the house I found Aunt Cleo had awakened and was heating a pot of water on the stove.

"Chrysostomos, you are up bright and early," she said while stoking the fire.

"Yes, Thea."

"Without anyone even telling you?" Aunt Cleo was impressed.

"Yes, I rise this early at home to do my chores. I know how they must be done."

"I see you do," she smiled. "We are so lucky to have such a talented little boy with us."

I smiled back, enormously pleased with myself.

Aunt Cleo made hot porridge for breakfast, and, after we all ate, I hurried to greet Uncle Russo at his store where I was told to simply watch him for a day or two. This continued for a week, but it was not long before I saw a number of ways I could make myself useful.

Uncle Russo had more supplies than Papa did, but his store was not as organized, and it seemed as though he could not remember exactly where things were. I decided to start helping by separating the bags of flour from the bags of sugar.

"Christo, what are you doing?" Uncle Russo asked.

"I am separating the flour and the sugar, Uncle Russo.

"Yes, a very good idea," he said a little absently.

Pausing a moment, he asked, "Why don't you separate the flour from the sugar?" as though his repetition enabled ownership of the idea.

So that is how my first workday began. During the four years that I worked in Uncle Russo's store, I learned everything there was to know about the business, including baking bread, ordering supplies, storing food, and keeping the store clean, which was my specialty.

The days were not difficult, but long and challenging, and in time I proved my worth. When I turned 13 in December of 1930 Uncle Russo would often leave me unattended in the store for hours on end. Oh yes, and at the age of 13 I had finally started to grow a bit as well. It was not long after this point that my family called to have Katina return home to help them with the tailoring they were doing for the Turks to eke out a subsistence. On Katina's last evening on the island, she and I talked for a while. Although no longer towering above me, at fifteen she was still slightly taller, though I had reached the respectable height of five foot four.

"Katina," I said, "you must let me know how everyone is back home."

"I will write you, Christo, but you must promise me that whenever we are separated you will write me, too."

"Okay, Katina, I promise."

When Katina returned to Imbroz, we began what turned into a thirty-five-year correspondence to one another through letters, the first of which I received a month after she had left.

We never broke our promise to each other. Over the years it would be through letters from home that I would keep in touch with my family.

• • •

When I turned thirteen Uncle Russo told me he would open a store for me if I stayed with him, but I missed my family and I knew I needed to go home. Although my stay had unburdened my parents of another mouth to feed, I wasn't being paid by uncle Russo for my work at his store either. Oddly enough, it was actually my great grandmother, Yiayia Theopisti, who supported my decision the most. Over the last three years we had grown very close and she sensed my longing to see my family.

"Christo," she called to me one day. "Come here my precious, and let me see you."

"Yes, Yiayia," I said, settling myself on the floor by her chair.

"God willing, you will be a wise and successful man someday," she told me. "You will have a family of your own and you will be respected by everyone you meet. I wonder," she smiled, "will you remember your old Yiayia then?"

"Of course, how could I forget you?" We both laughed.

"There is a big world beyond these islands, Christo." Though she would never see that world, I was determined to find my way in it.

"There is so much to see and do. You won't be truly happy if you stay here." I found the honesty of her encouragement both guiding and pleasantly surprising. I recalled Papa's advice and my plan to go to America.

"Yes, you are right."

"Of course I am," she said, bringing her face close to mine and looking into my youthful eyes. Her eyes were warm and thoughtful and they had nurtured a light of confident hope within me.

For a while we both sat in silence as though we felt the breath of change stirring in the air around us.

The next day I made arrangements to return home in the coming weeks. Papa wrote that he would send Captain Koutris to fetch me at first light on November 10.

• • •

The sight of Captain Koutris at the dock that chilly winter morning stirred memories. His graying hair and haggard appearance spoke of the chronic poverty and blight that had become a way of life at home. I lifted my bags for him to stow in the little boat. Aunt Cleo had prepared two baskets of assorted foods for my family. When I turned around to say goodbye, Uncle Russo—who never had shown much emotion—grabbed me in a heartfelt embrace and slipped some money in my pocket.

Take care of yourself, child," he said with misty eyes. "We will miss you very much."

My great grandmother gave me an extended warm embrace.

By now Thea Cleo was weeping. "Chrysostomos, my child, what will we do without you? It is so hard to say goodbye."

I kissed my aunt and thanked them both one last time. With a final bow, which would become a lifelong habit, I turned to board the small boat.

Once again it was Mount Fengari that for a moment captured my attention in the receding silhouette of the island, triggering thoughts of Papa and stories of the ancient Gods.

Papa and Mama, whom I missed so dearly, I soon would see at last. Uncle Russo, Aunt Cleo, and my great grandmother stood on the dock waving until they were receding into tiny figurines on a distant shore. For as long as they could see me, I waved back, watching them recede in the distance, unaware at the time that I would never see them again.

CHAPTER 6

Homecoming

The West and East came face to face
at the second-class coastal town of Mudanya
on a crooked road covered with dust
on the hot Marmara coast.
Despite the English flagship Iron Duke*'s*
ash-colored deathly turrets
that transported the Allied generals
for negotiations with Ismet Pasha,
the Westerners had come here to beg for peace,
not to ask for peace or to dictate the conditions....
These negotiations demonstrate the end
of Europe's dominance over Asia,
because as everyone knows,
Mustapha Kemal got rid of all the Greeks.

—ERNEST HEMINGWAY, 1922

THE MAN I WAS BECOMING had matured beyond his years, yet the thought of my return home reminded me that I was still a child. I was filled with youthful excitement to see my parents, Costa, and Sultana—whom I had left almost four years ago—and to reunite with Katina.

As the little boat made its way across the water, I snuggled up in the stern to get some rest, much as I had done four years earlier on my ride to Samothraki. This time, though, my body was much larger, making the trip home a bit more uncomfortable. Eventually lulled once more by the gentle rocking waves, I dozed into a dreamless, timeless stupor, only to be awakened a half-dozen hours later by Captain Koutris once again.

"Christo," he called out, "wake up, you're home. There is Imbroz."

Startled, I roused instantly and rubbed my eyes. Then, in the clear cool autumn air, I caught sight of my island home, still a few kilometers off. I could make out the port in the distance, and after a while I could see people standing on the docks. Although I could not make them out, I knew it was my family waiting for my arrival.

Finally I got close enough to see their faces. Sultana and Costa were waving. Approaching in the dim light of dawn I could see that Papa looked a little pale and somewhat older than I remembered, but his broad smile covered his worn appearance. As soon as we docked I grabbed my bags and scrambled ashore. Costa and Sultana reached me first.

"Chrysostomos!" I heard Mama's voice next. An instant later I was in her warm embrace.

• • •

On our walk home I noticed how different everything looked. Neglect and overgrowth were irregularly apparent. Before I left, the wounds to the land and people were fresh. Now I saw firsthand the sad, decaying remains of epidemic neglect and abuse. A broken wagon rusted on the side of the road. A fence was in disrepair, its posts leaning at angles. As we approached Panayia, the scene worsened.

All the houses along the road were vacant, their windows knocked out, their walls falling in upon themselves. Vegetation overgrew abandoned properties. I had never seen Imbroz with such a look of desolation. The dreary face it showed me that day would haunt me for the rest of my life.

Suddenly I spied our house, and there was Papa's little store which had been boarded shut. His convenience store had once been the bustling center of activity for our town, but now stood as a memorial to the blight that had enveloped the island. Papa sighed when I pointed out the "Closed" sign plastered above the entrance, and it served as a stark reminder that I was back on Turkish-occupied

Imbroz. Still, I couldn't help but be relieved seeing my family after such a long time.

It was late autumn in 1931, and a month later I would turn 14 years old. Out of necessity I had grown up more quickly than most. At that moment, though, I felt like the boy I had been deprived of being. The familiarity of home and family gave me a sense of warm security, and I wished the moment would never pass.

The next morning I slept in to the unheard hour of nine. Shortly after I awoke, Demetri Terzes came by to see me. He was a childhood friend from school who lived in our neighborhood. He was a little taller than I was, but we were the same age. Despite the passage of years, his bushy brown hair and dark eyes were unchanged and formed a contrast to my fair features, as was the case with most Greek boys I met.

Neither of us was sure what we were going to do with our lives, but we knew there was no future for us on Imbroz. Within two weeks I had made plans with Demetri and Yanni Apistola, another childhood friend who was three years older than we were, to go to Constantinople—Istanbul, as it is now known—to seek our fortunes. We would leave by the next Monday to catch a steamboat docked off the shore of Castro. We would take our chances in Byzantium, Constantine's City on Seven Hills. We could not afford to wait another month for the next ship.

• • •

The time for our journey came quickly. That Sunday, Mama made some porridge for breakfast, along with tea and *tsoreki,* which was normally saved for New Year's or Easter. Afterwards, we readied for church. Mama called out for Maria Karazou, Jimmy's aunt, as we walked across our yard.

"My goodness," Maria said, glancing at me. "You have become such a big boy, and I know your parents are very proud of you." She turned to Mama, "Jimmy is still away studying at Halki Seminary."

Then she turned to me, saying, "you will see him again one day, Christos, I'm sure." I nodded assuredly, not having the faintest idea of when we would ever meet again.

While Mama and Jimmy's aunt carried on with small talk during the walk to church, Sultana held Katina's hand and Costa held mine. The walk passed uneventfully and for a few minutes I forgot how brief my time at home with my family had been.

When we arrived at church the service had already started. Papa walked to our usual bench two rows back on the left side. The church was only about a third full. Since many of the younger parishioners had fled the island, the few who remained were older, and they looked more worn and gaunt than I remembered, yet many of their faces were still familiar to me. When they lifted their voices in song, I noticed that our once vibrant and plentiful choir had been reduced to no more than a handful of voices.

At once I saw Bishop Iakovos behind the altar. He walked a little more slowly and his hair and beard had turned completely white, giving him a rather saintly aura and cherubic look.

"Parishioners, my children," Iakovos began, "these are difficult times we live in, not only for Imbroz but for the world. The economic depression in Europe and America reaches throughout the globe. Our misery has been compounded by the loss of our small island's isolated and vibrant economy because of our Turkish intruders. We have endured their rule against law and God for ten years, and there appears to be no end in sight for us." He paused, gazing hard into the eyes of his congregation. When he continued, his voice was steely.

"I can remember days when this church was filled with worshipers," the Bishop went on, "and the handful of you who remain are the bravest of our brethren. Our gathering here on this day is evidence to God, our Lord Jesus Christ, that although the Turks have taken our lives, our properties, our language, and our schools, they cannot take our faith or crush our indomitable will.

"Although we are few in number, our resolve is immutable. As long as there is one Greek Christian alive on Imbroz, the traditions of our culture will survive. Even a flicker can become a flame. Our humility, our hope, and our honesty will sustain us in the face of this cruel conquest that has uprooted so many of our brothers and sisters. We will face this test by the Almighty together. Fate and necessity often expose life's fragility, yet our will confirms life's strengths."

His voice thundered above the congregation and people anxiously stirred, even as their faces were flushed with excitement and a unity of spirit. This was dangerous talk.

"In God's name we pray," he concluded. "In the name of the Father, the Son, and the Holy Spirit, Amen."

"Amen," the congregation responded in unison.

"Almighty God please watch over our Yanni, Demetri, and Chrysostomos and protect them in their journey to Constantinople, young men seeking their fortune, Amen," Bishop Iakovos prayed.

• • •

Katina planned a small farewell party for us for that evening. A few family members and friends came over to celebrate with us on the night before we left.

Mama was busy preparing Sunday dinner, which had all the makings of a special holiday. Mrs. Karazou came out on the porch to join me. "Chrysostomos," she said, "you will begin an adventure tomorrow going to Constantinople. Are you excited?"

"Yes," I answered confidently, smiling broadly. It would be an adventure, just as Jimmy's aunt said, and it would all begin tomorrow morning.

The evening passed quickly. Our little party had been warm and merry. No one seemed to choose to focus on the sadness of parting, preferring instead to focus on the prospects of the future for me, Demetri, and Yanni, who were also full of youthful exuberance.

Neither of them had even been off Imbroz, and their excitement was evident as they expounded all the feats they would accomplish in Constantinople, each trying to outdo the other, until their predictions of fame and fortune became so outlandish that even they were laughing.

As I watched them vie for the attention of Katina—and, indeed, anyone who would listen—I sat alone on the porch, feeling more uncertain of my future. From the darkness, Papa called to me and found my side.

"Chrysostomos, you remember the talk we had before you went to Samothraki?"

"Yes, Papa. You told me to go to America." I didn't ask him how he thought I might get there, but said instead, "I haven't forgotten. I'll find a way to America one day, Papa."

"Of course, you will," Papa reassured me. "When you get there, I would like you to help your brother and sisters. Try to stay together, whatever happens to us." The weight of my father's impassioned plea spread over me like a warm blanket.

"I will, Papa, I will." I nodded.

"Christo, I want you to wear this," Papa said.

He extended out his hand to reveal a quarter-sized brass and gold colored coin encased in a large ring. A smaller ring with a hook was attached.

"What is it?" I asked curiously.

"It is a very ancient relic coin. Some say it dates back to before Christ, and others claim it has pieces of the Cross in it," Papa told me. "It has been in our family for generations and now it is yours. Wear it all the time, next to your heart. It is a holy relic and God will protect you and watch over you every day of your life if you are wearing this."

My eyes were transfixed on the worn, tarnished coin. It appeared to have a faded, primitive rendering of a figure with a halo. "I will, Papa, I promise." Papa carefully placed a safety pin through the hook of the coin and into my t-shirt over my heart. The relic coin would stay pinned there for the rest of my life.

Our eyes locked in the sober sadness of a likely final separation between father and son. Papa realized his boy might be leaving for good. It was the winter of 1931. The times often required separation, and it had occurred so painfully twice in my early life.

"What type of work do you want to do when you get to Constantinople?" Papa asked, trying to change the subject.

To be honest it had never even occurred to me to think about what I wanted to do. "I don't know, but I'll find something."

"Yes," he nodded. "You will. And Chrysostomos," he went on, "wherever you go, always be honest and fair. Don't take advantage because of your position. No matter how high you go, be respectful."

"Yes, Papa." I smiled.

"One more thing," my father cut me off with a smile. "Walk like a king, with dignity and humility, and one day you will be as a king... and don't forget to bow." We both laughed.

I never forgot Papa's words to me that evening. Although the journey would be only a little more than two hundred miles east to Constantinople, it would be far different from the one I had made to Samothraki four years before. This time I was truly on my own.

Mama came out on the porch to join us. "My, such serious talk for such a young man, Yanni. Chrysostomos," she said, turning to me, "I have something for you, too." Smiling, she held out a beautiful jacket of pure silk along with a pair of trousers. "Here, try it on."

I turned and slid my arms into the luxurious jacket one at a time. It was a little big, allowing for my growth, and I was enormously proud to wear it. The trousers were also silk, and off-white in color. I knew she must have worked for months to make this suit for me.

"Thank you, Mama" I said, moved deeply by her kindness.

"Wear it in good health," she told me. "You will need a proper jacket in Constantinople. Now you have one."

Gratefully, I reached out to embrace her. I have kept the jacket and pants she made me all my life, just as I have the relic coin. These became the material keepsakes of my youth, connections to my past.

"Come now," my mother said, briskly pulling herself from my arms. "Let's go to sleep. Tomorrow is a big day."

"Thank you, Mama. Thank you, Papa." I went upstairs where everybody was asleep except Katina.

"Chrysostomos, do you think I will ever leave this island?" she asked.

"Of course, Katina, you will leave here someday. We will all leave eventually." She looked at me with wide and fearful eyes. Suddenly I realized she was almost a grown woman. She trusted what I said and I knew I had better do my best to make it a reality for her.

"You must promise me you will write me with all your news, and I will write you back," Katina said. "You are going to Constantinople, Chrysostomos. How exciting!"

"I will, I promise, and you must promise to tell me in your letters how Mama and Papa are doing. The truth," I entreated sternly for good measure.

"Of course, I will," she promised.

"I will be back," I said as I fell into bed, "but you must take care of them while I am away. I will find work and send you money. Don't worry," I assured her again.

Costa, who had been listening silently from under his covers, started to cry. "Will you take me to Constantinople with you?" he asked.

"Oh Costa, not yet. You are now the man of the house and need to stay at home and help Mama and Papa. But I will call for you when you are older."

"You promise, Chrysostomos?" Costa asked in a serious tone. "You won't forget?"

"I won't forget," I assured him.

"What about me?" asked Sultana, who had been listening intently from bed, as well. "Will you call for me, too, Chrysostomos?"

"Yes, Sultana, one day I will call for you, too!"

I opened my arms wide to embrace my three siblings, promising them I would never forget them. I had no idea how, but I had promised them all that I would send for them, and I was determined to keep my word.

Tired from an emotional day, I eventually slipped into my bed one last time before my departure.

• • •

The Aegean Sea

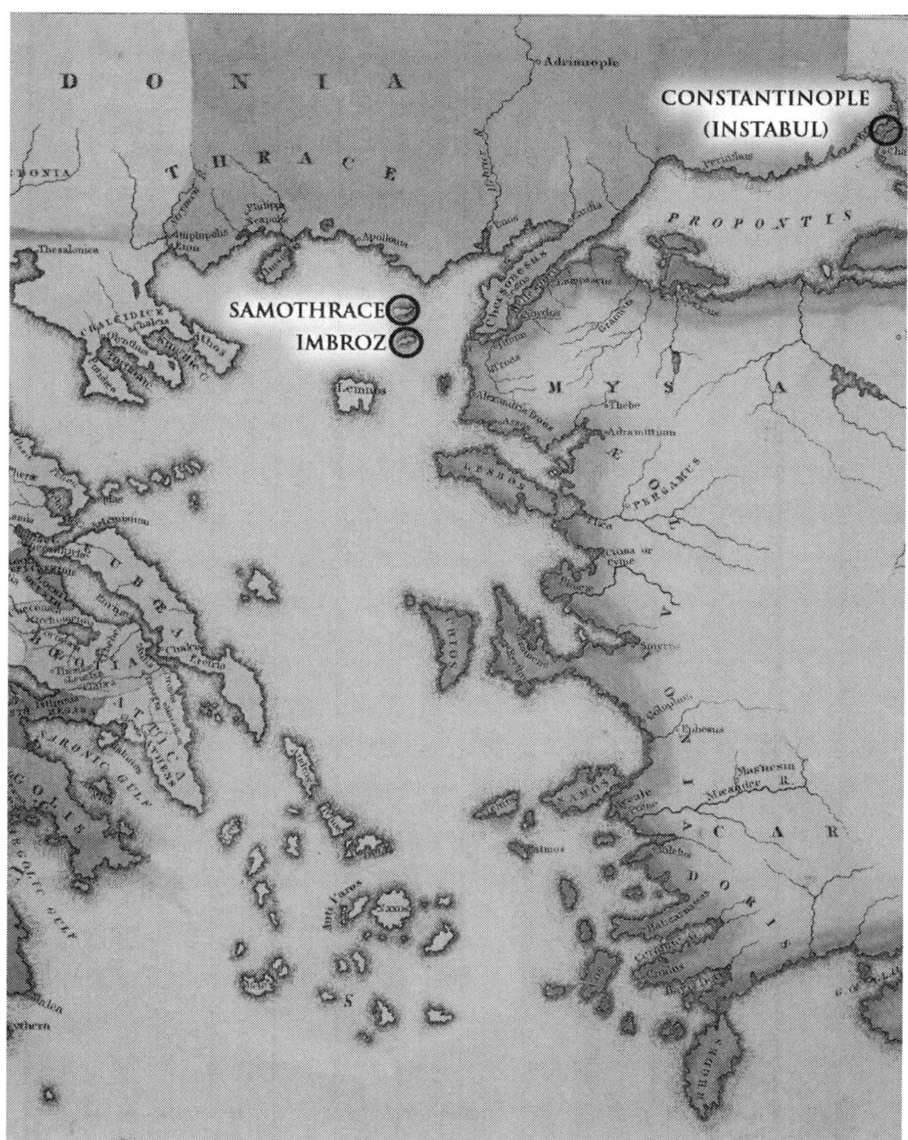

The odyssey of my life would truly begin.

All four of us were awake before the sun the next morning, but we waited until we heard Mama and Papa stirring downstairs before we rose and dressed. Soon enough Mama was calling us for breakfast. We had hot tea and porridge along with yesterday's leftover bread, which Mama warmed up on the stove. This fueled us for our walk to Castro where Captain Koutris would meet us to ferry my two friends and me three miles offshore to the steamboat that would take us to Constantinople.

Mama had packed my things, including my carefully folded silk suit, inside the same small, worn suitcase. I still had half the money Theo Russo had given me—the rest I had given to Mama—and Papa gave me boat fare. Costa took my hand and Sultana cried. A similar scene played out nearby with Demetri, Yanni, and their families. A few moments later we all boarded the boat and headed out to sea, three young compatriots leaving their homes to pursue their fortunes. As we moved away from shore, I watched as Mama and Papa's images fade into the horizon.

When I left Imbroz that day, such a long time ago, it was to find work and my way through a world in crisis. I clutched my medallion coin tightly under my t-shirt and glanced over at my friends, who both stared somberly back at me. Captain Koutris rowed us toward the steamboat, where the hopes and dreams for our futures awaited us. His words upon departing as I recall were "Going to America, are you? God bless you all and I wish you the best." We thanked him as we boarded the steamboat

• • •

The steamboat journey took a little over a day. We went through the Dardanelles and the Sea of Marmara to the mouth of the Bosporus and Constantinople. The journey in this larger vessel seemed much longer as it cut through small swells at about ten knots. The whole trip took us a day and a half to complete.

After we had been at sea for about four hours, we sighted the mainland. The wind had been at our backs and we had made good time. From that point on we kept land in our sight, seeing only a few towns.

The closer we travelled to Constantinople, the cooler the weather got. It was autumn and we all had sweaters and jackets on, knit by our mothers. The late autumn breeze over the water was chilling. There were few heavy clothes in our bags, though, as we hadn't endured the cold much on our small island.

We exchanged silent stares as we neared our destination, sensing the enormity of the change about to occur for each of us. Then, suddenly, there it was, the historic city founded by Constantine, a Roman Christian. This was the city that had served as the seat of Christendom for eleven centuries until the Mohammedan Ottomans conquered it in 1453.

Our uncertain futures waited as we approached the shore to dock. It was here, in the rightful home of Christians, that three young Greek boys would fight to find their way. The sun was setting as we approached Constantinople, and we could see the lights of the city in the distance.

Although in the last four years I had spent barely a month at home, I realized that my life's odyssey—in true Greek fashion—was only now beginning in earnest.

CHAPTER 7

City Lights

Gold and silver we will tell them
that they have from God;
the diviner metal is within them,
and they have therefore no need
of the dross which is current among men,
and ought not to pollute the divine
by any such earthly admixture;
for that commoner metal has been the source
of many unholy deeds....
And this will be their salvation,
and they will be the saviors of the State.

—PLATO, 380 B.C.

WHEN WE ARRIVED in the fall of 1931, the last remnants of the day were fading into the city's flickering lights. Like a glowing tapestry, the shoreline had no visible end. As the last rays of sunlight disappeared, the intensity of the manufactured lights magnified. Even the Bosporus Sea itself bore a faint, reflected glow. Lanterns were mounted on the boats we passed in the harbor as we entered the docking area. It was the first time any of us had seen electric lights—let alone a whole city illuminated by them—and the glittering sight enchanted us.

I gathered up my things and began to disembark with my friends. Before setting foot onto the soil of Constantinople, I instinctively said a prayer and pressed my hand against my relic coin. As we disembarked we paused uncertainly, bags in hand. None of us had ever seen anything like Constantinople before. It was breathtaking.

"Look at this!" Yanni exhaled loudly, his arms sweeping wide to embrace the scene. For a long moment we stood speechless, three island boys gaping at the city in awe.

Finally, Yanni turned to me. "Where are we going to go, Christo?"

"Well, first we should find a place to stay, I guess." My eyes travelled along the dock to a wooden shanty on the left. At the corner of the structure I saw the image of a large man standing in the dim light smoking a cigarette.

"We had better find a place soon," Demetri shot back. "It's already dark."

Yanni's eyes followed mine and rested on the man by the shanty. "Sir," he called out in his best Turkish. "Excuse me, sir, can you please tell us where we might find a boarding house?" Demetri and I looked at each other, not sure that it was wise for us to be talking to this stranger. As the man surveyed us a slight grin crossed his face.

"Go down to the end of this road," he said, his eyes glancing in the direction we were heading. "Then turn left and walk up the hill toward Pera. That's the Christian part of the city. Or, if you wish, walk a little farther south and you will be in Galata, the heart of the Muslim section." He paused. "Where are you boys from?"

"We're from the island of Imbroz," I responded in Turkish.

"Such a long way from home, island boys," he laughed.

"Yes, it has been a long journey, and we are very tired. A boarding house would be most appreciated, sir," I reminded him.

"A boarding house. Oh, yes. Well, in that case continue walking up the hill into Pera for about ten or twelve blocks and you'll see boarding houses. At the top of the hill, you can see the Bosporus on one side and the Sea of Marmara beyond the Golden Horn on the other. Up on a hill in the European side of town you will see Pera Palace, where diplomats and kings stay. Perhaps," he laughed, "you might find a room there or dine with the Pasha."

We ignored the teasing and I thanked the man in my best Turkish. As we scurried off, Demetri whispered under his breath, "You know, we named my dog Pasha and used to call for him in plain view of the Turks."

"That's funny," I said, checking behind my shoulder to make sure the man was out of earshot.

At the road's end, we turned to the left toward the Christian side of Constantinople. This was Pera, the wealthier half of the city. Ironically, most of the civil service jobs in the city at that time were held by Christians, and most of the commerce was handled by the Christian and Jewish minorities rather than the Turks. Even the Young Turks, who had slaughtered millions of Christians, couldn't run the city without them.

As we crossed the bridge that separated the Mohammedan and Christian sections of the city, I couldn't help but notice the beauty of Pera Palace. What appeared to be a grand dining room was visible to our right and overlooked the intersection of the Golden Horn and the Patriarchate in the distance as we crossed into Pera. Through the illuminated windows, I could make out elegant ladies and formally dressed gentlemen dining inside. I knew the older man back at the dock was kidding when he suggested we stay there, but I couldn't take my eyes off the hotel—it was so beautiful. I knew from the moment I set eyes on it that I would work there someday.

After a ten or fifteen-minute walk, the road became paved and we reached the more populated part of the city. Although the air was chilly and the temperature dropping, our brisk walk and our excitement from the bustling city made the cold hardly noticeable.

This great city, meant to reflect the glories of Christianity, was now, like my home of Imbroz, in the hands of the Young Turks. As the religious hub of the Byzantine period, Constantinople was full of shrines, historic relics, and temples for worship, many of which had been sacked, looted, and destroyed over time by the Mohammedan Turks.

The great Hagia Sophia, which had served as the Patriarchal cathedral for over nine hundred years during the Byzantine Empire, was even mimicked across its courtyard by the Blue Mosque with its six minarets. The cathedral itself was turned into a mosque by the Ottomans in 1453, and later a museum by the Young Turks in 1935. The leader of the Orthodox faithful was relegated to a small church in the Patriarchate compound about two miles away. The compound was a modest, walled-in block with a church and dormitories for the bishops—a type of Vatican City for Orthodox Christians minus the opulence and grandeur.

The Turkish presence was everywhere, from teahouses to Topkapi Palace—the residence of Kemal Mustapha's secular Turkey still seemed populated by the Ottoman sultans. Walking its streets, I wasn't sure how it all fit together, but I was sure that the Turks were responsible for my present condition. The city might now be called Istanbul, but in my mind it will always be Constantinople.

The streets were crowded with a multitude of people, some dressed in finery, others ragged and hungry. Beggars mingled with European aristocrats and greeted us at every corner.

"Do you have some money, please?" a voice rasped from the shadows.

A thin man in dirty rags appeared, his sharp hungry eyes fixed on us like those of a wolf on a nest of rabbits. We moved past him quickly. We were beginning to sense that, for as much splendor and glitter as the city held, it had an equally dark and dismal side full of misery and danger.

Eventually we came to a boarding house with a sign that read, "Room with a Tub." I suggested we look some more, but Yanni was tired and had already started to walk to the door. It was ten o'clock at night and we had had a long day and a half of travels.

Once inside we learned that the room indeed had a tub, but only one mattress. Yanni and Demetri haggled the landlord down from 900 to 850 lira. We paid half up front and took the room, thinking we could change the next month if we found something more suitable.

To those accustomed to indoor plumbing it may have been irritating, or even amusing, to discover that, though our room had a tub, there was no running water. However, in the hall outside our door there was an electric light bulb—an unimagined luxury. With light from the hallway illuminating the room, we pondered the single mattress, knowing that the three of us could never fit on it together.

Yanni and Demetri glanced at the tub, and then my way, visually measuring me. I knew that of the three of us I was the one—at five feet six and 130 pounds—who could most easily fit into the tub. Reluctantly, I dragged my bags across the little room, changed into my long johns, and climbed into my "bed." I rolled up some of my belongings, put them under my head, and covered myself with the small blanket Mama had packed, reminding myself that one day soon I would find better accommodations. With that final thought, I was soon sound asleep.

• • •

The next morning I was up at dawn. Letting the others sleep, I went down the hall to find a bathroom. I found a steel sink with an oversized basin and a commode. The commode was made of wood and had a pipe attached that dropped straight down to the sewer, which made the smell hard to mask. Still, it seemed quite an improvement over the outhouses back on Imbroz.

I threw some water on my face and hands and dried off with a hand towel my mother had packed. I returned to the room, grabbed my jacket, and decided to go out and have a look around. Breakfast would wait until Yanni and Demetri were up.

I walked down the three flights of stairs and out through the front door without seeing anyone. The street was empty except for the smell of coffee coming from an all-night coffeehouse a few doors down. I followed the scent inside, the aroma of coffee blanketed by the odor of cigarette smoke forming clouds above each occupied table. Most of the patrons appeared to have been there all night. A large man with an apron came up and asked in Turkish if he could help me.

"No thanks," I said, backing out the door. I was hungry, but I didn't have extra money for food.

Returning to the boarding house, I found a cup in the bathroom and filled it with water. Back in our room I divided up the bread, cheese, and olives Mama had packed for me into three separate piles, then roused my roommates.

• • •

Our food ran out in the first week, and we had little money more than the month's rent we had paid. Every day, from morning to night, we had looked for jobs with no luck. Work was impossible to come by, and the streets appeared filled with the unemployed, some looking for jobs and others for handouts.

During the second week I found a possible job in a grocery store about twenty-five minutes from the boarding house. The store was owned and operated by an Armenian Christian named Raki. "I am looking for a part-time delivery boy as well as someone to straighten the store, stock shelves, and clean," he told me. "How old are you?"

"17, sir," I lied, standing rigidly to convey maturity. I would be 14 in December.

"You're Greek?"

"Yes, sir, from Imbroz."

"I don't need you today, but come tomorrow at six in the morning," he said. "The person you're replacing fell sick, and I only need you until he returns," he went on, dictating the terms of the job. "Do you understand? We will provide you one meal while you're working, no food to be taken home, understand?"

"Yes, I do. Thank you, sir." I bowed slightly on instinct, struggling to hide my gratitude. "I will be here in the morning—at six."

My job at the grocery store included delivering orders all over the city—usually in Pera, but sometimes I was sent to the center of the Mohammedan side, which was about an hour walk one way.

I was paid 100 lira a week, plus tips. In order to stretch my monthly wage I ate almost exclusively at the grocery store for the entire first year. It was my first job in Constantinople and I was determined to make the best of it. I was told I was lucky to find work so quickly, and the more that time went on, the more I realized that was true. It was often said, and not in jest, that to get a job in Constantinople at that time you usually had to wait until someone died. In my case, the sick man I replaced never returned.

"Chrysos…" Raki struggled with my name.

"Christo is fine, sir," I offered.

"Ok, Christo, take this list of groceries to Mrs. Duma in the Turkish sector," he told me on my second day, "and be sure to collect."

Raki gave me directions and a grocery list. I went to the back of the store, collected the groceries and the bill, and was on my way. I might collect a tip at my destination, but many times I would get nothing.

As I quickly found out, it was very difficult to carry a bag of groceries down the city's beggar-filled streets.

"Hey, boy, come here!" A shriveled hand in a tattered garment beckoned within three feet of me. "Come here, can't you hear me, boy?"

"Sorry, I'm on delivery," I said in Turkish, quickly veering from the man's path, but passing close enough to smell his stench.

"Some bread, please, I am starving!" An unending stream of beggars littered the street.

"Please, some food! I've not eaten in a week. Please!"

"Hey, boy, what do you have there? Come here, let us see," a shabbily dressed heavyset man called to me in Turkish while his two friends smirked over my obvious unease. "Did you hear me, boy? I said come here!" A second later he began striding in my direction.

Sensing trouble I dashed quickly down the street, breaking into a jog. I was responsible for getting the groceries to their destination, and there was no way I was going to give them up to a street beggar. I heard the laughter of the men behind me as I darted away.

The beggars were a sad element of an impoverished and repressed society that had given up hope. Not all beggars in the Turkish section were old and feeble; some were relatively young and as healthy as I was. I felt sorry for them but I had no money to help them either. They served as a loathsome, frightful reminder of life that lurked around the fringes of the workforce. I reminded myself that it was a life that, for so many of us, was only a heartbeat away.

In Pera the streets were cobblestone, but in the poorer Turkish section they were mostly dirt. Finally, I found Mrs. Duma's row house. She answered my knock but ignored my greeting. When I put the groceries down and gave her the bill, she silently handed me the money.

"Would you like me to help you put the groceries away?" I asked.

Mrs. Duma shook her head and slammed the door shut. Despite the distance I had come, she never offered me a tip or a word of thanks.

• • •

Work with Raki was hard and demanding. I would try to arrive at first dawn, which meant I had to get up in the dark. In the morning I touched my toes to stretch twenty-five times, then cleaned my face, hands, and upper body by throwing water on myself in the bathroom since there was no shower. Finally, I pinned my father's relic coin on my t-shirt over my heart, buttoned up my shirt, and left our room.

When I arrived at work, Raki would usually have me do a series of chores to help open the store, many of which were familiar from my work with Papa and Uncle Russo. Afterwards, he would give me some bread and tea, and occasionally a piece of dry, light yellow *kasari* cheese. I performed my duties at the store quickly and eventually took over many of Raki's responsibilities. He always had me make the larger deliveries, and, although he had another helper, over time I became something of a manager.

The first month I was the only one working, but soon Yanni got a job working on a fishing boat in the Sea of Marmara. By the third month Demetri had a job at a butcher's shop. Yanni and Demetri were not lazy; it was just very hard for young Christian boys to find work in the city in the 1930s. By the third month I started sending money home in letters to my sister—a practice I continued for thirty-four years.

Dear Katerina,

I have a job in a grocery store working for an Armenian Christian. Enclosed please find 50 lira for Mama and Papa. Please give my love to everyone. Say hello to anyone you may see. I miss you all.

Love,
Chrysostomos

That year I sent about 500 lira to Mama and Papa. I also got three days off from work that year—the day before Easter, Easter Day, and a personal day to buy clothes. Although Raki wouldn't open the store to customers after church on Sunday, he always expected me to be there. The few purchases I made were for a pair of shoes, pants, two shirts, underwear, and some other essentials, all of which cost me 300 lira. I managed to save almost 400 lira.

In my first year I also started to collect menus and bought a notebook to write down French cuisine. In Constantinople the best restaurants were exclusively French and all the waiters spoke French fluently. I realized speaking French was a requisite for upward mobility in the city, so I began to teach myself the language.

My first menus were from the two most luxurious hotel restaurants in Pera. I studied the French on the menus for the next two years, using them like textbooks as well as for food presentation, and made notes in the margins. In this way my menu collection became something of a journal, and I would keep this journal updated for several years.

I meticulously pasted daily specials on the pages of my notebook, then carefully wrote out recipes in French. I had a good memory. If I saw or heard something once and focused on it, I would remember it. Collecting the menus of great restaurants and teaching myself French was more than a hobby. It was a way to improve myself, and was another step toward my goal of working at Pera Palace.

• • •

In the fall of 1933 I was approaching my 16th birthday and fairly conversant in French by this time, at least menu French. I went to a club in Pera that a friend had recommended and was immediately hired as a waiter. Although I didn't particularly like the late hours or the clientele, my schedule would give me days off to spend time at Pera Palace to study its operations. Besides, the club was a popular spot and I would be able to make more than twice the salary I was making at the grocery store.

The next morning I went to Raki and gave him two weeks' notice. It would be my policy to leave every job on good terms so that, if need be, I could return. Working for Raki was my first job in Constantinople and I had been with him for over two years. During the first week of my notice Raki tried to talk me out of leaving, but my time with him—long days carting heavy deliveries for miles—was over. Still it was my habit to leave on good terms. In fact there has never been an employer, starting with Papa and Uncle Russo, that I couldn't return to or who did not want me to stay.

My new salary, with tips, had doubled. I immediately made arrangements to move into a small apartment as well. The apartment had access to a sink with running water, electricity, a hot plate to cook on, and a semi-private bathroom. I gave Yanni and Demetri notice. They were both working and could easily afford the rent without me.

Before I left, I took one last look at the tub I had slept in for almost two and a half years. Since I had arrived in Constantinople I had grown about four inches, which made my nights sleeping in the tub increasingly uncomfortable. I slept with knees drawn up first on one side, and then the other—but usually I was so tired from my days at the grocery store that it didn't matter. It was hard to believe that in my new apartment I would have a real bed, which was an unimagined luxury for me.

I was sure I would continue to see Yanni and Demetri after I moved, but my busy work schedule meant I saw less and less of them as time went by. I left my old apartment and began my new life in high spirits reflecting back on my first arrival in Constantinople. No longer was I awed by the city of crossroads, by the mixed crowds of haves and have nots, by the colors and lights, for I had become a Constantinopolitan myself, a city boy. I wrote happily to Katina a couple of weeks later.

Dear Katerina,

I have left Raki and gotten a job as a waiter in a club in Pera. I have also moved to a new apartment. My new address is at the top of this letter. I am now able to send more money. Enclosed you will find 150 lira to give to Papa. Regards to everyone.

Love,
Chrysostomos

My spirits were renewed daily by my desire to succeed and help my family at home. Although not yet 17 years old, I was confident my life was moving in a positive direction. The starkly vacant structures of Byzantium stood as a reminder of the culture that had thrived for eleven centuries. They were now ghostly, drab, vacant edifices. I had navigated the realities of the city. For me, Pera Palace stood as an oasis of civility for me. That is where I belonged.

CHAPTER 8

Waiter at Last

Out of the mud two strangers came
and caught me splitting wood in the yard,
and one of them put me off my aim
by hailing cheerily "Hit them hard!"
I knew pretty well why he had dropped behind
and let the other go on a way.
I knew pretty well what he had in mind:
he wanted to take my job for pay.
—ROBERT FROST, 1936

THE NIGHTLIFE OF CONSTANTINOPLE in late 1935 was fast and furious. I was making good money at the club, but I was already restless. It would be better to work daytime hours, I decided, rather than late at night. The drinking and carousing at the club was not something I enjoyed, anyway. I had never forgotten my goal to work at Pera Palace, which was about a twenty-five-minute walk from my new apartment. For some unknown reason, I associated it with my future success and, as such, I was spending nearly all my extra time there.

I left early each morning for the club, passing Pera Palace on my way. I would often stop and watch a small army of waiters and busboys setting up the dining rooms for lunch. Mirrored walls reflected large marble columns and dazzling crystal chandeliers that hung elegantly over each table. Chairs upholstered in velvet were drawn up to the tables, which were covered with white linen and adorned with polished silver and freshly pressed satin napkins. I stared in awe at the waiters who were serving Pera's legendary cuisine on gleaming china.

I would sometimes leave for work extra early just to watch the wait staff readying the room for breakfast, as well. I often wore the silk suit that Mama had made for me and eventually I got to know a few of the waiters by sight.

In the tradition of a fine French restaurant there was a captain who supervised the waiters and staff, as well as a *maître d'* who greeted the guests. The staff was also multi-cultural, composed of Turks, Greeks, Armenians, French, Russians, Africans, and Italians. However, all were manicured to fit seamlessly into the colorful tapestry that was Pera Palace.

One day the captain noticed me standing in the service entrance.

"What can I do for you?" he asked in French.

"Nothing, sir. I'm just watching, with your permission," I said in my best French and offered him a polite bow. The captain was a big man, with a dark handlebar mustache, jet-black hair, and a broad face. Although he spoke French, his name was Memet Kahele, and he was unmistakably Turkish.

"Where are you from?" he asked in Turkish. Evidently, my "menu French" had not been that persuasive. Nonetheless, with my blue eyes and sandy colored hair it was not readily apparent that I was Greek.

"I am Greek, from Imbroz."

"Oh, an island boy from Imbroz. Are you looking for a job at Pera Palace? I don't need anyone," he said without waiting for an answer.

"I actually have a job at a club nearby," I told him. "I was just stopping by to watch," I responded.

"You can watch," the captain told me curtly, "but stay out of the way of my staff. Stand to the inside of the door—over there." He gestured with his hand to the wall directly inside the service entrance door while his keen eyes surveyed me.

"How old are you, anyway?" he asked abruptly.

"20," I answered quickly. I would turn 18 in mid-December.

"Well, we don't need anyone," he said, turning to walk away, "but you may keep checking with us. Maybe you will be lucky." Pausing, he appeared to lose interest, turned and left.

"Yes, sir," I gasped, and bowed respectfully. I quelled the excitement rising inside me. Jobs were no easier to come by in 1935 than they had been three years earlier, and many of the busboys were older men who had worked at Pera Palace for over twenty years.

• • •

The next day was my day off at the club. I arrived earlier than usual at Pera Palace. I stood in my suit for an hour and watched the end of the breakfast service and the setup for lunch. I know Memet saw me but he said nothing. I came again half a dozen times over the next two weeks, usually wearing my homemade suit. Even though a busboy's wage at Pera Palace, including tips, was a little less than I was currently making, I did not mind. I would not be a busboy forever, I decided, and waiters at Pera Palace did very well.

One day as Memet passed I bowed politely. "Nothing today," he said briefly. This continued over the next two weeks and I began wondering if I would ever be hired. I diligently returned time and again, though, whenever my time allowed, and soon two weeks stretched out to three months. Then, the unthinkable happened.

From my post at the right of the service door I saw Memet come out of the kitchen and start mopping the marble dining room floors. By now, I knew everyone's job and, in the past, an older gentleman had always done the mopping. A quick glance around confirmed his absence. I removed my silk jacket exposing my only white long sleeve shirt. On impulse, I strode over to Memet, bowed, and in one smooth movement took the mop from his hands. Without speaking, he submitted and released the mop to me. Finally, I had a chance to be of some help and show my worth.

I mopped the white marble floor of the Agatha Christie Ballroom in long straight lines as quickly and efficiently as possible, being careful to follow the wet mop with a dry mop so that customers would not slip and fall. I had spent so much time watching the old man who normally did this job that I knew exactly what to do without being told.

When I finished, I immediately took the mop and the bucket into the kitchen, a large bustling room with shiny stainless steel sinks and ovens and a white porcelain floor. Later, I would rinse, clean, and dry the mop, but right now there was no time. An assistant to the cook tipped his head toward a small closet.

Customers were beginning to come for lunch and the setup had not yet been completed. I moved quickly, arranging silver place settings and napkins at the tables. I had watched this procedure so many times I felt I could do it blindfolded.

After finishing the lunch setup I went back into the dining room. People were being seated by the *maître d'* while the waiters, in their black jackets and bow ties, stood patiently by their stations, some with hands folded behind their backs, others with crisp, white linen towels folded carefully across their bent forearms. This was the customary, formal manner of Pera Palace waiters.

The customers, meanwhile, had not noticed the anxious and hurried preparation, which is how it should be in good restaurants. I gleefully moved in an orderly manner to other tasks. After my long wait I was committed to a flawless performance.

Since no one had stopped me, I proceeded to fill glasses with ice water and placed them on a tray. Then I lifted the tray with the palm of my hand underneath, placing my other hand on the rim for balance. I stood to the left of each guest as I carefully placed a glass of water to the front left of each plate. I also started to clear the tables of departing guests and reset them exactly as I had seen it done so many times—with a dinner fork, a salad fork, a knife, and two spoons.

I smiled and bowed politely at each guest who looked my way. The tasks I performed that day were fluid and required little if any assistance by the regular staff. Busboys normally wore white jackets, but my plain white shirt and light-colored pants seemed to blend in enough so as not to arouse comment.

I knew Memet was eyeing me and I knew I was on trial. Since the time he had allowed me to stand by the door and observe, I had felt certain he would afford me a chance one day and here it was. A mistake might mean an end to my potential employment, so working as much from instinct and common sense as from experience, I spared no effort to do every task quickly and correctly.

After lunch, Memet approached me. "Are you hungry?" he asked. "You may go to the kitchen and eat now if you are." The question was rhetorical in those days, since everyone was hungry, but the offer of food was clearly evidence of his approval.

Regretfully, I shook my head. "No, thank you," I said politely. "I am late and they will be expecting me at the club."

Memet looked at me carefully. "You are very diligent," he said, his face betraying nothing. "Why don't you come by tomorrow at the same time?"

"Yes sir," I said. It took me a minute to understand that Memet had offered me a job, at least for another day. It was too good to be true. Being hired as a busboy in the Agatha Christie Ballroom of Pera Palace at 17 was a tremendous milestone in my young, hard life.

• • •

If Constantinople was the crossroads where East meets West, Pera Palace was Grand Central station. It was an important and very cosmopolitan hotel at the height of its celebrity. Pera Palace was a melting pot of espionage and intrigue, where the haunts of the European aristocracy dined, where heads of state and diplomats held clandestine rendezvous, where vestiges of the White Russian Army intermingled with wealthy Bulgarian and Armenian traders.

Pera Palace had dedicated suites to both Ernest Hemmingway and Greta Garbo, who visited in the 1920s as did many other notables. The posh dining room I had worked in that day got its name because Agatha Christie is said to have written *Murder on the Orient Express* in an upstairs room, now known as the Agatha Christie Suite. Everything about the place bespoke an opulent, first-class hotel restaurant. Filled to capacity, the Agatha Christie Ballroom and its bar seated over two hundred.

I could barely believe I had a job there, and the joy in my heart was indescribable. I gave the club a two-week notice and then began my career at Pera Palace. I learned later that the old man who had not shown up for work that day was named Albert Lamare. He had worked at Pera Palace for twenty-eight years and had died the night before. The saying had proven true—it literally had taken someone to drop dead before I got a job there.

• • •

On my first full day, Memet followed me into the kitchen where the breakfast cook was changing pans on the cooking line to prepare for lunch. The chef was to the side, taking freshly baked bread out of the oven and placing it in a warmer to serve for lunch. He had been preparing sauces, condiments, and soups from scratch for the luncheon menu. In those days, all chefs worth their salt prepared everything from scratch.

"Victor," Memet called out to the chef, "show Christo how to wash the dishes. He will help you clean up and prepare for lunch. Oh, and give him a white jacket before he returns to the floor." From the outset, I was to be somewhat of a handyman for Memet. His habit of putting me in service where I was needed complemented my quick mind and allowed me, over time, to master most of the restaurant's tasks, including food preparation.

Victor nodded and beckoned me over to a linen closet where he held up a smart-looking white jacket just about my size. The jacket had gold buttons down the front and completely covered the plain white shirt I was wearing.

After cleaning up the breakfast dishes, I returned to the dining room—this time properly attired in my jacket—and began to clean and set up for lunch. The area used for breakfast extended into two other rooms for lunch and dinner.

Lunch that first day was very busy. Besides my regular busing duties, Memet sent me on errands to fetch things from the laundry room and kitchen. After lunch I was given a dinner menu. It was required that a waiter memorize the French luncheon and evening specials every day and, though not required for busboys, it was a practice I embraced. I understood most of it and learned it by heart.

No member of the staff ate or drank during a meal service, but after lunch Memet took me to the kitchen and said something to the chef in French that I did not quite understand, something about leftovers. I soon was pleased to discover that leftovers did not mean food left on customers' plates, but soups or specials *du jour* that did not sell during meal time, all expensive and quite perishable. The restaurant was careful and efficient in this regard.

Gourmet meals were a benefit the entire staff enjoyed, even down to kitchen helpers and dishwashers. For many employees the food was a bonus that supplemented their wages and bound them to the mystique of the grand hotel. For the hotel it was an efficient way to have items consumed that were not ordered by customers It also had the benefit of allowing us to become familiar with the restaurant's cuisine, thereby making the waiters more authoritative when giving recommendations to customers.

"Christo," Memet told me finally, "you may go home now, but be back at six thirty in the morning."

"Yes, sir," I responded crisply. It was almost eleven thirty.

Without a word I bowed respectfully and left. I didn't even know what my pay would be. It was two weeks before I learned it would be about 200 lira a week, which I had been making at the club, although some months I could make more than that amount, dependent on the tips that waiters would give bus boys. It was customary for the waiters to share a nominal amount of the tips with the busboys.

Since it often involved preparation in the kitchen, my workweek was eighty to one hundred hours or more. I didn't get a day off during my first year, but I had no complaints. Memet's rules were simple: *I will give you a job and l will feed you, but you must arrive promptly every day and you cannot leave until I tell you.* This was fine with me.

In mid-December I would turn 18, yet I was led to believe by others that my maturity and poise far surpassed my years. I had been working for almost eight years and now I was working at the finest restaurant in Constantinople.

• • •

I didn't get to sleep that first night until well after midnight, but I was up at first light, very hungry and a little stiff from my long first day of work. Having no shower facilities, I washed my face, teeth, and underarms. The light fuzz on my face did not yet require shaving.

I touched my toes to stretch twenty-five times, dressed, pinned the relic coin on my t-shirt, and said a prayer of thanks to God. I left for work before six o'clock, hoping that I would be offered breakfast at the restaurant. When I arrived at Pera Palace it was barely six thirty and no one was there except the chef and his assistant.

"Good morning, sir," I said, bowing respectfully to the chef.

"You're here early," he commented.

"I'll start setting up for breakfast," I offered, donning my white busboy's jacket. The large crystal chandeliers had not been turned on in the dining room, but there was adequate light from the windows to do my breakfast setup. Within minutes a waiter arrived, a 40-year-old Greek named Aristis Plaka.

For several moments Aristis watched me setting up with an experienced eye. "What are you doing?" he asked me finally in Greek.

"Setting up for breakfast, sir," I responded.

"Make sure you crease the napkins like this," he said, making a fold and then applying pressure with his palm as if to iron the fabric.

I bowed my thanks and continued working.

A few minutes later Memet arrived. As soon as he saw me, he called me over. "Christo, Good morning."

"Good morning sir," I responded, a little nervous.

"Today is Saturday and we are having our buffet. I want you to come with me so that I can show you how we set it up."

He took me to a room off the dining room in the front of the house where there were long folded tables.

"These tables will be set up in a line like this," he said, motioning with his hands along the back wall of the room. "Allow room so customers may pass on both sides, Christo," he added, gesturing to another busboy. "Pedro will help you, and Aristis will supervise," Memet said with a side-glance. Aristis acknowledged begrudgingly with a head bowed over his morning coffee.

"Yes, sir," I responded automatically.

The tables were long and a little difficult to move, and we had to be careful not to bump them into anything. After setting them up and covering them with spotless white tablecloths, the chef's helper and I brought out large ornate chafing dishes from the kitchen, filled them with hot water, lit paraffin wax beneath them, then placed food trays on top.

By the time we had finished arranging the buffet, the chandeliers had been turned on, more than half the waiters had arrived, and guests were being seated. Another long workday had begun.

• • •

My 18th birthday came and went in December of 1935 and I seemed to have mastered all my assigned tasks at work and a few others as well.

I was working seven days a week, week in and week out, with my workdays stretching into fourteen hours or more. At first I was sore and tired from the rigors of my job, but after a while I grew used to my grueling schedule and even became proud of it. Although I planned to ask for a day off, I wanted to make sure that I was secure in my job first. I wanted to become irreplaceable.

I became quick friends with our chef, Victor Francois—a Frenchman trained in Paris who was fluent in German, English, and Turkish, and even conversant in Greek. Although the two of us normally spoke to each other in Turkish, he often helped me with my French.

He was a very skilled chef and prepared everything daily from scratch—breads, desserts, condiments, dressings, soups, and sauces—nearly an unheard of production method these days.

Some nights when I did not have time to eat properly, Victor gave me kitchen leftovers to take home. My diet was certainly much improved when I joined the staff at Pera Palace. I think possibly that the restaurant business attracts poor rural boys for this reason.

After I became established a few weeks later, I wrote my sister.

Dearest Katerina,

I have changed jobs and I am working at the restaurant in the Pera Palace Hotel where all the aristocrats of Europe dine. I am presently a busboy but I hope to be a waiter soon. Enclosed you will find 200 lira. Did you receive the money I sent last month? Hope everyone is well. Love and regards to Papa, Mama, Sultana, Costa, and anyone who might ask for me.

Love,
Chrysostomos

Six weeks later I received a response to my letter. It was good to get word from Katina and it was a relief to be able to send money home regularly.

Dearest Christo,

We were so excited to receive your letter. You are in our thoughts every day. We are all so proud that you found such good work. Please write again with all your news. Regards to Yanni and Demetri. Do you still see them?

Love from your sister,
Katerina

• • •

As time passed I continued to collect and study menus daily as an opportunity to improve my French and to expand my knowledge of food. My menu scrapbook served as a chronicle of my interest in the restaurant industry—a fascination born of necessity that proved very useful in my current job.

"Christo, you see how this is done," Victor told me in French, explaining a recipe to me one day. "The sauce must start with the correct *roux*." Victor's soups, sauces, and soufflés were what filled our dining rooms with customers. Never take shortcuts with food, he insisted. Always use the best ingredients and you will have the best results.

Increasingly, Victor or one of his helpers would ask me for a hand in preparing the food, and I became his apprentice of sorts. My ease in learning and eagerness in the kitchen made me an instant success.

"Christo, can you please help me prepare these Lyonnaise potatoes?" or, "Christo, I have a roast for the large party under the chandelier. Would you please baste it for me?" The requests went on and on. My knowledge of food grew considerably with Chef Victor in the kitchen, as did my respect for proper preparation.

The long hours and hard work of my first few months at Pera Palace were paying off. My self-taught French lessons were paying off, too, with Victor speaking French to me daily. I was an insatiable sponge and my energy and interest were inexhaustible. I had no doubt that one day soon I would be a waiter.

As time went on, I also continued to be the person whom Memet called upon most frequently. "Christo, where is the small cocktail table?" he would ask. "Please find it right away," or, "Christo, we have a party of twelve in the small dining room. Please do the setup." Even the waiters joined in. "Christo, will you please bring my wine from the kitchen?" or "Christo, check with the kitchen for my fruit bowl for that table in the corner." I stayed very busy and was in high demand.

• • •

It was January of 1936, and Memet had promised me a day off after the New Year. The lavish parties had tapered off some, perhaps due to the global depression, but the hotel remained full and something always seemed to come up to prevent me from taking a day. I finally did get my holiday in early spring.

That day there were many things I had to do. I posted a letter to Katina and enclosed another two hundred lira to Mama and Papa. I also went shopping for a new pair of shoes, two pairs of black slacks, two new white shirts, a bow tie, and a black waiter's jacket. It cost me almost two months' pay, but I viewed it as an investment in my future.

On my way back from the shop I stopped by the Patriarchate, which housed a Byzantine Orthodox church and the Patriarch—the spiritual leader of the Eastern Orthodox Church worldwide. The church was a small sanctuary with inconspicuous white walls on the outside and a blue rounded dome. The inside glistened with ancient gold relics and stained-glass windows, and the walls were adorned with brightly painted icons.

Although the Christian population had been purged in the genocide, I marveled how the immutable Patriarchate remained standing by the sheer indomitable will of its bishops, a Christian refuge from antiquity in the center of a Mohammedan world. Its walled-in block containing the Partriarch's church and dormitories for the bishops and monks served as a quaint admonition from the Hellenic period that had been erased. Although rich with icons and memorabilia, its modesty stood in sharp contrast to the opulence of the Vatican in Rome.

I thought of Jimmy, knowing he was still at the Halki Seminary. I offered a prayer thanking God for my good fortune and one for my family's health and welfare. It never hurt to pray.

Later that evening Demetri, Yanni, and I went to see a performance of the *Whirling Dervishes*, a Mohammedan sect who, as part of their religious ceremony, spun endlessly round and round. Yanni brought a bottle of *ouzo*, a Greek liquor with a distinct licorice flavor. It was as good an excuse as any for three teenage boys to reunite. We drank the liquor before the show. All three of us watched wide-eyed and captivated by this timeless ceremony. Upon leaving we spun in laughter until we all had fallen dizzy on the ground.

We then treated ourselves to a hot meal and some cold beer. We had much to celebrate together. We feasted and swapped stories and eventually, with the aid of alcohol and the food, we fell with the setting sun into a silent and reflective camaraderie.

No one spoke of homesickness, nor, strangely, even of Imbroz, but we all felt it. It was at the root of our bond together. As the night's darkness fell, we gradually shook the spell, and sadly said our farewells. Demetri and Yanni headed back to their room and I went home to get ready for work the next morning.

• • •

Rejuvenated and refreshed from my day off, I arrived at the restaurant early the next morning as was my habit. I wore my new white shirt, black slacks, and shoes, and I set up the whole dining room for breakfast by myself, all the while reliving the fun memories of my night out on the town.

When Memet arrived I gathered my nerve, looked him directly in the eyes, and addressed him in my best French.

"I would like to become a waiter," I said, staring into his eyes and trying not to flinch.

"In time you will wait tables, Christo," he promised.

That night, by chance, two waiters did not show for dinner. As I was well aware by now, necessity often invites promotion in the restaurant business. With Memet's blessing and Aristis's assistance, I waited on my first party that evening. They were an older couple, distinguished in appearance and expensively dressed. The older man wore a white dinner jacket, and his wife, her silver hair piled luxuriously high, wore a beautiful ruby-studded pearl necklace. They appeared to be German, but their French was perfect.

I bowed and asked for their order as if I had been a waiter all my life. I was being watched; I was on trial. At Pera Palace everything had to be done right. The man turned to his wife, "What will you have, my dear?"

"What would the young man recommend?" she replied.

"Tonight, we have *Potage creme d'Orge*" I said smoothly, "as well as *Langousta en belle vue sauce remoulade, Sigara borek, Perdreaux rotis pommes frites, salade verte, Kadin gobagi au kaymak, Corbeilles de fruits*, and *Café*."

"That sounds perfect," she responded with approval.

"Then I'll have the same," her husband added.

This was my cue to bow. "Right away," I said sharply in French and headed to the kitchen.

It was a waiter's task to be inconspicuous and make the meal delightfully uneventful. The dinner I served the German couple went well, and afterwards I collected my first tip as a waiter, 100 lira—the same as my full week's wage when I was working for Raki.

My second party that night consisted of two elderly couples whom I recognized as frequent patrons of the restaurant. One of the men had been a general in the White Russian Army fighting the Bolsheviks. I stood at the right shoulder of one of the gentlemen and bowed. "Monsieur, may I take your order please?" I asked politely.

The man facing me across the table apparently recognized me as one of the busboys. "Well, you are a waiter now," he commented pleasantly in French. "What is your name?"

"Chrysostomos, sir," I replied, surprised that he had noticed me in the past.

"You are Greek then, is that right? Yet your French is so good."

I felt myself flush with pleasure. "Thank you, sir." A smile broke across my face and I bowed politely, beaming over his compliment.

That night my station included four more tables. Busing and cleaning up after dinner, as well, I made upward of 500 lira in tips. At last, at the age of 18, I had become a waiter at the Per Palace.

• • •

I had been working at Pera Palace for three years. It had become Memet's habit to call out my name when he needed me, and one night it occurred in a most unexpected circumstance. In late November of 1937, there was a group of Turkish dignitaries chatting with a young woman about twenty feet beyond us.

"Christo," Memet called in a low voice.

"Yes, sir?" I bowed.

"I want you to take His Excellency's party." It took me a moment to fully grasp whom he meant. Then I saw him: Mustapha Kemal Atatürk, the "Father of Turkey." My view was a little obscured by the figure of the beautiful young woman he was talking with, but there was no mistaking him, a slight man of about my height, with a dark complexion.

"Yes, sir. Right away," I said with a sharp bow, and Memet turned to take me to the party. "Your Excellency, Christo will have the pleasure of serving you this evening. Lemel is not here tonight."

"This way, Your Excellency," I said crisply, barely making eye contact. I bowed and gestured toward two tables in the far corner of the ballroom Memet reserved for special guests. Atatürk was a nationalist and a member of the Committee of Union and Progress that twenty years earlier, along with the three Pashas and others, had erased almost 4,000,000 poor nameless Christian souls. It was quite unusual for a Christian to have this assignment.

"Your Excellency, what can I serve you this evening?" I offered, glancing in his eyes after a very deep bow.

Atatürk barely acknowledged me with a glance, never pausing in his conversation with the young woman. I did not recognize all of the men in the party, except for one from newspaper photos: Ismet Inönü, who commanded Turkey's armed forces as the Chief of Kemal Mustafa's General Staff. He also had negotiated the Treaty of Lausanne that ceded my small island to Turkey more than fourteen years earlier. I remember Papa mentioning him. An older man sat between him and Atatürk. I believe it was Ibrahim Temo, a founder of the CUP. I thought he had died. My pulse quickened with thoughts of these men, and the horrors they had orchestrated, the killing of so many innocents, yet I tried not to betray my nerves as I seated them.

Before the rest of the party was seated, a large man among them issued an order. "*Raki* and *hors d'oeuvres* for the Father of Turkey!"

"Right away, Pasha," I responded with a bow. *Raki* was a popular licorice liquor in Turkey. A few moments later, while I was pouring it, the same man exclaimed, "Leave the bottle!"

I bowed and withdrew to bring the *hors d'oeuvres* to tide the group over until dinner was served. Again, the same man threw his fists on the table, demanding, "Bring another bottle!"

"Bring a bowl of chickpeas and pilaf," Atatürk added, breaking away from his conversation with the young woman for a moment to gaze into my eyes.

"Right away, Your Excellency," I replied with a sharp bow. Atatürk suddenly acknowledged my presence with a bold stare.

"You're not Turkish, are you?" he queried with a penetrating stare.

"No, sir, I am not." In that moment, while gazing into his piercing eyes, my life as well as the lives of my family and kinsmen flashed across my mind.

Images from the harsh, stifling violence imposed by this ruthless man years earlier flashed across my mind after that one moment when our eyes locked. I had every reason to hate him, and yet, surprisingly, I felt no hatred. Instead, I felt a soul-wrenching sadness for all the poor souls lost as I looked at him—a slight, aging man, clearly feeling the effects of liquor and the flowery fragrance of the young woman who, at that moment, was the object of his attention. This was a different time and my duty was to serve him as a customer of Pera Palace, and I did.

Over the next hour or so, the "Father of Turkey" and much of his party fell increasingly under the influence of drink. They did not linger after dinner and, as Mustapha Kemal staggered toward the exit later that evening, he clutched the perfumed young woman for support. Atatürk, the man credited with the creation of so-called "Modern Turkey," staggering out of the ballroom, was a powerful image. The cold, dark stare we exchanged for a moment when our eyes met was one that would fix permanently in my mind. About a year later, on November 10, 1938, he died at the age of 57.

• • •

There wasn't time nor money for me to return home that year, but I finally felt that I was established enough to make good on my promise to bring my little brother Costa to Constantinople. I was filled with pride and pleasure when I wrote to Katina to invite him. Costa wanted to be a tailor and had been helping Mama, Papa, and Katina sew clothes back home on Imbroz.

By the end of November, I had a reply. Costa would arrive on the evening of December 15, 1937—my 20th birthday. When the day came, Memet gave me the dinner shift off so that I could meet Costa.

When the boat docked, I saw Costa walking down the plank. My heart ached as I watched him carry a small, worn suitcase that I recognized as Mama's and Papa's, and a somewhat larger duffel bag with pull strings slung over his shoulder. He had grown considerably in the six years since I had last seen him, and he was almost as tall as I was, but Costa didn't look like me at all. Where I resembled Papa, with my sandy hair and blue eyes, Costa had Mama's brown hair and brown eyes. My brother and I had not spent much time together and I was looking forward to his stay.

"Costa, over here." I waved to get his attention.

"Christo, Christo!" His small figure broke into a brisk run and he nearly toppled me over with an embrace.

He was wearing his best clothes: his only white shirt and a jacket Mama had made for him.

Reaching for his duffel bag I said, still grinning, "I'll take you to my apartment now. I have the evening off, so we have time to get you situated. Then we will go out for dinner."

Costa was 16 years old and thrilled to be in Constantinople with me. "I can't believe I'm here," he exclaimed over and over, his voice laden with excitement.

"Christo, this is the first time I have ever left our home," he said as we began walking.

"Is that so?" I asked him in mock surprise. "Well, you look so much a man of the world I would never have known that." Costa nodded proudly, the humor lost on him and his face full of wonder as he took in all the sights on the walk back to my apartment.

Besides the luxury of a sink and bathroom with a shower, my apartment had a closet and chest that also fit Costa's clothes. In the middle of the room was a small table with one chair. I had even bought Costa his own mattress, placing it against the wall at a right angle to mine.

"My own bed," he exclaimed, dropping his suitcase in excitement and jumping onto the mattress as we entered.

"Tell me, Costa," I began, eager for news of home, "how are Mama and Papa?"

"They are fine," Costa said, who was now reclining on the bed. "Papa was proud when he learned you waited on the President of Turkey."

"Yes, I did. His regular waiter was not in," I replied.

"You know, there are not many Greeks left on Imbroz anymore," he continued. "Turks are coming over from Turkey and taking the abandoned properties that Greeks have left behind. The Turks are the police and the government. Slowly they will take all the property, Papa says, but," he added brightly, "a few of Papa's friends have been talking with the Turks and there is some discussion of reopening a Greek school on the island."

"What about the churches?" I asked.

"Some of the churches have closed, but ours is still open."

"And Bishop Iakovos, is he well? Does he still visit Papa?"

"Yes, Christo, and he and Papa still talk late into the evening—about everything, you know, just as they used to." It was reassuring somehow to know that some things don't change. I smiled and watched Costa recline completely on his bed, looking content.

"How are Uncle Dimitris, Uncle Russo, and Aunt Cleo?" I asked.

"They are fine. You are a celebrity. Did you know that?" Costa sat upright and spoke proudly in a tone that was half-serious, half-joking.

"Is the money I'm sending home enough?" I asked next.

"We have enough to get by," he told me. "Mama, Papa, and Katina also make a little money sewing clothes for the Turks, and Papa still has a few gold coins, so we have managed."

Costa looked at me gravely. "Last winter was hard though. Most of Papa's sheep were stolen. We would not have made it without your help, and now here I am," he excitedly said.

"Did you ever doubt that I would send for you?"

"Of course not." We both chuckled with joy.

"We've talked for over an hour, Costa. Let's go get something to eat," I said with a smile. "Aren't you hungry?" I asked rhetorically.

In all my years in Constantinople, I had only eaten out a couple of times, and never at a fine restaurant. Tonight, I would treat both of us to dinner.

We left my little apartment around eight o'clock and explored the streets a bit more, with me pointing out everything of interest I could find.

"Look, Costa," I pointed in front of us. "On the hill there you can see Pera Palace where I work, and to the left, on the Golden Horn, is the Patriarchate."

"That's where you work?"

"Yes," I replied. "There are some beautiful Byzantine churches, too—there on the hill. And, can you see the tower? It's part of the old walls of Constantinople, built by Constantine himself. Even with so many of the ancient relics lost and destroyed, the city is still steeped in Christian tradition."

Costa's eyes were as wide as saucers as he took in the sights around him. "There will be time to explore during the day. Would you like to have dinner at Park Hotel?" I asked.

Costa hesitated. "I've never eaten at a restaurant," he said.

"Don't worry, you are with me and you will enjoy it." I was enjoying playing host, and perhaps the earlier praise made me want to live up to—and surpass—expectations.

Park Hotel was just east of Pera Palace overlooking the Bosporus and Sea of Marmara. Park shared the limelight in Constantinople with Pera Palace in terms of the clientele it attracted. Waiters often moved back and forth between jobs at the two, and I had heard the cuisine at Park Hotel was also excellent. What better time to sample it than with Costa on my night off?

"I'll order for you, Costa. The menu is in French."

"I didn't know you spoke French!" Costa exclaimed.

Again, a rush of pleasure filled me. I had worked hard to learn the language and was proud of my accomplishment. "You have to speak French to be a waiter at a place like Pera Palace or Park Hotel," I explained. "The food is French, you see, and—"

I broke off abruptly and pointed to the right.

"Look, there are the docks where you came in today. On the west side is the Asiatic section of the city. Straight ahead is Park—over there, see it?" Within a few minutes we were walking up to the entrance.

Taking in the glitter of the entryway and ornate dress of diners around him, suddenly Costa hung back. "Christo," he said uncertainly, "I'm not dressed up enough to go here."

"Nonsense, Costa," I reassured him. "You look fine, truly."

The *maître d'* greeted us with a smile. "Good evening, gentlemen."

"Good evening," I responded giving him a respectful bow, recognizing that I knew him from Pera Palace. He had worked as a waiter when I was a busboy. Evidently, he came to the same conclusion.

"You have been here before?" he asked, looking at me carefully.

"No, sir. I am a waiter at Pera Palace."

"Yes, of course. What is your name?"

"Chrysostomos, sir," I said. "We came to have dinner."

"Certainly, right this way, gentlemen." We received a little extra attention that evening—an unadvertised perk between waiters.

I could tell Costa had no idea what to do. After we were seated, I told him in Greek, "Costa, take the napkin and put it on your lap. Also, when the salad arrives, use the outside fork. It's a salad fork, and the outside spoon, the round one, is the soup spoon."

"Oh, yes, I see." Costa gazed down at the white tablecloth and then back at me, wide-eyed. "Thank you for bringing me here, Christo."

"Just enjoy your meal." That evening we certainly enjoyed our dinner. We had soup, tossed salad, and veal, followed by *strudel au pomme* for dessert. The foods were rich and new to Costa, who ate everything, including a second serving of bread.

After dinner we walked along the Bosporus for a few blocks. "Tomorrow morning I'll take you to Mr. Babayan." Prior to Costa's arrival, Memet recommended I talk to Mr. David Babayan, a well-respected Armenian tailor in need of an apprentice. "He's supposed to be one of the finest tailors in Constantinople. I'm taking the morning off." Papa and I wanted Costa to have a trade so it would be easier for him to find work.

"Christo, thank you. One day I will make it up to you, I promise," Costa said after dinner.

"You are my brother," I reassured him. "Brothers don't have to thank each other; it is my pleasure." Costa was only five when I left for Samothraki, what seemed like a lifetime ago, and I had not spent any significant time with any of my family, except perhaps Katina, since I was ten. Over the next few weeks, despite our busy schedules, Costa and I got reacquainted with each other.

"Christo," he said one day, "I don't know how you work so hard. You leave at dawn and you don't get back until ten o'clock at night, day after day. Aren't you tired?"

I laughed. "It's not that bad, Costa," I told him. "I have a half-day off on Sundays and one full day a month off now. In my first year at Pera Palace I had no days off. Besides, next summer I plan to take a week's holiday and go home with you."

"Still," he said, shaking his head, "the hours are so long—"

"It is not so hard when you have good reason to work." As I said it, I realized just how true it was. Somehow knowing that others depended on me inspired me to do more than just enough to get by.

In the next fourteen months that Costa lived with me while learning to become a tailor, I developed a deeper affection and appreciation for my little brother. We talked freely of the difficulties Mama and Papa experienced aging on the island. The Turks had taken the town records, including the property deeds. It would be difficult, Costa told me, for Mama and Papa to verify right to their property if the Turks ever contested their ownership.

Many properties were abandoned and had been converted to Turkish ownership without recompense to the rightful owners. These things I already knew, but until now I had been shielded by my family from the direct extent of the hardship. Nonetheless, I felt powerless to do anything but work and be productive for their sake and mine.

• • •

By January 1939, Costa would soon return home to Imbroz. For the past year I had paid all the expenses for both of us, including Costa's room and board. I had also sent money home and managed to save eight hundred lira. Before the trip I was able to buy gifts for Mama, Papa, and my sisters.

"Costa, soon you will be a tailor," I told him, "and you will make a better living. You'll have a trade and one day, when I'm in America, I'll send for you to make me a suit." We both laughed.

"You will do well there, I know," he said. I would miss my brother dearly and set out on our trip home with mixed emotions.

"When you go to America and become rich and successful you will need a good tailor." We both laughed. Suddenly, he turned serious. "Please send for me, Christo. Promise you won't forget me."

On a Monday morning that summer, Costa and I boarded a steamship that made a brief stop at Gallipoli and then anchored offshore of Imbroz. There, once again, Captain Koutris picked us up and rowed us ashore.

"Hi boys, are you ready to go home?"

"Yes, Captain Koutris," we responded in unison.

The deep lines in the Captain's leathery face reflected the ravages of his long, hard life, but he was happy to see us. I felt the same excitement as I had as a 13 year old boy being rowed back from Samothraki Island, but as we drew closer the blight I saw extinguished my excitement.

The deep pastoral colors, the flowers, the bustling economic activity were all long gone. What remained was a drab vacant island rife with weeds, abandoned structures, and a desolate barren landscape. The Turks referred to the process as "Turkification."

The week I spent at home passed uneventfully with none of the pomp or celebration I remembered. My sisters greatly appreciated their presents. My parents, now in their mid-sixties, moved familiarly through their days a little more slowly. I could tell that the specter of war was taking a very heavy toll on Papa, though. He feared the Turks would use the war to revive the horrific Christian persecution. The lines in his face were the only evidence of the smile that used to come so quickly.

"Tell us, again," Katina asked at dinner one night. They were fascinated by the transition through my various jobs over the past few years and the cast of characters I had met in Constantinople.

Mama and Papa sat smiling at me, effusive with pride.

"Christo, we are so happy for you." Mama said, holding back tears.

"My son, a waiter at Pera Palace. Bravo, Christo," Papa added.

"I waited on Ataturk," I said, "Ismet Inonu, too, and there were others." The room went silent.

Spending that week with my family was very important for me. Witnessing their toilsome, meager lives on Imbroz gave me a renewed resolve to move forward, away from the labored and numbing monotony of the Turkish occupation of my tiny island—which was such a sharp contrast to the robust pace I had thrived and matured in while serving in the Agatha Christie Ballroom.

My departure from home was emotional. As I waved goodbye to my family at the dock, I began to realize that although my considerable energy could change much, there was nothing I could do to change Imbroz or my family's plight. Nevertheless, what I could do, I did without reservation. I had to move on.

CHAPTER 9

Amele Taburu

I saw a man this morning
who did not wish to die;
I ask, and cannot answer,
if otherwise wish I. . . .
Achilles came to Troyland
and I to Chersonese;
he turned from wrath to battle,
and I from three days' peace.
Was it so hard, Achilles,
so very hard to die?
Thou knewest and I know not—
so much the happier I.
I will go back this morning
from Imbros o'er the sea;
stand in the trench, Achilles,
flame-capped, and shout for me.

—PATRICK SHAW-STUART, 1918
(IMBROZ, BEFORE DYING IN GALLIPOLI)

BACK IN CONSTANTINOPLE my busy schedule was shortened. Winter had arrived and the clouds of impending world conflict had significantly darkened horizons throughout Europe. Complacency was quickly becoming transfused with chaos and fear. Yet Pera Palace seemed as impervious to the start of the war as it had been to the global economic depression. It remained an oasis of sensibilities and civility. While I worked there I felt insulated from the irrational cruelty of life.

It was late January of 1939 and by now I had been working for over seven years but, at 21 years old, I was still the youngest waiter at Pera Palace. Although my financial freedom and success were gratifying, storm clouds of war were brewing over Europe. I could only wonder how they would manifest in Turkey and how they would affect me.

In the spring of 1938 Hitler "reunited" Austria with Germany. In a misguided attempt to appease Hitler, Great Britain's Prime Minister Neville Chamberlain signed the Munich Agreement later that year, ceding the Sudetenland to Germany, while promising "peace in our time."

As time passed it was becoming apparent that Hitler was not likely to be contained by appeasement, though. Having created an unquenchable nationalistic fervor, Hitler was primed to invade his European neighbors in his quest to mimic the Roman Empire. Europe braced for war. Although an ally of Germany in World War I, Turkey seemed committed to her neutrality this go-round.

My first night back at work I was summoned by the *maître d'* and told to report to the head bellhop to assist in moving a newly arrived guest and his entourage into the hotel. A half-dozen limousines pulled up and then I saw him: Ahmet Zagu, otherwise known as King Zog, King of the Albanians. The last Ottoman king, he had abdicated his throne for a handsome payment in gold bars from Italy's Prime Minister Benito Mussolini.

Even though the walk to the hotel safe was only one hundred feet from the front door, it took two bellhops and me almost two hours to unload the wealth of Albania into a vault under the watchful eye of his armed guards. When all the gold was safely stored, the King spoke to one of his aides, who then approached us giving each of us one hundred Turkish lira as a tip. At the time, 326 Turkish lira equaled one U.S. dollar. After all that gold, it seemed almost a pittance. Never underestimate the price of an Ottoman king.

I felt I was watching history unfold. The departure of King Zog, one of the last artifacts of the Ottoman era, from Albania served as another reminder of the crises unfolding across Europe and spilling into the Balkans. King Zog was an anachronism, yet at the same time he was quite at home in modern Turkey, where he fared well after Mussolini declared Albania an Italian protectorate.

Time passed uneventfully, in a seamless bubble at Pera Palace, my haunt of habit.

• • •

Over the next two years the war ravaged Europe, eventually raging eastward into Russia. Between September of 1939 and May of 1940, Nazi Germany vanquished country after country across Europe. By the summer of 1940 Hitler had conquered most of the continent and Britain stood alone. Yet I was impervious, isolated in my cocoon of civility and refinement at the top of the world. All that would change shortly and abruptly.

Despite the horrors of the enveloping war, Pera Palace was usually filled to capacity. Although Turkey was finding it increasingly difficult to maintain neutrality, she had mostly limited her participation in the struggle to a war of espionage. Most of the intrigue in Constantinople around this time revolved around the Pera section of town and in the Palace itself. Secrets were exchanged over morning coffee and tea, and clandestine political agendas were often hatched in the cocktail lounges in the evenings. Rulers, diplomats, and the very wealthy all frequented Pera Palace. It sat at the crossroads of East and West and was a melting pot of sorts for the elites. In that sense, the wait staff had a front row seat to history, although sometimes this proved a little too close for comfort.

The strengthening winds of war soon came battering against my door. On the morning of March 11, 1941, the British had just begun landing troops in Greece to assist the Greeks in their successful resistance against the Italian invaders. The British Ambassador, Hugh Montgomery, had arrived at Pera Palace for a scheduled meeting with the Turks, hoping to gain assurances of their continued neutrality.

It was a typical day at the Palace—a sparse group of socialites were carousing outside in theater attire waiting for a taxi, a British gentleman was enjoying a leisurely smoke on one of the overstuffed chairs in the lobby, and a weary traveler speaking in broken Turkish was desperately trying to communicate with a bellhop. The familiar dance of glamour and service was in full, perfect step, a dance all the performers knew to absentminded perfection. The Ambassador was part of tonight's scene, another important guest whose needs were being served.

On occasion, when the *maître d'* was out, Memet would allow me to greet guests, even though I was only 23. I would attribute that to my maturity and mastery of the French language, but this night it might have just been good luck.

"Christo," Memet called for me. "I need you to do me a favor."

"Yes, sir," I replied.

"I need you to take Mr. George Rendel, a British envoy and minister, to his table after he checks into his room for the evening. Can you handle that?"

"Yes," I replied, with more certainty. I waited for the minister at the bottom of the glittered staircase in the center of the lobby, just outside the ballroom, as I watched him and his entourage ascend to their rooms. After waiting a few minutes, I helped put the baggage in the room beside the lobby.

Then, just in the nick of time, Memet signaled me to return to the ballroom at once. I bowed respectfully and returned to finish preparations for lunch. Moments later I was knocked to the floor by a deafening blast. I crawled under the table to seek refuge with the few early luncheon guests in the ballroom. I felt the floor beneath my feet shake violently while dishes and silver went crashing off trays and tables. The ear-splitting blast shook the entire building, and the world as we knew it tilted slightly while a million shards of glass from the chandeliers and windows above furiously rained down on a stunned group of patrons. A split second of suspended animation preceded more sustained, panicked screaming as thick black smoke rolled through the lobby, into the corridors, and out onto the street.

After a stunned second, I crawled out from under the table and ran into the lobby, but the police and hotel security had already descended on the scene and blocked off the area. I hurried with other staff to get clean linens and hand towels for the attendants to care for the injured until the ambulances arrived.

Arriving medics saved whom they could, but the blast had killed six people—including a porter who was a friend of mine—and injured seventeen. The explosion was in the luggage room but had enveloped the whole lobby where I had been waiting moments earlier. The British party with Mr. Rendel had remained unharmed as they were upstairs in their rooms during the bombing. It had been rumored that the Nazis placed luggage with bombs in and around the British party's luggage.

A few days after the so-called "Rendel bombing," food service continued with little interruption, but it took months to repair portions of the internal and external structures damaged by the explosion. After that, nothing was the same. Up to that point I thought Pera Palace had been impervious to depression or the ravages of war, but now the grand finery of the 1930s was gone and I once again felt powerless in the face of the brutality of savagery. The impermeable stronghold of the privileged had been penetrated by the violence of the war that surrounded it. Its aura as a reclusive oasis had been scarred and would not be restored quickly.

The years of war were finally showing wear and tear on the opulent Pera Palace. Her decline seemed to draw Memet with her, and soon, after thirty years of service, he would quietly retire. The bombing also prompted Olgalik, Victor's assistant chef, and Regas, a young busboy I had befriended, to eventually take jobs at Park Hotel. Many of our customers had gone to Park as well.

• • •

Immediately following the bombing I would receive a letter from the Turkish government. I remember that fateful spring morning in 1941 well. I reported to work by six o'clock as usual to help with setup and kitchen preparation to find most of the staff standing to greet me when I entered.

"To what do I owe this surprise?" I joked as I entered the ballroom.

Memet walked forward with his eyes downcast, handing me a notice addressed from the Turkish government. His countenance suddenly changed as I opened the letter, my hands now visibly shaking. I had been called up to serve the motherland. The notice simply stated that I was to report to Ankara within thirty days to serve in the Turkish military by notice of Turkey's new Prime Minister, Ismet Inönü, whom I had waited on almost three years earlier.

The Turkish military reinstated a compulsory draft of young Christian males. The *amele taburu,* or work battalions, were instituted by Turkey days before the outbreak of World War I in 1914. They were essentially forced labor camps for the purpose of ridding Turkey of young Christian males, mainly Greeks and Armenians. Although they were stopped by the Treaty of Lausanne in 1923, Kemal Mustapha's successor, Ismet Inönü, reinstated them in 1941, just in time for my conscription. By now, it was no secret that these camps were nothing more than a convenient means to enslave and often exterminate the young, healthy, Christian male population.

Memet knew from my reaction that the notice wasn't good. "Thank you" was all I could muster in response.

The workweeks flew by before my time came to depart. I went through my duties that last evening at Pera Palace without emotion, all life drawn from me. I felt sullied by the realization that the eight years I had spent working my way up to a decent standard of living would be dashed. I was being plucked from the solid security of Pera Palace and forced back into the dark world of Christian persecution. All of my efforts to rid my life of hardship now seemed pointless as I was being dragged right back into it.

As I went through the motions of my duties at work for the next few days, the passion I always felt to approach each workday was gone, replaced now with a suffocating feeling of desolation so deep and black it had no beginning or end. I posted a letter to Mama and Papa telling them the news. It pained me deeply to have to tell them that I was being forcibly conscripted by the Turks instead of going to America.

Dinner service my final evening was finally over and only three parties remained in the ballroom. Andreas, the head waiter, beckoned me into a side dining room. I wearily crossed the room, with little curiosity as to why he summoned me.

Memet, Victor, Olgalik, Aristis, and Regas were all waiting there.

"We wanted to show our support and let you know you will be missed by all of us," Aristis began.

Overwhelmed, I barely uttered "thank you" when he went on, holding a shot of Greek *ouzo* high above his head. "I propose a toast, wishing you luck and health and a speedy return to us."

"Hear! Hear!" the entire staff shouted, their echoes merging into a murmur of personal well wishes.

Victor, the old French chef from whom I had learned so much, approached me afterwards, fighting back tears. "You will be in my prayers, Christo. Take good care of yourself," he said earnestly.

"I will," I responded automatically.

Aristis tearfully embraced me. "God be with you," he exclaimed.

After all of the embraces, tears, and words of support, we parted company for possibly the last time. The small group was dwindling as people headed home when Memet approached me. His eyes were bright and tearful as they stared into mine, and he silently extended his hand.

"Goodbye, Christo," he said softly. He grasped my hand for a very long minute, finally uttering, "I will keep your job. Please come back."

I don't even know if I thanked Memet. In a fog I bowed politely, arousing an echo of the small bow I had made to him on our first encounter years earlier. I only remember rushing outside to fill my lungs with the night air. I needed to breathe, not think. I patted my forehead with a clean handkerchief and took a few deep breaths. Returning from my lost thoughts, I finally came back in from the dark, made arrangements with Regas to send my final pay and a few valuables to my father, and went home for a final restless night.

I gathered my belongings the next morning, placed them outside the door, and took one last look at my apartment—the sink with running water, the private bathroom with plumbing, the electric light. I turned off the switch and closed the door. How quickly and completely life can change, and all because of one letter.

• • •

With my relic coin pinned to my t-shirt and the rest of my belongings in a seaman's bag, I embarked on my three-hundred-mile journey southeast to the military compound in Ankara by train early one morning in April of 1941. Upon arrival a day later, I presented my paperwork.

A few moments later I was herded into a room with other inductees, and in short order our heads were shaved, our clothes were off, and we were forced into a shower and deloused. The Turkish gendarmes then issued us two shirts and two pairs of trousers each. Military boots were in short supply and the conscripts seldom received them, even though the temperature often plunged to below zero in northern Turkey. Some of us were given unloaded rifles for appearance's sake. The Turks would not dare give a Christian conscript ammunition, for fear he would turn the weapon on them. Shortly afterwards we were arranged in some semblance of formation and addressed by a Turkish gendarme.

"You are in the Turkish military," he shouted. "It doesn't matter where you came from, whether a village, an island, or a city; you will all serve the new Turkey now. Any insubordination or treachery towards the Turkish government is punishable by death. Desertion is punishable by death. You will do what you are told for as long as you are told, no matter what you are told. Europe and much of the world is at war. Even though we are neutral, we have many enemies, and, if need be, you will sacrifice yourself to defend our country."

Over the following senseless twelve weeks we would endure forced marches of twenty or more miles, and motionless sentry duty for hours under the false pretense of training. If any Christian conscript could not keep up or collapsed, he would not be heard from again. We were also kept in constant and indentured servitude to the

Turkish "regulars" who, we had no doubt, would use the slightest infraction as an excuse to shoot us dead and suffer no consequence. Time passed.

In April of 1941, Hitler's army invaded Greece just after Mussolini's failed attempt in late 1940. The time the Germans spent conquering Yugoslavia and Greece delayed their attack on the Soviet Union by a couple months and would cost them victory at the gates of Moscow, and a year later in Stalingrad. A month earlier, with milder weather conditions, the German tanks may have prevailed before the Russian winter set in, and Stalin would have been forced to surrender. The world would have been a very different place.

It was in June of 1941, with nearly all of Europe securely in German hands, that the onslaught into Russia began with Germany's launching of Operation Barbarossa with 3,000,000 German and Axis troops. Great fear and uncertainty had gripped the people of occupied Europe and the civilized world. Although Turkey would remain neutral, the Turkish army accelerated its compulsory conscription of young Christian males throughout Turkey under the fog of World War II.

Then in the late fall of 1941 we were herded into train cars to travel over five hundred miles northeast to the Russian border, presumably to serve as "border guards." We were trucked the last hundred miles or so. When we arrived a week later, we were immediately forced to start digging in the earth for roadbeds. The reality was that we would work on a chain gang building a road to nowhere in what would soon be the frozen tundra of the Russian border, and we would be told to stand guard without ammunition or weapons.

It was early winter of 1941. Although we were given heavy jackets, for the most part we were inadequately dressed for a freezing winter. Some men had shoes with holes in them, many did not have gloves. Meanwhile, the Turkish regulars had thick wool coats, fur hats, and sturdy boots.

The hardship I had known on Imbroz was nothing compared to the fear and misery I would shortly live every day. When the winter weather came, some died quickly from the harsh elements, frozen like statues in their tents where they lay, while many others faded slowly before perishing.

Little progress on the road we were to build was ever actually made, but the Turks never really seemed to care. They only cared that we got up in the morning, marched to the construction site, and banged picks into the frozen ground all day and every day. To further complicate our difficulties, as the year wore on we would soon see the full force of winter with wind chills as low as twenty degrees below zero.

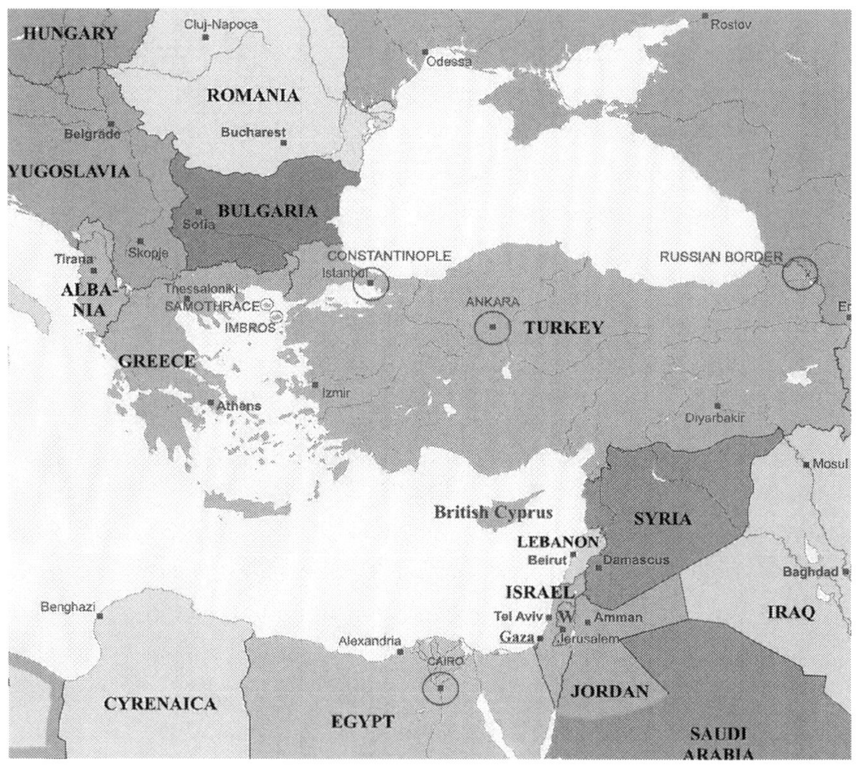

Off to the Russian border with the work battalions.

The Russian border is where I spent most of my enlistment while battles were raging in Russia to the northwest. Most of the casualties among Christian conscripts in the work battalions assigned to the northern border where I was stationed were due to illness and the conditions. Between the severe climate, inadequate nutrition, and the merciless Turkish regulars, survival itself was the principal daily chore.

• • •

It was December 1941 and the dead of winter was suddenly upon us. It seemed like we existed only to provide creature comforts and serve the Turkish gendarmes until we froze to death. Whereas I once served sumptuous meals to the rich and fashionable, I now did the bidding of coarse men in brutal conditions, yet my service skills served me well.

Our work battalion had about a half-dozen vehicles in which the Turks rode and behind which the young Christian males marched on foot. The Turkish gendarmes were housed in structures ranging from shanties to the near palatial, determined by rank and availability. No matter the accommodations, though, all the Turkish troops were provided with wood-burning stoves or fireplaces for warmth, and it was our job to deliver the daily supply of firewood.

The Christian conscripts, on the other hand, lived in two-man pup tents, provided we could chop through the frozen crust to get adequate dirt to lay them. At the end of each long day, we would attempt to pitch the pup tents and lay our tired, cold bodies onto the hard-frozen ground. With a shortage of blankets, we insulated the tents by collapsing them and covering them with snow and dirt, when we could, to provide some relief from the frigid cold. We often slept back to back in a feeble attempt to provide some thermal retention.

At dawn we were aroused from a shivering sleep by the banging of a paddle on a steel pot. After a cup of strong Turkish coffee, we would walk a quarter mile to the road site and begin digging in the frozen tundra. We bore the shovels, picks, and saws on our backs, while the Turks bore the guns.

Even though my short life was difficult and had prepared me for hardship, the days I spent in the far northern reaches of Turkey were some of the most difficult of my life. During my twenty months on the Russian border, more than half the young Christian boys I served with perished.

• • •

"That ought to do it, Christo. I've packed dirt on the outside. That should keep us warm."

"Yes, Gregory, I hope. I pray for us," I replied.

"You know, Christo, the Mohammedans kill dogs because they believe a dog revealed Mohammed's whereabouts. They also revere spiders because they believe a spider wove a web to protect Mohammed."

"I believe it," I responded, not at all surprised by any of these oddities. "The Turks are the most uncivilized people on planet earth."

My tent-mate was a young Greek conscript from Telenos, the island adjacent to Imbroz. Gregory didn't have a pair of shoes when we began, but I found him a discarded pair of boots. Although small, they at least offered some protection throughout the winter.

"It is so cold, Christo."

"I know. Let's hurry to dinner," I said. "We can go to the fire and warm up." Dinner was a tasteless oat mush cooked on an open fire.

"If they're able to get one going," he replied.

We worked quickly in the frozen ground of the tundra, using the backs of our shovels as ineffective picks.

"Look, they got it going." We hurried toward the fledgling flames on frostbitten toes and with shivering breath.

Although I was dressed better than most and wore socks, heavy shoes, gloves, a military-issue jacket, shirt, and pants, the frozen air and wind still pierced my flesh like a thousand knives. Still, I felt I was one of the lucky ones. I had a thick wool scarf that Mama had packed for me years ago that now covered the lower portion of my face and ears, up to the military-issue cap. Many of the boys had no scarf, and they used whatever scraps of cloth they could find to wrap their faces.

"What is this stuff they feed us? I think they put sawdust in it."

"I think it's oats, Gregory. I'll use my container, and then give it to you."

Gregory nodded. I had a clean tin can that I would hold out to get my scoop of food.

"Next," called out George, the large cook. George looked Turkish, but was actually Greek. Usually at least one armed Turkish gendarme stood by watching at mealtime. In a twisted perversion of fairness, the gendarme would shout out if it appeared that one of us received more of the slop than another. No such protests were uttered if one of us was deprived of shoes or a jacket, or froze to death in our beds, however.

"Move along!" the cook droned on.

Many of the boys held out their hands since they had no containers. I quickly ate the tasteless gruel, then washed my can and spoon with snow and gave them to Gregory.

"Thank you, Christo."

"Go quickly, before they pour out the rest of it," I urged.

After dinner we began the cold two-hundred-yard walk back to our tents. Once packed inside our tents for the night, we often pulled down the center posts, allowing the tent to fall down on top of us for additional warmth, then wished for snowfall to further insulate us from the frigid wind.

• • •

We spent much of the pre-dawn day before going to work on the road site searching for wood to build fires in the Turkish quarters. Afterwards, some of us made the Turks tea and porridge. None of us minded this duty, which actually sheltered us temporarily from the elements. We were the lucky ones.

Over time, because I was experienced at preparing and serving food, I was assigned to stand guard at the Pasha's quarters where, apart from the duty of actually guarding, I prepared breakfast and sometimes dinner for the Turkish regulars. This duty spared me some time from the farcical road construction detail and allowed me the luxury of two or three hours a day out of the elements. The rest of the time I spent caring for the livestock and trying to keep from freezing to death.

"Christ-sto," my tent-mate Gregory said as we returned to the tent, "I'm so cold, I can hardly move." I gave him my scarf to wrap around his neck and face. This was the second day of a blizzard that had stopped all roadwork and confined us to our tents for shelter.

I was very worried about Gregory, who lay shivering uncontrollably under a thin blanket. I had noticed that Gregory was growing increasingly despondent of late. I had seen too many others give up hope and succumb to the elements.

"I'll go up to the Pasha's house now and start his fire," I told him. "You should come with me. It will be warmer there." I did not want to leave Gregory.

"I can't," Gregory replied. He peered at me from beneath his blanket, my scarf wrapped tightly around his head and ears. "I'm telling the truth" he said, "I'm too cold to move."

"If you stay here," I told him, "you'll freeze. Get up, Gregory, please—you must keep moving."

"You go ahead," Gregory said, pulling his blanket completely over his head. "I'll come along later." He moved his legs a little to show me he would keep moving.

Soon the Turkish soldiers would be looking for me if I didn't show up. I knew there was little chance Gregory would make it to the Pasha's quarters without further prodding from me, yet my weakened intuition sent me to tend to my responsibilities.

"I'll come back for you after I get the fire started," I told him as I pulled my jacket over my head and pushed out into the snow. My feet were numb as I struggled through the drifts toward the gendarmes' quarters.

The howling wind buffeted me, and snow whipped at the exposed parts of my face, stinging my cheeks and eyes. The storm that morning was so intense I could not even tell if dawn had broken. The faint light from the gendarmes' headquarters guided my way for the quarter-mile walk.

I paused at the gate. The blizzard outside had extended the night's eerie darkness. Two days before the storm struck I had made a stack of firewood and kindling and covered it with leaves to keep it dry. When the toe of my boot struck a log, I kicked away the snow and collected an armload of wood. I carried the wood to the house and pushed open a side door. The execution of my chore would temporarily insure my survival.

"Who goes there?" a Turkish gendarme named Osmond barked from a bedroom.

"Ch-Ch-Christo, sir," I replied, forcing the words from my frozen lips. "I've come to light the fire."

"Well, come in, then. Hurry up and close the door!"

"Yes, sir, right away," I answered quickly, hoping that the gendarme wouldn't notice that I was early and send me away. I wasn't sure that I could last another hour if I were forced back outside.

It was cold in the Pasha's house, but at least the walls cut the harsh wind. First, I sought out a kerosene lamp to light the darkness. Striking a match with frozen fingers was a time-consuming chore. I then knelt by the hearth and clumsily arranged the kindling, my hands so stiff I could barely move them. The wood was frozen, too, making the fire more difficult to start. Eventually, however, I coaxed a few flames to life and fed them more kindling until I had a nice blaze going.

"I will make some coffee," I called out to the stirring soldiers.

"Forget that," a voice bellowed from a back room. "Tend to the animals before you tend to the coffee." The voice belonged to a sergeant, a Kemalist with no love for young Christian conscripts.

My heart sank at the thought of going out again into the elements. "Yes, sir." I paused before the fire for as long as I dared, maybe a minute, absorbing a final breath of warmth before heading back out into the blizzard. Feeling had just begun to return to my extremities when, stepping into the cold, I was slapped once again by a piercing blast of frigid air.

The animals were in a shed about two hundred feet from the Pasha's quarters. Beside the shed was a haystack, now so completely covered with snow that only the handle of the pitchfork appeared above the drifts. I kicked away the snow as best I could and forked some hay into a wheelbarrow, which I had stood on end next to the pitchfork so I could find it.

Then I cleared a short path and dragged the wheelbarrow into the shed. I fed the animals—three or four sheep, a goat, a donkey, two horses, and a half-dozen chickens—and broke the ice in their water trough with a shovel to allow them to drink. Then I headed back toward the quarters, taking a quick detour to my tent to check on my friend.

"Gregory," I called, "pushing open the tent flap. "Come on, get up! I've started a fire in the house and you can help me with the breakfast." Although not permitted, Gregory direly needed the warmth.

Inside the tent I was greeted with silence. "Come on, Gregory, please," I persisted. "You'll freeze if you stay here. Besides, I've got sentry duty today and I may not be able to get back here. You need to come with me now."

"You go on, Christo," Gregory told me, his voice so thin with cold I could barely hear him. Beneath his blanket I could see that he was trembling. I reached down and touched his shoulder. I grasped at him, trying to pull him off the ground, but I was so weak I could hardly stand myself.

"Please, Gregory," I pleaded one more time. The winter had already taken the lives of several young men, their heads split open like coconuts by the cold.

"In a minute," Gregory said. "You go ahead. I'll be right behind you." He sounded calm, and I reluctantly agreed to go ahead again without him on his promise that he would follow straight away. I had already been gone too long and I feared the Turks would notice. In the frigid interior of the tent I felt my own strength fading. Hesitantly, I patted Gregory's shoulder one last time and left the tent to make the trek back to the Pasha's quarters. By the time I reached the kitchen door I had icicles on my eyes, mouth, and nose.

I slapped at my face with a numb hand, kicked the snow from my boots, and entered the house where I stoked the fire and broke the thin film of ice that had formed on the buckets of water I had brought in the day before. Then I moved to fill the kettle on top of the fire with water and set about making coffee and the morning porridge. My limbs began to sting with a welcomed soreness.

I realized suddenly that today was December 15, 1941, my 24th birthday, and I reflected that I had spent most of my working life preparing food and serving others—at Papa's, Uncle Russo's, and Raki's stores, in the club, at Pera Palace, and now for the Turkish gendarmes. It had served me well, for here on the Russian front it put me in a job that provided me with adequate sustenance and some shelter. In fact I truly believe it is very likely that the only reason I survived my conscription to the Russian border was because I could prepare and serve a good meal.

The Turkish officers and regulars were rising now. I served them at a small table in the next room, then I prepared coffee, porridge, and biscuits for the Pasha. When I was done, I loaded the food on a tray, which I handed to gendarme Osmond to take to the Pasha's room. Gregory still had not arrived, and I was very concerned, but I had to finish my duties before I could check on him.

Some minutes later while I was scrubbing pots, the Pasha called out to me from his room. "Christo, bring me more bread and some cheese."

"Right away, sir." I turned away from the pots and sliced some cheese and bread, which I arranged on a plate and carried to the Pasha's room. I paused outside the door to knock, then entered and served the plate to the Pasha with a respectful half-bow.

"Who has first watch?" Sergeant Osmond bellowed as I left the Pasha's room. Standing guard was another form of senseless torment.

"I do, sir," I told him, "but I would like to check on Gregory first as he is not feeling well."

"Nonsense!" Osmond snapped. "Finish your work and stand your watch."

I simply nodded, betraying no emotion. "Yes, sir," I said, and retreated to the kitchen.

After the officers finished breakfast I cleaned up the dishes, fed the fire again, and made my way through the snow to the front gate. I had gotten warm while preparing the Pasha's breakfast, and the slug of frigid air that greeted me when I left the house cut through me with renewed impact.

Instead of standing at attention by the gate I marched back and forth—I took three steps to the left, turned, and walked back three steps to the right, over and over again, worrying about Gregory and trying, to no avail, to keep my extremities from going numb.

My eight-hour shift was torturous. Halfway through I was permitted a half-hour break, during which I was allowed to stand in the side doorway where, partially screened from the wind, I could drink coffee and smoke a cigarette.

Afternoon finally arrived with no discernable change in temperature since dawn. I waited an hour past my time for relief, but there was no sign of Gregory, and Sergeant Osmond would not permit me to leave my post to check on him. After a second hour passed I finally got permission to check on my friend. With all the haste I could muster, mixed with a large measure of dread, I made my frozen way through the snow to our tent.

Though fearing what I might find, and with severe frostbite myself, I did not hesitate to pull back the tent flap. "Gregory, I'm here," I announced my return as I pulled back the parchment of the tent. At that moment my heart sank. As I approached him the hairs on the back of my neck stood on end.

"Gregory?" I whispered in vain as I pulled back the blanket and revealed his face wreathed with icicles, a pallid, waxy mask of death.

"Gregory, Gregory!" I yelled, falling to my knees and shaking him gently.

"Oh, Gregory." I sobbed and offered a prayer to God as I covered his lifeless face with the blanket.

I was so cold and tired myself I thought I would be next. Surviving another hour was all that was on my mind. I barely made it back to the Pasha's quarters to report Gregory's death to the sergeant. With an unexpected show of compassion—perhaps due to his having lost a second man who could serve him creature comforts—Osmond ordered me inside the house.

"You may fix dinner for the Pasha and his officers," he told me, "and one of the regulars will stand watch until a replacement is found for Gregory."

That evening I prepared and served dinner with anger, fighting back my tears. I was overcome with sadness for Gregory. I think I felt that if I didn't grieve for him, no one would know or even care that he had passed away. He deserved so much more than that.

As soon as I could, I slipped away to the tent and removed his body, literally frozen stiff, and placed it near the livestock shed. Because it was impossible for me to dig a grave, I covered him with leaves and dirt as best I could. I made a small cross from kindling, placed it at his feet, and said another prayer over him before returning to the Pasha's quarters to wash the dishes and thaw. This would have to do until the weather broke.

No one noticed my absence and, even less, the death of my friend. I don't believe I have ever felt more sadness in my life than I did the night my tent-mate Gregory lay lifeless in a coffin of snow by that little woodpile in the middle of a vast wasteland. The senseless loss of Gregory's life that day tested my Christian faith to the limit.

When the dishes were done that night I was allowed to remain for a while in the house. The temperature outside was well below zero, and the wind made it deadly. I nodded my thanks and made my way to the warmth of the kitchen fire to clean up some more, and eventually fell into a restless sleep in the corner of the kitchen under my military-issue jacket.

When I awoke I was still numb with sadness. Even though I knew I could not send the letter until I returned to Constantinople, I found ink and paper and immediately began to write to Gregory's family to tell them what had happened. I felt inadequate as I wrote, but it was the least I could do. After I finished I folded the letter, placed it in my shirt pocket, and returned to my pup tent alone. Gregory was one of many young Christians who froze to death in the service of the new secular Turkey. The harsh conditions the Germans would encounter during Hitler's battle for Stalingrad in 1943 were something the *amele taburu* on the border had already experienced during 1941 and 1942. I was one of the survivors of those two terrible winters.

• • •

In December of 1942, after more than twenty months at the Russian border, I was sent back to the army base at Ankara where I was unceremoniously given in back pay the rough equivalent of three pounds sterling, and formally discharged in January of 1943. I was also handed a dozen letters I had written to my family that were never delivered because they "lacked the appropriate postage." Turkish humor was no less cruel than Turkish reason.

I made my way from Ankara back to Constantinople and wrote my family immediately, telling them of my discharge and asking them to write to me at Pera Palace in Constantinople until I found a place to stay. I also posted the letter I had written some months earlier to Gregory's parents on Telenos, as I felt sure they had not received any news of their son's death. I enclosed his Christian cross.

I was underweight and malnourished when I finally returned to Constantinople to pick up the pieces of my life. I drifted around the city for two days before finding a place to stay near the Patriarchate. I mustered up the strength for the forty-minute walk across the Golden Horn on the Galata Bridge to visit my old job.

I stood by the Pera Palace entryway, peering in to watch the wait staff set up for dinner. I spotted a young waiter I didn't recognize. I felt the same way I had years ago when I saw the Palace for the first time, somewhat disconnected.

New waiters had taken my old station, but they recognized me and placed me in another station. I was so happy to be back—to be alive—that I didn't care. I left early my first day to settle into my new room, confident that, as soon as an opportunity availed itself, I would be reengaged.

Afterwards, I went to the Patriarchate to pray. The Patriarch's small church was my safe place. While I prayed, I clutched the relic coin that Papa had given me so long ago and which I still kept pinned inside my t-shirt over my heart. It was my habit. I thanked God for watching over me and protecting me during my conscription. I prayed for my family, for the inhabitants of my small island, and for Gregory and all the other young Greek soldiers who had frozen to death in *amele taburu*. Man's inhumanity to man is a great mystery of evil.

I was 25 years old when I returned, and, although physically weak from my ordeal, my spirits were high. As I prayed in the Patriarchate that day I realized just how fortunate I was to have survived. To have returned at all was a blessing from God. To have returned with my health and a job still waiting for me was a miracle.

To this day I still have the three pounds—the hardest money I have ever made.

CHAPTER 10

Dare I Dream

Men since the beginning of time have sought peace....
Military alliances, balance of powers,
leagues of Nations, all in turn failed,
leaving the only path to be
by way of the crucible of war....
If we do not now devise some greater
and more equitable system,
Armageddon will be at our door.
—GEN. DOUGLAS MACARTHUR, 1945

THE FEW WEEKS I SPENT doing odd jobs around Pera Palace gave me some time to regain my strength. I was still feeling the effects of exhaustion from my time in the work battalions and was so thankful for the opportunity to be back in my old haunt, but after the bombing things had changed.

I had been away for two years and I hardly knew anyone at Pera Palace. Memet had retired. The old chef, Victor, had also retired. His assistant Olgalik, whom I had befriended, had gone, too. Olgalik was a Russian Orthodox who had previously been a colonel in the White Russian Army and had escaped to Constantinople in 1919 when the Bolsheviks took control of Russia. Although he was thirty years my senior, we quickly became good friends. He had learned to cook while working in the restaurants of Constantinople and had become quite accomplished, though, truth be told, he lacked that certain *je ne sais quoi* of his French predecessor.

There was also Regas, the new busboy about my age I had become fast friends with before my conscription. Regas had come from a different village, but was also from Imbroz. Both Olgalik and Regas had left Pera Palace shortly after the Rendel bombing and my conscription and were working at the fashionable Park Hotel dining room.

When I finally met up with Olgalik, he persuaded me to join Regas and him at the Park Hotel. "Christo, after the bombing at Pera Palace, during the time you were conscripted, business had considerably slowed, so we went to work at the Park Hotel dining room," Olgalik said. Newer than Pera Palace, the Park Hotel also featured elegant first-class French cuisine. Olgalik went on to explain that after the bombing apparently many of our old customers had gone to the Park Hotel. It was a decision that would change my life.

• • •

On the first day I arrived at Park Hotel I reconnected with my friends Olgalik and Regas. I was told to assist the *maître d'*, who also was Greek. His name was Ted Theologos. He was about five years older than I was. Once again, I immediately threw myself into work. I remembered the evening Costa and I had dined at the Park almost four years before when he was doing his apprenticeship. Costa had been conscripted into the Turkish military in the late winter of 1943 and was stationed at Ankara in 1944 for two years.

In 1944 the work battalions had been suspended once again, so Costa avoided the life-threatening experience on the Russian border I had endured. The prejudice of the Turks against Christians was fickle and ran in cycles, but the certainty was that it never ended.

"Christo, we will have cream of asparagus soup for lunch today," Olgalik called out in perfect French.

"Okay, Chef, I will let them know." I called for Regas as I walked into the ballroom.

"Yes, Chrysostomos?" he responded in Greek.

"Let me show you the proper fold in the napkin. You see?" as I demonstrated.

"Thank you, yes." I remember how Aristis had said the same to me, a busboy of 17, nine years before.

"Very well, finish the lunch setup."

"Yes, of course, Chrysostomos." Hearing Regas speaking my name in perfect Greek made me feel like I was back on Imbroz. I thought of my family and my carefree childhood before the Turks. I thought of Jimmy at the Halki Seminary and what sort of life he may be living worlds away from me.

I felt personal solace when I learned that the complexion of the world conflict was changing to favor the Allies. The German war machine had buckled under a frigid Russian winter that I knew only too well. Tens of thousands of German soldiers had frozen and starved to death on the frigid bank of the Volga River in and around Stalingrad the previous winter, but not before killing a million Soviet soldiers in the battle. The Germans were finding the Russians to be a formidable foe on their own soil.

It seemed only a matter of time before Germany would be defeated, and, in June of 1944, the Allies launched an all-out assault on the beaches of Normandy and began to drive toward Germany. All men who thirsted for freedom were encouraged. The world had begun to change in anticipation of Germany's eventual surrender. New alliances were frantically being forged and the Americans reestablished diplomatic relations with Turkey. The Turks were eager to change their posture in preparation for an Allied victory. As Germany grew increasingly weak, communism became the new threat, and, bordering Russia, Turkey became a strategic ally overnight.

• • •

During the fifteen months I spent working at Park Hotel I met and served many wealthy and politically powerful people, but one fateful meeting was more noteworthy than the rest.

One evening in November of 1944, a month before my twenty-seventh birthday, I was serving Mr. Hüseyin Ragip Baydur, the newly appointed Turkish Ambassador to America. We had the occasion to get to know each other as he had chosen me to wait on him a number of times during the preceding year. He had been Ambassador to Russia from 1929 through 1934 prior to his appointment to the United States and this was the first time I had waited on him since he had assumed his new position.

At first the evening seemed no different than any other.

"Christo," he said after he had been served his appetizer, "you understand, don't you, that I've been appointed to go to America to serve at the Embassy in Washington?"

"Yes, sir," I responded mechanically, pouring him some wine.

"As the new Turkish Ambassador I will be taking some people with me."

"That's nice, sir."

He continued on, and I was uncertain what more he wanted of me. "Christo, I want to ask you if you would like to accompany me as my aide, my butler."

I had to repeat back what he said to me to believe it. He was speaking so casually that the full import of his words escaped me at first.

"To America?" I gasped.

"Of course, to America," the Ambassador laughed. "Where else would Washington be?"

"But, sir, I am a Christian," I said.

Our eyes met. I saw his warm anticipation of this response.

"I can take whomever I want, Christo," he reassured me. "I have spoken to your boss requesting permission to ask you. In addition to managing my appointments, you would also be in charge of planning my meals and entertainment schedule. . . ."

I never even heard his next words. *America* was all I could think about. Can this be true? My mind flashed back.

I remembered myself as a young boy with Papa. I heard him urging me to go to America, and I remembered how I promised him that someday I would. A chill ran up my spine and a lump swelled in my throat. I had been hit full force with the mighty blow of good fortune.

"We will leave in the second week of February," he continued. It seemed the entirety of what he had just offered me was lost on him.

"We will go first by plane to Cairo, and then by ship to New York. From there we will take a train to Washington. There will be others in the group. A chef named Olgalik will be my cook. You will assist my secretary with my itinerary during our travel and in coordinating my meals and functions...."

He paused, looking at me in some amusement as I stared back intently. "I assume you accept my offer, Christo?" he asked.

"Yes, yes, sir!" I exclaimed, finally finding my voice and bowing formally. "Yes, I wish to go with you to America," I repeated with a respectful second half-bow.

"Good," he nodded, "then it's settled. The pay will be 800 lira a week, and, of course, you will have room and board at the Embassy. Do you have any problem with that?"

"No, sir, none at all," I replied hastily, shocked at the notion that anyone could possibly have a problem with such an offer. Suddenly I realized that I was staring wide-eyed at the Ambassador, an ear-to-ear grin splitting my face. My cheeks and face flushed and I glanced down, struggling to retain some composure. At long last my opportunity had arrived. What an irony, I thought, that the ambassador of my oppressor would be the ticket to America. Papa's wish for me and my dream would finally be realized. Serving my enemy had served me quite well.

• • •

It had taken fourteen long years after leaving Imbroz before the age of 14, but my dream was about to be realized. After the long years of six and seven-day workweeks of service, and a cruel conscription in the Turkish military, it seemed that I was finally about to seek my fortune in America—the land of freedom and promise. I wrote to Katina immediately telling her the good news and letting her know that I planned to visit Imbroz in late January of 1945 for one final time before I left for America. She responded just as quickly.

Chrysostomos,

Costa is back from Ankara and working as a tailor thanks to your help. Papa has lost everything but his pride—yet you have sustained him and us and now your dreams are our dreams. It saddens me to tell you this now but Bishop Iakovos has been arrested. Five Turkish gendarmes came with guns pointed, accusing him of making subversive statements against Turkey. Oh Christo, after all this time we don't understand why. We all love you and are so proud of you. We are so excited about your return.

Love,
Katerina

The arrest of Bishop Iakovos at the end of 1944—twenty-one years after the signing of the Treaty of Lausanne—underscored the ongoing persecution still being endured. I soon learned that Bishop Maxim, Metropolitan of Chakidonos, had also been arrested, as well as two members of the Holy Synod, the ruling body of the Church at the Patriarchate. Rumor had it they had been imprisoned in Bursa. I wondered how Jimmy was. Even though the chaos of World War II was winding down, nothing seemed to bring civility to the Turks.

Still I was so thankful to hear that Costa had been released safely from his conscription and was working at home with my family to sew clothes for the Turks. The year 1945 would see more good news on that front, with the Allies winning in both the European and Pacific theaters. The end of war was in sight, but the extreme discrimination that was endemic against Christians throughout Turkey was not. I made my final arrangements to leave Park and embarked on my trip home to Imbroz.

• • •

After disembarking the steamship from Turkey, my thoughts were focused on my family when I boarded the tiny boat with Captain Koutris and we rowed ashore to Castro one more time.

"Greetings, Captain Koutris, how are you?" I called out enthusiastically.

"I'm all right, young man," he responded with a smile. I was now 27 years old.

The Captain was more haggard and worn than ever. His appearance, chiseled features, and detached solitude did not readily lend themselves to the feelings of warmth, family, and home that he had always evoked in my memories. It had been five years since Costa and I had taken our short trip home, and fourteen years since Captain Koutris had first rowed Demetri, Yanni, and me to catch the ship to Constantinople. The truth was that much had changed, yet much had stayed the same. We were happy to see each other.

"Look at you. You are a grown man now. You remind me of your father."

"Thank you, Captain."

"What's this I hear? You're going to America with the Turkish Ambassador!" His sharp piercing eyes looked youthful on his wrinkled rugged face. He stood with a black Greek fisherman's cap set squarely on his head.

"Do I remember a young boy of ten going to see his uncle and aunt on Samothraki telling me telling me he would go to America?" his dark eyes staring with an uncharacteristic ear to ear grin.

"Yes, Captain, the second week in February I will be flying with his excellence to Cairo, where we will board a ship for New York." I was smiling ear to ear with my news, causing the stoic Captain to laugh for the first time, slap me on the back, and say, "Well done, son!"

There was nothing I wanted more than to be like my father, and Captain Koutris's words were gratifying. The rest of our time at sea passed quietly as we approached the shore, and the surging, painful anticipation of my visit home dissipated upon my arrival. There at the worn and splintered dock of Castro I saw my family.

In the cold air on the dock I embraced Mama and Papa for a long moment—our first embrace since I'd brought Costa home five years before. They looked older. Papa's hair and moustache had turned fully white, although his eyes and warm smiled remained as I had always remembered them. Mama seemed smaller but she greeted me with outsized cheer. Costa, Katina, and Sultana shared in our embrace before we all walked home. I was positive and determined and planned to spend every minute with my family.

That week I spent at home passed quickly.

"We have invited everyone to join us this Sunday," Katina said the night before I was to return to Constantinople. That next day Uncle Dimitris, Mrs. Karazou, and even Captain Koutris joined us for dinner. I had written home about the Ambassador's offer, so by the time I reached Imbroz everyone had heard the news. What a special day.

Captain Koutris raised his drink to toast me, tears in his weathered eyes. "Good luck, Christo. May the seas be calm on your journey."

My favorite Uncle Dimitris stood next. "Everyone on the island is so proud of you. May God bless you with happiness and success in America."

Papa spoke next with his usual warm smile. "Hold your head high, Christo, and forget what we have endured. Rise above it and make a way for yourself. Take what you know from us and hand it down to the next generation. That way a part of us will always be with you. God bless your travels and keep you safe."

"To Chrysostomos!" Everyone stood and raised their glasses.

Jimmy's aunt met me with a final embrace. "Jimmy sends his regards. I'm sure your paths will cross again one day."

The next morning my family returned me to the dock one last time.

"You and Mama and Katina, Sultana and Costa," I said to Papa. "I will bring you all to America."

Shaking his head Papa smiled and said, "Christo, don't worry about Mama and me. We are not leaving. We will be with you always, but we will not leave the island." He glanced over to my siblings. "But your sisters and brother are another matter," he added.

"Chrysostomos, we are very proud of you." Mama embraced me one final time.

I fought back my tears when I gave each of them a final embrace and boarded Captain Koutris's boat. As we rowed away, I took one last look at my family—again parting was difficult not knowing when I might see them again. I watched until their images faded into the distance.

When we reached the steamship for Constantinople, Captain Koutris took his hat off and made a respectful bow, which I returned. We both laughed.

At age 27 I had spent fourteen years, just over half my life, two hundred miles away from home and due to my work and responsibilities was only able to visit my family twice. Now my childhood dream, hatched with Papa on the porch of our small home, had finally become real. The odyssey of my life would finally take me to America.

CHAPTER 11

Flight to Freedom

In an age of fops and toys,
wanting wisdom, void of right,
who shall nerve heroic boys
to hazard all in Freedom's fight,—
break sharply off their jolly games,
forsake their comrades gay
and quit proud homes and youthful dames
for famine, toil and fray?
Yet on the nimble air benign
speed nimbler messages,
that waft the breath of grace divine
to hearts in sloth and ease.
So nigh is grandeur to our dust,
so near is God to man,
when Duty whispers low, Thou must,
the youth replies, I can.

—RALPH WALDO EMERSON, 1863

THE TIME HAD ARRIVED, but my journey to America almost ended before it began. In late February of 1945 the Ambassador's itinerary was set. We would depart Ankara by plane for Cairo, Egypt, where we would stay for ten days on business. Then we would board a passenger steamship bound for New York flying the flag of the Isthmian Steamship Company, and within a month we would be in the New World.

I joined Ambassador Baydur and his entourage and boarded a twin-engine passenger plane that held about forty people for our two-hour flight to Cairo. It was my first trip on an airplane, and I watched in fascination as the ground fell away beneath us, clutching the armrests of my seat, relaxing only when we reached our cruising altitude. Though it was my first time travelling by air, it would prove to be memorable for another reason.

After our ascent I noticed that my window was being showered as if it were raining. When I glanced at the porthole across the aisle, however, the window glass on that side of the plane was dry. Could it be raining on one side of the plane and not the other? I peered out a porthole three seats up on the same side of the plane as mine and saw no rain. Alarmed, I turned to Olgalik, who sat across the aisle.

"Look at the rain on my window," I said, but his gaze showed he did not understand its significance.

"Oh, Christo," he responded, shaking his head, "I'm sure it's nothing—just a little moisture."

"I know that," I said impatiently, "but why just on a few windows?"

Then I realized that the rain-splattered windows were directly behind the right wing of the plane. Moreover, the droplets were not clear in color. It suddenly occurred to me that the droplets might be fuel, not water.

"Stewardess!" I called to the attendant who stood with her back to me several rows forward. "Madame, please!"

She turned and I gestured her closer. "See the rain hitting my window?" I asked in Turkish.

"Yes," she nodded.

"Well, it's not rain. I believe it's gasoline."

"Oh, I don't think so, sir" she smiled.

"Look at the windows in front of the wing," I told her a little frantically, "and the ones across the aisle. They're dry, but the wet ones are behind the wing—where the fuel tanks are. Please, go tell the captain."

She glanced at the windows where I was pointing. Then she nodded. "Okay," she said, "just stay calm," but I noticed that her smile had disappeared and she moved rather quickly up the aisle toward the cockpit.

A few minutes later an officer from the cockpit followed her down the aisle. "Excuse me, sir," he said as he bent over me to peer out the window, then returned to the cockpit without a word to me.

A moment later the captain's voice came over the loudspeaker. "Ambassador, ladies and gentlemen," he said in Turkish. "It has come to our attention that we must return to Ankara. Please remain calm. Thanks to an alert passenger, we are not in danger," he assured us. "It appears there is just a minor fuel leak. We estimate our return time to be thirty minutes. Thank you for your patience."

No sooner had the captain made his announcement than I felt the plane veer to the right to begin a sharp descent. Just my luck, I thought to myself. When the maneuver was completed, the stewardess returned to my seat. "Sir, the captain has asked for your name," she said.

"Christo Chrisostomides," I told her.

While waiting back in Ankara, Olgalik talked about my lifesaving discovery to anyone who would listen. Meanwhile, mechanics on the ground realized that the gas cap had been left off the tank near the right wing. The plane was refueled, the cap tightly sealed, and we boarded the plane again for another try at Cairo.

Once we were airborne the captain explained to the passengers that, without a gas cap, fuel was profusely spraying from the tank. "Thanks to Mr. Christo Chrisostomides's alert detection," he went on, "we avoided a serious problem."

"Bravo, Christo!" the passengers burst out in a unanimous cheer. Suddenly the entire plane, including the Ambassador, turned to face me. "Stand up, Christo," Olgalik said, pulling on my arm. Blushing a little, I stood amidst rancorous clapping and cheers and offered my fellow passengers a brief bow.

"See why I have him on my staff?" the Ambassador joked, and the passengers, in the exuberance that usually follows relief, laughed and chattered, continuing the celebration.

Knowing the problem was solved I allowed myself to relax back into the seat, still rather enjoying my first—now second—plane trip.

I would not allow anything to ruin this, my long awaited, though delayed, trip to America.

• • •

This time our flight to Cairo was uneventful. When we arrived we were picked up at the airport and ferried to a downtown hotel. During our ten days in Cairo the Ambassador and a few aides were scheduled to make a side trip to Portugal.

In the hotel after unpacking, I sat on the edge of my bed to reread my passport. "Chrysostomos Chrisostomides," it said. "Not valid for more than one journey to the United States unless revalidated. Authorized by the Department of State, Telegram No. 125, January 27, 1945."

There was a sense of exultation in the air and shortly I would become part of it. Like Europe, I would soon be freed, liberated from the oppression I had known since I was a boy.

These exhilarating thoughts rushed through my mind while I sat on the corner of my bed in that Cairo hotel. I looked at the passport that would take me to a new and better life. "God bless America," I whispered softly. I had not yet set foot on American soil, but I had my passport and American visa in my hand and a lifetime dream in my heart. Most importantly, I now had the means to make that dream a reality.

During the next few days I accompanied the Ambassador to several receptions around Cairo. I also planned a function that we held in a room at the hotel for the Egyptian diplomatic corps, the American Ambassador to Egypt, and other assorted dignitaries. I planned the food and drink, and Olgalik prepared the meal. Later in the week I accompanied the Ambassador and a couple of his seasoned aides on his brief state visit to Portugal.

When we returned to Cairo, we had a couple of days to relax before embarking for America. Olgalik and I decided to see the Sphinx and the Pyramids on the outskirts of the city. When we arrived at the stables at seven that morning the temperature was already more than eighty degrees. Dressed in khaki pants and a white t-shirt I was still uncomfortably warm.

A young boy approached us with two camels and outstretched hands. We paid him and took our places on the seated camels, heaving forward as they straightened their legs and snapping back when they stood upright. Olgalik and I quickly found that riding a camel was very different than riding a horse or, in my case, a donkey.

With the young boy as a guide, we continued on a path of sand, the colossal formations looming before us as we travelled toward them.

"Christo, I am not a young man," Olgalik said. "I lost my family and a good part of my life to the Bolsheviks, just as you lost so much to the Ottomans. Yet I, like you, feel the excitement of a child when I contemplate my trip to America."

"America, the land of freedom, will soon be our home," I told him.

"We are a bit like vagabonds who have lived for a long time in exile in Constantinople," he laughed. "And now we will go, compliments of the Turks, to our new home. It is a bit more than ironic, is it not?" We both laughed.

The young boy guided us back to the stables so we could visit the Sphinx on foot. When we motioned to get off our camels, he exclaimed, "One price to get up, one price to get down." That was my first and last camel ride.

• • •

The next morning was our last full day in Cairo and I had a number of things to do for the Ambassador before we left. I rose at dawn, showered, and dressed carefully, pinning the relic coin over my heart on my t-shirt, and said a prayer. Then I packed my belongings and went downstairs.

I had begun collecting stamps as well as menus during my years in Turkey. I found several interesting Egyptian stamps that morning and I placed them in my stamp book near the ones I had recently acquired in Portugal. I then began the activities of the day, which included attending a farewell party for the Ambassador hosted at the

American Embassy. That evening porters carried our baggage in large cases to the dock to load aboard the ship.

The next morning we boarded the *Isthmian* steamship and began our journey to America. It was a large vessel with cabins for passengers on the three upper decks, and cargo stowed deep in its holds. The Ambassador stayed with two of his aides on the main deck. Olgalik and I shared a small cabin with bunk beds directly under the Ambassador's suite.

I had grown up close to the sea. I had fished in it, swum in it, and boated across it, and had never once become seasick. Poor Olgalik was not so lucky. During our three weeks at sea he spent barely a day or two out of bed. Most days we ate in a galley below deck—or I did, at any rate. Olgalik had little appetite. The galley food was palatable but unexciting, which under the circumstances suited Olgalik quite well. On two occasions, the Ambassador invited us to the first-class dining rooms, which provided us a respite from the monotony of this plain fare.

During our first week at sea we ran into a nasty storm that pummeled us with gale-force winds and threatening swells. For over twelve hours the vessel rocked violently like a toy boat. Everyone was sick and stayed below deck. The captain turned the ship into the swells so that they broke over the bow, washing along the decks all the way to the stern. Everything that was loose had to be tied down.

I wondered during the storm if the boat would hold together. When the storm finally abated we were off course by one day, yet we were only four days outside New York harbor. The calm sea and clear sky marked my passage from the tempest of my old life to the fair weather of promise before me. Olgalik and I spent our last days aboard ship on deck playing *tavoli*, known as backgammon in America, and absorbing all the sights and sounds.

On the morning of our approach to the harbor we were all on deck at dawn eagerly straining to see the Statue of Liberty. Like children, we anxiously awaited the gateway to better days. Olgalik and I were so excited that we could barely talk. Gradually, the city's dramatic skyline appeared on the horizon and then suddenly, at the mouth of the harbor, luminous in the pearly light of sunrise, there she was.

The sight took my breath away and gave me chills of excitement. Thousands of immigrants pass by the statue seeking a better life every year, trading oppression and sacrifice for a future of hope. I stood at the bow of the ship, humbled by the sight of the statue beckoning us towards America, and I silently hoped she had room for two more.

I glanced over at Olgalik who stood near me at the rail.

"She is beautiful, isn't she?" I said.

Olgalik looked at me and smiled. "Yes, Christo, she is," he replied. A single tear dropped down the side of his face.

"We are here," I muttered as we both laughed with tears in our eyes.

Standing nearby, tearfully crossing themselves in whispered praises, were Elias and Ann Melas, an older Greek couple. They would be joining Olgalik in the Ambassador's kitchen. As I quietly joined them, I saw Olgalik silently signing the cross as we all stared at the New York skyline. At long last we had arrived in America.

Because we were part of the diplomatic corps we were permitted to disembark directly and board a train bound for Union Station in Washington, D.C. When we arrived we were greeted by representatives from the State Department, then driven to the Turkish Embassy on Massachusetts Avenue. The city appeared to be very clean and manicured, standing in stark contrast to the filth and debris of Constantinople and the other old cities I had passed through. I was awestruck. My new home was more than I had expected.

Papa, Mama, at long last we are here, I whispered as I clutched the relic coin under my t-shirt.

I was overwhelmed with the feeling one gets upon coming home from a long journey, and I knew that the feeling would fill me for a lifetime. Even though I had never set foot in America before, I felt like I was home at last.

Part II: New World

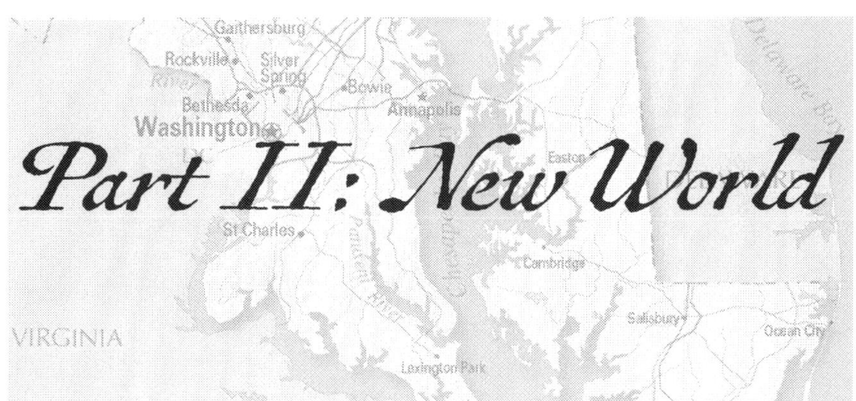

CHAPTER 12

Reunited

He that is thy friend indeed,
he will help thee in thy need:
if thou sorrow, he will weep;
if thou wake, he cannot sleep:
Thus of every grief in heart
he with thee doth bear a part.
These are certain signs to know
faithful friend from flattering foe.
—WILLIAM SHAKESPEARE, 1599

THE TURKISH EMBASSY on Massachusetts Avenue had luxurious rooms buttressed by sturdy white columns. Crystal chandeliers hung from the ceilings and fine Persian rugs covered the marble floors. My room had a full bathroom and my window overlooked Embassy Row at Sheridan Circle in Washington. Although my wage was modest, the Turkish government spent lavishly on its Ambassador, so his staff was quite literally living in luxury. As soon as I unpacked, I sat in the chair before the small desk in my room and began to write a letter home.

"Christo?" My writing was interrupted by the Ambassador, whose room was down the hall from mine. The letter would wait.

I promptly stood, slipped into my jacket, and walked into hall.

"Yes, Your Excellency?" I responded in Turkish, offering a slight bow as he entered the room.

"Tomorrow I will make a formal visit to the White House," the Ambassador informed me. "While I am gone you will prepare for a reception we will hold here at the Embassy tomorrow evening.

Have Olgalik prepare a full complement of *hors d'ouvres* and pastries. There will be many dignitaries among the guests, Christo."

The Ambassador paused in his flurry of orders to look at me. "Even Vice President Truman will attend," he said.

"Yes, sir. What time would you care to dine tonight?"

"As soon as you can manage it, Christo," he told me. "Make it something small and light, and I will have it in my room."

"Yes, sir." I responded with another bow and hurried off to find Olgalik.

There was a great deal to be done for the Embassy reception, and I spent the next couple of hours making plans. When I returned to my room, I finished my letter to Katina and went to bed.

Dearest Katerina,

Each room in the Embassy is larger than our tiny home. No room is as warm or beautiful as our home which I miss dearly....

Christo

The next day would be filled with preparations. It would be the first full day of my new duties in America, and it would include serving the Vice President of the United States.

• • •

Guests began arriving shortly after seven o'clock and among them was a small group of men escorting Vice President Truman. The Ambassador greeted the entourage personally upon entering. As Truman's gaze passed over me, our eyes met for a brief second. His face confirmed my impression of a serious and modest man who appeared to lack the insecurities and superiority of the Turkish leaders to whom I had grown accustomed. I was filled with awe by the humble demeanor of the Vice President.

A month later on April 12, 1945, President Roosevelt would die and Vice President Truman would become President. Although

Roosevelt had many critics, he was generally viewed as a great man, and his death would be seen as an irreversible loss to the free world. It was sad to think that President Roosevelt did not live to see the victory he had worked so hard to achieve.

Yet I was intrigued and pleased to learn that the new President had begun working as a haberdasher, much like my brother and family. It is evidence of the greatness of America that a man could make his way from a clothing store to the White House. The new President would guide the nation in the final months of war.

Germany surrendered unconditionally a short time later, on May 8, 1945. Hitler was defeated and the western world was overwhelmed with joy. The entire staff, including the Ambassador, listened to the radio as President Truman and British Prime Minister Churchill announced to the world the end of World War II in Europe. The western world began an uncontained celebration of Hitler's defeat. I celebrated right along.

• • •

In the summer and fall of 1945 there were many diplomatic functions I helped plan between Turkey and her newfound ally as talk of the spread of communism increased. The Turkish Ambassador represented the Turkish government in the negotiation of many matters. He offered an interesting perspective as Turkey's former Ambassador to Russia, and was of particular interest to the Americans. Toward this end there were many social and political functions, all requiring my assistance.

The fact that Turkey shared its northern border with the Soviet Union and stood between the Soviets and a warm water port meant that she was of great interest to the Allies. Even before the surrender of Germany was ratified, the lines of the Cold War with Russia had been drawn. The sands had shifted.

"Christo, the Ambassadors of France and England will join us at dinner tonight, so make sure the menu is continental."

"Yes, Your Excellency," I replied, offering my trademark bow.

"Oh, and Christo, this letter came from your father," he added, placing the letter in my hand with a smile.

"Thank you, sir." Bowing, I slipped the letter into my pocket and hurried through the day's tasks so that I could retire to my room to read Papa's letter in leisure.

I discovered that evening that the letter was dated April 11, 1945, more than four months earlier.

My Dearest Son Chrysostomos,

We are receiving the money you send. I kiss you and I pray that God will be with you always. Rest assured that by doing the following four things you will be loved by God and honored and respected by your fellow man; you will live a happy life: (1) your expenses should not exceed your income; (2) self-interest shouldn't separate you from family; (3) if your country calls, go to her aid, no matter how high you rise in life; and (4) never lose your humility.

Your Father,
I. Chrisostomides

The letter was classic Papa. I wondered if the family tapestry with more of Papa's wisdom still hung on the wall inside the door of our small home on Imbroz. Although I had grown, for a brief moment Papa's words had me feeling like a child sitting on our porch listening attentively to his wise words.

Meanwhile with Germany's surrender a great weight seemed to have been lifted off the nation. The infectious mood of optimism and rebirth after Hitler's defeat was captivating. Along with the euphoria of that summer came rumors of the super "doomsday" bomb that President Truman planned to drop on the Japanese.

The explosion of two atomic bombs in August would end hostilities in the Pacific in a gruesome display of man's destructive ability, unleashing the threat of future nuclear war. Man had developed a weapon that could bring an end to his very existence.

• • •

One cold morning in the middle of December I received an unexpected birthday treat. I was in the Embassy lobby when the doorbell rang. The secretary was nowhere to be found so I crossed the lobby, swung open the door, and found myself face to face with a bearded, Orthodox priest in his mid-thirties. He was over six feet tall and had curly hair under his raised headwear, and familiar brown eyes. Around his clerical collar was a heavy gold chain, and hanging from it was a gold Orthodox crucifix about three inches long.

For an instant the priest and I gazed blankly at each other. Then he smiled warmly. "Jimmy," I whispered under my breath.

"Chrysostomos, my friend—how are you?" he asked.

I couldn't believe it. It was Jimmy Coucouzes, my childhood friend. Astonished, I had not seen Jimmy since I was ten years old—eighteen years ago. We had both grown up but his stare and his height made it unmistakably Jimmy.

"Father," I said bowing, smiling warmly and properly kissing his hand to show respect.

Jimmy pulled his hand from mine and chuckled.

"Come in, please," I said, ushering my old friend from the doorway into the lobby.

Once inside, Jimmy patted me on my back and smiled. "Christo, it is so good to see you!"

"And it is wonderful to see you, too, although I must admit that I am surprised to see you here."

Jimmy told me he had arrived in America four years before to attend Harvard after graduating from seminary, and he was now teaching at Holy Cross Greek Orthodox Seminary in Boston, Massachusetts. He had heard of my conscription into the *amele taburu* a few years before and was worried.

"I came down from Boston on business, Christo. I learned you were at the Embassy and I couldn't leave without seeing you. It has been a long time, my friend."

"It has been too long," I said, thinking how ironic it was that we would both be reunited in America.

"Remember the ball we played with?" he inquired.

"How could I forget that ball, it was so misshapen and hard to kick." We both laughed.

"Have you spoken with your aunt?" I asked.

"Yes, things will never be the same on Imbroz," Jimmy replied. "How are your parents?"

"I write them but you know how difficult things are."

Later that morning, after Jimmy and I had toured the Embassy, we settled in a small reception room. We talked about Imbroz, our families, and our journeys to America.

"Do you like your new duties here at the Embassy?" he asked.

"Very much," I assured him, "and I stay very busy. But I miss my family, of course. This may interest you, Father. Katina writes me to ask if I can find a husband for Sultana. I understand that Taki Hatzikiriakidis is here in America—do you remember Taki?"

The Hatzikiriakidis—or Hatzi—family was among our neighbors on Imbroz, from the seaport village of Castro. Jimmy and I sometimes played with Taki. The Hatzi family had been in New York since 1938. They left behind large holdings of land on Imbroz for the safety of America. Taki was 21 when his family left the island. He enlisted in the U.S. Navy to gain citizenship, and served in the Pacific during the war.

"Of course, I remember him," Jimmy told me. "Taki has been in America since before the war. I believe his entire family is in America now. You have heard, I suppose, that he is serving in the Navy though, and I have no idea where he is stationed."

"Do you suppose you could get his address somehow?" I asked.

"Of course, Christo," Jimmy laughed lightly. "I would be happy to help Sultana. And tell me, what of Katina? How is she?"

"She is fine. You know, my parents are older now, and she is a great help to them." The truth was I was worried about her and I wanted her desperately to have a life of her own.

• • •

To my delight Jimmy stayed to have lunch with me, and for dessert I made sure to serve him *loucomades,* a deep-fried doughball immersed in honey and sprinkled with cinnamon—his favorite Greek pastry.

"You remember your father advised us to go to America?"

"Of course I remember, Jimmy."

"Well we did it, Christo. We made it to America. Isn't life strange?" he mused with a smile ear to ear on his face. A long, still, solemn moment of solidarity passed. Then Jimmy broke the silence.

"But I have kept you from your duties long enough, Christo," Jimmy said, rising reluctantly from his seat, "and I have a train to catch to Boston."

We stood and Jimmy clasped my right shoulder. "I will not forget today," he told me.

"Nor will I, Father," I said, as I accompanied him back to the Embassy lobby.

At the door he turned to face me. "May God bless you, Christo, and always be with you."

"Thank you, Jimmy," I bowed.

"It has meant a great deal to see you again, Christo." he said.

In parting we both shared a prideful, lingering smile that acknowledged our reunion in America and the mere improbability of the difficulties we had traversed on our separate but parallel paths to get here. Standing outside I felt a slight breeze, yet the warm sun shone down upon me as I watched Jimmy descend the steps to hail a cab in front of the Embassy. I lingered outside after he left, trying to hold on to the moment for as long as I could. Yet something told me our paths would cross again.

• • •

Finally, my young friend Regas, still at Park Hotel in Constantinople, located Taki's mother, Urania Hatzi, in New York and eventually Taki's address was forwarded to me. Regas was from

Castro, the village Taki and his mother had left. Greek grapevines are quite extensive and often effective.

I played my role in the matchmaking process successfully, for within a month Taki wrote my father asking if he could have permission to court Sultana.

Papa agreed, and soon enough Sultana and Taki Hatzi were officially corresponding and engaged. That was the way things were often done in the Old World. The fact that our families were acquainted with each other and that Taki was now established in New York and could provide a good home for Sultana was paramount. Taki wanted to go to Imbroz to get Sultana, but Papa advised strongly against it in a brief letter:

> *What if he is conscripted into the Turkish Army? That would jeopardize all our hopes and dreams for the future, what we are working so hard to accomplish. It is best if Sultana comes to America....*

After receiving Papa's letter, I immediately began saving money to finance Sultana's passage to America and making arrangements with the Embassy for her visa.

Shortly after Papa's letter, Ted Theologos arrived at the Embassy from Constantinople. I had convinced the Ambassador to have him work with us at the Embassy. Ted carried himself well and worked hard, and I believed he would be an asset to the Ambassador, and to Olgalik, as well.

I greeted Ted with real enthusiasm and satisfaction. It was also rewarding for me to share this opportunity with someone who had endured similar hardships. It was a big event when someone from our small corner of the world made it to America, and I wanted to make sure he knew it. The post–World War II group of immigrants appreciated the opportunities of America as much as any other immigrant group in America's history. America had been spared the pure evil that blanketed Europe, Asia, and parts of Africa.

• • •

It was the early summer of 1946, a few days after Ted's arrival, and I was preparing a new menu in the kitchen with Olgalik when I was called to the Embassy foyer. I couldn't believe who was waiting for me—again, it was Jimmy.

"Greetings, my friend," he said.

"What a surprise, a pleasure!" Pleased to see my childhood friend twice in a year. "Will you stay for dinner with me?"

"I cannot," he replied regretfully. "I have a train to catch back to Boston. I could not leave the city, however, without saying hello again."

"Then perhaps you will share some coffee and *loucomades* with me?"

At the mention of his favorite pastry, Jimmy smiled. "How can I refuse such an offer?"

Within twenty minutes Olgalik had prepared us coffee and fresh *loucomades*. Soon after the treats were served, Jimmy and I retired to a quiet room to exchange news. He was excited to hear of the engagement, and heartily agreed that Sultana should come to America instead of risking Taki's conscription by the Turkish army. I also told him about Ted's arrival from Constantinople, and for several minutes he talked about other Greeks who had recently come to America.

"And what is your news?" I asked Jimmy finally.

"Chrysostomos, I have been called by the Bishop of Constantinople, Athenagoras, who was also from Imbroz, to return to the Patriarchate in Constantinople, and I would like you to ask the Ambassador for assistance with my visa. I would ask if the Ambassador can mitigate or eliminate the fees involved, and in general allow me an uneventful passage and a timely arrival. Do you suppose he could do that, as I have very little money?"

"I will talk to him. When do you go?" The Bishop of Constantinople is the religious leader of the Eastern Orthodox Church, the Pope's equivalent for Orthodox Christians.

"I am uncertain of the date I will leave, but I will write you when I return to Boston. The point of my trip is to visit the Patriarchate for sabbatical, but I will try to return to Imbroz for a while. The Bishop of Constantinople may have something else in mind."

"Is there anything you would like me to tell your parents?"

"That I think of them and pray for them every day," I told him. "Now, let's have some more coffee and I'll ask Olgalik and Theologos to join us."

Moments later we were all together.

"Any news of Iakavos?" I asked Jimmy.

"After the arrest of old Bishops Iakovos and Maxim a year ago, the Holy Mount and the Holy Monastery of Great Lavra on Mount Athos were taken over by Turkish settlers. All the elders who protested were exiled. Finally, Iakovos and Maxim were released from prison." The news of Bishop Iakovos's release was happily received. He was much older now and did not need to be in prison.

After an afternoon of catching up over Turkish coffee and honey-laden warm *loucomades,* I reluctantly escorted Jimmy to the door to meet a taxi I had called. "Are you sure you can't stay for dinner?"

"No, no, my friend, I must return."

It was difficult for both of us to let go of the time we had together. Before he turned to enter the cab, I gave him a bag filled with *loucomades* that Olgalik had prepared for his trip back to New York. Jimmy had a sweet tooth. I waved goodbye from the door of the Embassy. After so many years apart, I felt lucky to be reunited with Jimmy in America twice, even if only for a few hours each time.

• • •

A few weeks later I received a letter from Jimmy telling me that he had seen Taki, and inquiring for the latest news regarding Sultana's arrival. Shortly after Jimmy wrote, I received another letter from Papa in May. The news wasn't good.

Dear Chrysostomos,

We received Sultana's papers—the letters, immigration papers as well as the Ambassador's letter—for which we thank you very much. We *also received the check for $100 for Sultana's fare. Unfortunately, we have another problem and will require your further assistance. On April 9 we brought Katerina to Constantinople. She was in urgent need of an operation for her appendix. The operation was performed on April 10. She was hospitalized for ten days. Afterwards, I took her to the Romana Hotel where we are staying. I sent a telegram to Imvros requesting that Sultana come to Constantinople and ready herself to embark for America.... Katerina has recovered.... Please send more money to us in Constantinople as these events were unexpected.*

With love,
Your father

Once again I was reminded how easy it was to forget the difficulties of day-to-day life in the world I had left behind. The transfer of money overseas was still a major challenge in those days. I immediately made arrangements to send money to my friends at Pera Palace, who could change dollars to liras. It took a couple of weeks, but as soon as possible I sent Papa another $100.

• • •

The time had come for Sultana's arrival. Taki and I made the trip to Norfolk, Virginia, to meet her and, as soon as she cleared customs, I called out to her. When she heard my voice she scanned the crowd, looking for me.

"Christo!" she exclaimed in an excited squeal when she saw me.

A moment later she threw her arms around my neck and kissed me. "I made it! I can't believe I'm here," she said breathlessly.

"Welcome to America!"

It had been nine years since Sultana and Taki had seen each other, and for a moment they looked a little embarrassed. "Hello, Sultana. We are going to take you to New York where you will stay with Urania, my mother," Taki told her. In a shy but hopeful gesture, he took her hand in his.

"Okay, Taki," Sultana smiled warmly. I could see them both visibly relax, and we made our way through the bustling crowd to find a taxi.

It was a happy day for everyone. I had brought my little sister to America, and she and Taki would soon be married.

Shortly after Sultana's arrival, I received another letter from Jimmy with news of his long-awaited trip.

Christo,

I am leaving by airplane for Constantinople.... Maybe I will be able to go to Imvros. My visa is for a return trip in September. Thank the Ambassador for taking care of my travel fees. Should I see your parents, I will give them your warmest regards....

Archimandrite lakovos

It was strange to see Jimmy sign in the name of our old Bishop on Imbroz. His new title also reflected his advancement. Apparently, he had been appointed to supervise a group of priests, a sign of what was to come, no doubt.

Life is full of surprises, I thought. Fancy two young island boys reuniting after eighteen years at the Turkish Embassy in America. Unimaginable, but so it happened. I had arranged a letter from the Ambassador for Jimmy after his earlier request and had promptly mailed it to the Patriarchate. As it turned out his request for assistance on his return trip never materialized. It would be much longer than September before I heard from or saw Jimmy again, and then once again under conditions I would never have expected.

CHAPTER 13

Elenitsa

Nature's first green is gold,
her hardest hue to hold.
Her early leaf's a flower;
but only so an hour.
Then leaf subsides to leaf.
So, Eden sank to grief,
so dawn goes down to day.
Nothing gold can stay.
—ROBERT FROST, 1923

THE WORLD SEEMED RATIONAL and I finally felt in control of my destiny. The crisis period seemed to be over. It was now the fall of 1946. Opportunity replaced despair; freedom replaced servitude; dignity and value seemed renewed. The dramatic change from war and chaos to the light of order and productive improvement was everywhere.

The sense of hope abounded. For a brief period the mood in Imbroz had changed as well. Many of my friends were also getting married, and my parents' letters were filled with all the details.

> *Eranthia is coming to America as a tourist. It seems her aunt has someone in mind to get her engaged to.... One of the Dimitriadis daughters was engaged to Dimaria's brother.... Katina Kouletbrianow is engaged to an Australian... a kind and good gentleman....*

Greek scuttlebutt was about to prove enormously beneficial to me. Elias and Anna Melas, who worked with me at the Embassy, had a Greek friend in Altoona, Pennsylvania, Mr. Mastos, who was, in turn, a close friend of Mr. Anton Anthony in Cumberland, Maryland. Mr. Anthony had a daughter, Eleni Antonia, who was 24 and single. Eleni was a high school graduate with two years of secretarial school, and she worked for her father.

Through the Melas-Mastos grapevine I was invited to dinner at the Anthonys' in Cumberland one evening in late fall of 1946. To make the situation less awkward Mr. and Mrs. Melas, who had never met the Anthonys, were also invited, and the three of us planned to make the trip to Cumberland by train.

On the day of the dinner I was up at dawn. I showered, touched my toes twenty-five times, pinned my relic coin to a fresh new t-shirt, said a brief prayer, and then dressed in a fine, brown, double-breasted suit. I heard Eleni was beautiful, so I wanted to look my best.

The train from Union Station to Cumberland was slow, and the trip was long enough to make me slightly nervous. When we finally pulled into the station in Cumberland we were greeted by a middle-aged, bespectacled man with brown receding hair, perhaps two inches shorter than my five feet eight inches.

"Good day," he called out in Greek as he spotted the three of us on the platform. He extended his hand to Mr. Melas and acknowledged Mrs. Melas with a smile.

"Greetings, Mr. Anthony," Mr. Melas replied, "may I introduce you to Mr. Chrysostomos Chrisostomides?"

Mr. Anthony turned to me and offered his hand while studying me. "Hello, young man. I have heard many good things about you."

I shook his hand. "The pleasure is mine," I said respectfully. The four of us chatted briefly as Mr. Anthony herded us to his car. The drive to his house took us through the town where he owned and operated an ice cream parlor called the Royal Confectionary. An energetic man, Mr. Anthony also operated the Eat Well Grill during the summer season.

"I have worked hard all my life," he told us as we drove, glancing at me in his rear-view mirror. "God willing, we are doing well, but it isn't easy."

"I imagine not," I said earnestly. He turned to me and asked, "You know about hard work, Christo?"

"Yes," I told him, smiling in return. "I know about hard work." It is an immigrant's badge.

"I see," he said turning away with a smile. He too was an immigrant.

• • •

When we arrived at the house, we were met by Mr. and Mrs. Gus Mastos, and by Mrs. Anthony, a small woman who was about 50 years old and had noticeable difficulty walking due to arthritis.

"Come, Christo," Mrs. Anthony said as we entered the front door. "Sit beside me on the sofa. You are from Turkey, are you not?"

"I am from Imbroz," I responded, sitting comfortably beside her.

The realization that I, too, had grown up under the shadow of the Turks seemed to trigger a response in her, and she opened up to me. "I am also from Turkey. From Rankia, Christo," she told me. I nodded in recognition. Rankia was a town located near Tekirdağ on the Marmara Sea in Turkey, about halfway from Imbroz to Constantinople.

"I was a girl of 14 when we left more than thirty years ago. Papa lifted my mother and me into a small boat with two other families. The Turks were trying to stop us, but Papa stood his ground. He stayed behind and pushed our boat off, protecting us even as the Turks grabbed him." Mrs. Anthony stopped, catching her breath.

"He said, 'Go! Go!' The Turks hit him over and over, Christo. We were helpless. I turned away for I could not bear to watch. I heard a gunshot. When I finally did look back, I saw him floating face down in the water. That was the last time I ever saw my father." Her voice trailed off as she looked mournfully into the distance. Even after thirty years, the anguish of losing her father in that way was still fresh.

"I understand," I said softly, and I truly did, as only another Christian from Turkey could have. She seemed comfortable with me right away.

Lightening the mood a bit, Mr. Anthony took me by the arm.

"What may I offer you to drink?" he asked hospitably. "Gin and tonic?"

"That would be fine," I told him.

He nodded and began mixing the drink.

"You know, Christo," he said, handing me a glass, "I came to America in 1908. I was 16." Mr. Anthony was ten years older than Mrs. Anthony. He paused a moment, reflecting, I supposed, on that long-ago time.

"I am not educated and I could barely speak English," he continued. "Still, I was proud to serve my new country in the U.S. Army during World War I from 1917 until armistice in November of 1918. I was lucky to survive. In the twenties, I settled in Cumberland and I married Alexandra."

I nodded in acknowledgement.

"In those days, Christo, when I was starting out, I had a horse-drawn ice cream cart that I pulled all over town. I used dry ice to keep the ice cream cold." He eyed me seriously. "And then the thirties came. They were hard years. Many people lost everything, but we got by." He broke conversation briefly to remove his thick glasses and clean them with a handkerchief.

"Come, Christo," he said, finally ushering me back toward the living room. "My daughter Eleni will be down shortly and I want to introduce you."

As we crossed the foyer I put down my drink and picked up a family picture on a side table to catch a glimpse of her.

"Eleni!" Mr. Anthony called more quickly than I had anticipated. "Come, I wish you to meet my young friend here, Chrysostomos Chrisostomides. Christo," he went on, turning to me, "my daughter Eleni."

I conspicuously placed the photo back, hoping no one noticed, and turned to see her. Eleni extended her hand to me. "It is nice to meet you, Chrysostomos," she said in perfect Greek.

I stumbled slightly to take her hand. "It is a pleasure to meet you, Eleni," I said, bowing while bringing her hand toward me for a respectful kiss. "Please call me Chris."

In the next instant, Mr. Anthony herded us toward some chairs at the dining table where we sat facing each other.

"I understand you work for the Turkish Ambassador?" Eleni asked.

"Yes, that's correct."

"You must meet a lot of people."

"Yes, I do."

There was a moment of silence, but Mrs. Anthony cut in. "You must be hungry," she offered as she brought a platter of food in from the kitchen. Usually I would be the first to help prepare for dinner, but tonight I was their guest.

"Yes, thank you."

During the meal I was so completely captivated by Eleni that I nearly forgot to eat.

"What's wrong, Christo?" Mrs. Anthony teased me good-naturedly. "You don't like my cooking? What sort of Greek are you?"

I turned my attention to my plate for the rest of the meal.

When dinner was over, Eleni and I returned to the living room for coffee and dessert. As the evening wore on we chatted about my family and my time in Turkey. By the end of the night—with the aid of a few more gin and tonics, and the encouragement of Mr. Anthony and Mr. Mastos—I was singing "You Have the Most Beautiful Eyes in the World," a popular Greek song.

I couldn't tell if Eleni was amused or embarrassed, but I welcomed her laugh either way. "I will call you Elenitsa," I said softly to her when we were alone. *Elenitsa* is a Greek nickname for Eleni, or Helen.

"Okay," she smiled in approval.

• • •

The next few months I spent every day off I could get visiting Helen. One weekend in the spring of 1947, Taki and Sultana came down to Cumberland by train. When they arrived, Helen suggested we all go to a drive-in theater that had just opened in town. This was a wonderful novelty for us. Imagine, watching a movie while sitting in a car. Afterwards, we went to Royal Confectionary where Mr. Anthony treated us to ice cream floats and sundaes—although Taki and I would have preferred a cold beer.

The weeks flew by into summer. Sultana and Taki's wedding arrived on June 20 in New York. Jimmy was still in Turkey, or he would most certainly have performed the service himself. My heart ached over the absence of Mama and Papa, too, but I was proud to represent my family at the wedding, which turned out to be a beautiful occasion, filled with joy and laughter. We celebrated with traditional Greek food, music, and dancing that extended well beyond midnight.

When I returned to Washington after the wedding, I immediately set out to have one of my own, catching the next train to Cumberland.

"Elenista, will you marry me?" I asked at once when I arrived.

"I cannot marry." Her response knocked me off my feet. "I may not be able to have children, Chris," she explained.

"Helen that doesn't matter to me," I protested.

"It's unfair to you," she insisted. "Chris, a few years ago, I had peritonitis, which required surgery. They ended up removing part of my ovary. I may not be able to give you children."

I would not let the subject rest. "I knew from the moment I met you that I wanted to spend my life with you, Helen." There was a silence that seemed to go on longer than it did.

"Okay, I will marry you."

• • •

That summer I had made up my mind to leave the Embassy and immediately began to train Ted Theologos to take my place.

I knew the Ambassador valued my services highly and I was grateful for this opportunity, but I also knew that advancement at the Embassy was limited. Besides, it was my goal to have my own business. In order to accomplish that and to be financially secure enough to support a wife and start a family in America, as well as helping my family back on Imbroz, I would certainly need to find another job. Olgalik had recently introduced me to a man named Blaise Gherardi de Parata, one of the owners of the Place Vendôme, and later Rive Gauche, two exclusive French restaurants in downtown Washington.

With my experience in French and fine dining Blaise was anxious to hire me as a waiter, and I was confident it was a better opportunity than staying on at the Embassy. The upper class of Washington, as I understood it, tipped very well. Blaise had also promised to help me obtain permanent citizenship—an offer I could not refuse.

Once Ted had learned my job duties sufficiently I gave the Ambassador notice that I would be leaving by August 1, a one-month notice. He did not take it well.

"I plan to get married," I told him, "and I cannot devote as much time to the Embassy. I will have a family and responsibilities…"

The Ambassador cut me off. "No, Christo. When you marry, I will give you a suite of rooms. You may bring your wife here."

"Your Excellency, it wouldn't be fair to you. I may eventually have children and I would not be as available to you as I am now. There are others who can serve you better now. Ted knows my job and…"

"Out of the question!" he said emphatically. "You are close to completing three years here and I can accelerate your pay increase. And, Christo," he turned more serious. "You think about it. Think about losing your diplomatic status. If you leave here you will be deported." With that, he turned abruptly and left the room. I had thought about it, though, and there was no turning back.

• • •

That summer I wrote my parents with the news of my engagement. We had decided to marry on January 11, 1948.

I continued to be extremely busy, as the Ambassador's list of social functions grew. We did not discuss my departure again, but I had arranged with Blaise to begin work within two weeks at Place Vendôme. Meanwhile, most every weekend found me journeying to Cumberland to see Helen.

I also asked Blaise to help me notify the Immigration and Naturalization Service, or INS, that I was leaving the Embassy. We promptly sent a letter to INS, and on July 25, 1947, I received a response along with an application form, and a general information form that we completed. I brought in documents that I had and we sent everything back with my application for citizenship. The only document that was absent was a certification from the Turkish police that I was a person of good moral character and had no prison record.

I put a deposit on an apartment in a house in Falls Church, Virginia, and paid the August rent in anticipation of leaving the embassy. It had one bedroom, a kitchen, and a bath—with a separate entrance. I was only renting, but it would be my first rental in America and I certainly wanted to make a good impression. I planned to take possession on August 1.

The next week, I received a note from Katina and Papa congratulating me on my engagement.

• • •

Though I had not intended to continue working at the Embassy, the Ambassador asked me to stay and oversee one last function in mid-August. I agreed even though I had paid a full month's rent and would not be occupying the rental until mid-month. By that time I thought his stance toward my deportation would have softened somewhat, but he was still less than thrilled that I was leaving. With Olgalik's help we served *creme d'asparagus*, rockfish with a special sauce, pilaf, artichokes *au gratin*, and fruit for dessert. I helped Olgalik prepare while allowing Ted to oversee the event.

The evening went very well and the next day I moved out of the Embassy.

As I was packing I heard a knock at my door. "Come in," I answered.

The Ambassador stood at my door with his arms crossed. "Christo, are you sure you must go?" the Ambassador asked quietly.

"Yes, Your Excellency. It has been my privilege to serve you."

For a moment the Ambassador was silent. Then he cleared his throat. "I wish you well, Christo," he said. "Is there anything else I can do for you?"

All the Ambassador's initial anger had been replaced with resignation and, I thought, a little sadness, despite his earlier threats about revoking my visa. I had received my application for citizenship, along with my birth certificate and baptismal documents with Jimmy's assistance. I had just submitted all my paperwork to begin naturalization, a process that would end up taking over five years.

I thanked the Ambassador and bowed. In an uncharacteristic response, he offered me a partial bow in return and then embraced me. Although a Mohammedan Turk who was thirty-five years my senior, we had developed an affection for each other. I would always be grateful for the enormous opportunity he had given me by bringing me to America. He turned to leave.

"Oh, Your Excellence, there is one more thing. The immigration department requires a testament from Turkey that I had no prior record with the police. I never had a police record. Could you help me obtain that document please?"

"Yes, of course, Christo, I will do so immediately," he said as he turned to leave.

Unfortunately, he never did. Apparently the Turkish government would not cooperate with my desire to change my citizenship, despite forcing Turkish citizenship on us. That afternoon I left the Embassy.

• • •

On April 13, 1948, I received a notice from the American School of Naturalization of the District of Columbia requesting that I obtain notarized signatures for my naturalization application and include my marriage certificate. We complied. Helen wrote a letter referencing the file with the material requested. I started to attend immigration classes monthly in Washington, D.C., the next week. On April 29 I received notice from the Immigration and Naturalization Service with regard to my application for citizenship. It stated:

> *You entered the United States on April 22, 1945.... Our rules require that you prove good moral character for a period of at least five years immediately preceding the date of the filing of your application. Therefore, it will be necessary for you to secure a certificate of good conduct from the police authorities in your native country.*

The authorities were requesting that I obtain a certification of good conduct from the police of my native country, which was absent from my preliminary application and which the Ambassador had promised to obtain on my behalf. This was bad news. I highly doubted that certificates of good standing were anything the Turkish gendarmes would consider issuing, particularly to Christians.

The notice had been sent to my father-in-law's house, and I picked it up on a weekend visit.

Anton wanted to help me. He had an affidavit notarized and sent to the INS on May 2, 1948. It said, in part:

> *I hereby certify that Chris John Chrisostomides has been employed by the said Anton Anthony... at a salary of forty dollars ($40.00) per week; and that said Anton Anthony did further make oath that he is a person of good moral character.*

I appreciated Anton's assistance. Even though I had married a U.S. citizen, the INS would not recognize my application for citizenship without the certificate of good standing. They sent a letter on August 5 asking if I had obtained the certificate from the police authorities in Turkey. Apparently the United States only cared about my moral character.

• • •

One afternoon Anton took me aside so we could talk. "What are your plans?" he asked.

"I'll stay in food service, where I have some experience," I told him. "I would like to own my own business."

My father-in-law smiled. He liked that answer. "When you find a business I will help you."

Anton was not wealthy, but since leaving the Army after World War I he had been a small-business man. No one had ever offered me financial support before. I was humbled not only by his kindness, but by his belief in me. It made me all the more determined to succeed.

• • •

In January of that year Helen and I had married in a small, traditional Greek ceremony at the Church of Saints Constantine & Helen in Washington. Father Thomas Daniels performed the service. Mr. Mastos, who had arranged my initial introduction to the Anthony family, was my best man. On my side, Olgalik, Ted and Anna Theologos, the Melases, and, of course, Taki and Sultana attended. Helen and her family had invited about thirty people.

After our wedding we had a simple honeymoon in New York with Taki and Sultana. After the weekend we returned to our little apartment, and that evening I went to work at Place Vendôme. I was often working lunches as well as dinners, so I frequently left home at ten thirty in the morning and did not return until one the following morning. There was a new pleasure in serving people during these long hours because now, for the first time in my 31 years, I felt freedom.

• • •

Six months later Anton loaned me money which, along with my savings, allowed me to open the Apollo Restaurant. That night Helen told me she was carrying our baby. Beaming with pride and overcome with joy, I folded her in my arms.

"Chris," Helen began calling me by my American name shortly after our marriage, "it's a miracle." I agreed.

"If this is a boy, I would like to name him Anthony, for my father," she continued. "Would that be okay?" Generally, the oldest son in a Greek family is named after his father's father, but if Helen wanted to name our child, that was fine with me.

"And if we have a second son," she promised, "we will name him Jon, for your father."

"One baby at a time." I laughed.

Helen lifted her eyes to mine. "Thank you, Chris," she said. "My father will be so proud."

I was sure Papa would understand if we named the boy after my father-in-law, but I stopped mid-sentence as another thought struck me. "Helen, what if the child is a girl?"

She laughed at me. "No use talking more about it until we know."

Suddenly, I smiled. I was about to become a father and a restaurant owner all at once. I named the restaurant Apollo for the Greek god of sunlight, prophecy, music, and poetry.

• • •

Opening the Apollo was not easy on my Spartan budget, but a little financial creativity proved very helpful. First, I financed the purchase after a five-percent down payment over ten years with the current owner. Then I put down a little under $1,000 on equipment and furnishings, leaving me with a balance of around $200 to finance the day-to-day operation of the restaurant.

"Chris, what if something happens? We hardly have any money as it is. If we lose our investment, we will have nothing. Then what?" Helen began to worry.

"Nothing is going to happen, Helen. It is an opportunity for us. For the first time, I will have a chance to create something. Yes, I will have to work hard, but I have been doing that all my life. This is our opportunity to make something better for our lives."

"You will be just like Daddy—working all day, never around for me or the children." That didn't sound so bad. Since I was ten years old, I had been serving others. Finally, I had an opportunity to do something for my new family and myself.

"Why can't you get a regular job like everyone else?" I was an immigrant with a fourth-grade education on a work permit going to citizenship classes. My options were limited.

We never did see eye-to-eye on this issue, despite how hard each of us tried to get to know one another's point of view. Helen did not want to be left alone, this was clear, but she never understood that success has its price. Even years later, we would have the same circular arguments over my long hours, a source of contention that that would become less of an issue over time. Every marriage has its issues, though, and some become like broken records, so familiar that eventually the anger and passion behind them fade to an almost comfortable predictability. Due to present-day work obligations at my start-up though, we were still in the full force of emotions on the subject.

"How can I get a regular job like everyone else when the restaurant business is all I know? Trust me, Helen, I'm doing this for you, for our family."

After spending most of my adult life as a restaurateur, I can say that successful business ventures are a function of four disparate yet requisite parts: hard work, experience, persistence, and luck. After spending years powerless under the control of the Turks, I took enormous pleasure in the newfound control of my own fate. It was inspiring, especially for an energetic and ambitious young man, for I had a chance at economic freedom. I had earned the right to risk, and, God willing, I would succeed.

• • •

In 1949, Falls Church was a growing suburb about eight miles outside Washington, but its true growth spurt would not begin until the second half of the next decade. A further complication was that business in general that summer was unusually slow. Still, I managed to pay a few dollars to all my creditors and buy some more time. The following month business improved somewhat.

As the days and weeks passed, a few more customers came in, and within three months I had thirty to forty customers a day, averaging about forty cents per sale. In order to pay the bills, my evenings were spent waiting tables at Place Vendôme while the restaurant continued to build business.

Restaurants are somewhat deceptive. To the casual observer the food business may appear to be a well-run operation, but, behind the scenes, it is a bustling, time-consuming profession that takes constant attention. Regardless of whether you have one, ten, or a hundred customers a day, you still have to undergo all food and set-up preparations. The only thing that changes is that as your customers increase the food cost per customer drops. Making a profit is not always certain but day in and day out, you have to show up.

Though it was against my instincts to have a partner in business, I soon decided to call Taki in New York since I knew he was looking for an investment opportunity. He had saved money while in the Navy, which he added to funds his family had managed to take with them when they had left Imbroz a decade earlier. Taki offered to invest in the Apollo in exchange for a fifty-fifty partnership. We sealed our agreement with a handshake.

Taki's investment in the Apollo allowed me to repay my father-in-law and the balance on the equipment loan, leaving only the property mortgage as outstanding. Equally important, I was now able to arrange to rent a two-bedroom apartment with a proper kitchen so my new son would have his own bedroom.

• • •

The apartment was at 347 Gundry Drive, Falls Church, about a half-mile from the Apollo. Considering the long hours I worked, this proved to be very convenient. Taki came to work before lunch and stayed until closing, while I would open at five in the morning and work breakfast and lunch. Finally, after six months, we were making adequate money to pay our debts and take home a meager wage. I also continued to work at Place Vendôme in the evenings to supplement my income.

After the move into our new apartment in January of 1949, Helen was nearing full term. "Chris, I don't think I can manage it," she said tearfully one night. "We have to finish the baby's room—we haven't even gotten a crib. At any time, I might have to go to the hospital and where will you be?" she lamented. "I have been all alone. It's so hard, Chris."

"Now, now, Helen, don't you worry. The baby isn't due for a few more months. I will be there when the time comes. You will call me, and I will be right there. Tomorrow, I will get the crib."

On March 30, 1949, Helen gave birth to our son, Anthony. It was not an easy delivery, however, and Helen remained in the hospital more than a week after the birth. The lengthy hospital stay was costly, creating yet another monthly debt and making it increasingly difficult to continue sending money to Imbroz, but my wife was safe, and we had a healthy son. There was much to be grateful for. I now had both a family and a business in America. My only problem was whom to pay when, and how much. The line of my creditors seemed never ending.

Every morning at four-thirty when I pinned my relic coin to my t- shirt, I gave special thanks to God for my son and prayed that He would bless and watch over my new family. Responsibilities that might have seemed stressful were a breeze, given the extreme stress of my past. Yes, life in America was a far cry from the life-and-death struggle that was endemic during my first 27 years.

A month or two later Helen and I called Father Daniels, who had performed our marriage ceremony, to schedule a baptism for our son. Helen asked two of her close friends, Ted and Eleni Papadeas, to be godparents to Anthony. Afterwards, our guests gathered at our apartment where we celebrated with *hors d'oeuvres* and drinks. Indeed, it seemed to me I had much to celebrate. After all, my son was born in America.

• • •

Some months later, in June of 1949, I returned home to find two letters. One was from my father. Helen was asleep, so I put on my pajamas and sat down at a small table with a night light to read it. Papa was by now over 70 years old.

My dearest children Chrysostomos and Elenitsa in the U.S.A.,

Greetings... We received your letter as well as the beautiful photographs which made us very happy. We are again sending you our heartfelt blessings for a long and happy life together with the arrival of little ones.

You, Christo, should always treat your wife with love and respect. You, my daughter Elenitsa, should be guided by the three virtues of obedience, patience, and attentiveness. Both should relate to each other with devotion, temperance, and tolerance. When you practice these virtues in your lives, you can rest assured you will have God's blessings and your fellow man's respect.

With love,
Papa

Papa's words of wisdom and counsel still resonated with me after all this time and connected me with him as I started my new life with Helen. I felt Papa's presence that evening in a realization that my old family, although far away in Imbroz, shared with me fully in thought, word, and spirit.

The other letter was from the United States Department of Justice. Its message was not so uplifting. It ordered me to report to court to defend why I should remain in the United States. It read, in part:

By virtue of the power and authority invested in me by the laws of the United States, I hereby command you to take into custody said alien and grant him a hearing to enable him to show cause why he should not be deported. Pending further proceedings... the alien above-named may be released from custody upon his own recognizance if you are confident he will appear when and where wanted.

Albert Del Guercio
District Director

I had been served a warrant ordering the INS to deport me.

CHAPTER 14

Blessings

I fall, I stand still…
I trudge on,
I gain a little…
I get more eager and climb higher
and begin to see the widening horizon.
Every struggle is a victory.
—HELEN KELLER, 1902

THE NEXT MORNING I left home early to ask Blaise for help with my warrant. He called the INS and informed me that I was to go for a deposition on July 5, 1949, with the acting chief examiner, Eleanor Enright. The week of August 16, 1949, I received a hand-delivered copy of a letter written by Enright and a note from John L. Murff registering my application for permanent suspension of deportation. Attached was Enright's affidavit on my interview, which stated:

> *The alien's assets are about $1,000. It is apparent that the alien's deportation would result in a serious detriment to his spouse and newborn son. A check of the appropriate local records, as well as those of the police department of Imbroz, Turkey, has failed to reveal an arrest or criminal record. It is recommended that the deportation of the alien be suspended. It is further recommended that if Congress approves the suspension of deportation, the proceedings be cancelled and the alien be charged to the quota of Turkey.*

I questioned whether the Turks even knew what "good conduct" was. This lack of documentation had resulted in my being served with the warrant of deportation, which was later suspended. Thanks to post–World War I laws, such as the Immigration Act of 1924, the amount of immigrants coming into the United States was capped with different quotas for each country. Although relieved that I might somehow be counted into that total, my requirements to obtain citizenship still remained unclear.

• • •

I continued to attend my naturalization classes. During my sixteen-hour days of working two jobs, Helen took care of Anthony. By the time I got home, Anthony was asleep. Many late evenings I simply stood by his crib and watched him. I was so proud of my son.

Though predictable, the lack of response from Turkish officials regarding good conduct was frustrating and worrisome. My only hope seemed to be to persuade the INS to waive the requirement. In my reply to the immigration authorities I detailed my efforts to obtain the requested paperwork and expressed my concerns that the Turkish authorities would not cooperate. Helen wrote the letter for me.

I also talked to Blaise, my boss at Place Vendôme, and he agreed to help. He confirmed to the authorities that I was gainfully employed and married to a U.S. citizen. After the testimonials from Blaise and other American friends, I continued my monthly classes at the naturalization school in Washington to satisfy my citizenship requirements. Because it was my first formal schooling since fourth grade, it was both enjoyable and enlightening. Perhaps for this reason I was more excited than most of my classmates to attend, and studied dutifully any information I was given. Learning about the history of my new country became my passion.

One evening before going to bed I opened a letter from the INS. It was September 22, 1949, two years and two months after I had made my initial application. The letter stated, in relevant part:

The alien is eligible for suspension of deportation under Section 19(c)(2) of the Immigration Act of 1917, as amended.... Upon the basis of the entire record, I recommend that deportation of the respondent be suspended.

Signed Samuel M. Reichman, presiding Inspector.

I smiled, and as I got ready to go to bed, I kissed the relic coin attached to my t-shirt and whispered *Papa, we did it.*

"What was that you said, Chris?" Helen asked half asleep.

"Nothing, dear. I will tell you later."

A week later I received a copy of the order signed by the Commissioner of the INS with an attached note from John L. Murff, officer in charge, which stated in pertinent part:

wherein you will note he has ordered your deportation suspended. You will be advised in due course of time of the action taken by Congress in your case.

• • •

Before I knew it, we were buying a cake for Anthony's first birthday party. My son's birthday was another milestone in my life's journey, for it was the first time I had participated in the American tradition of a birthday celebration. In the old country we celebrated name days of saints, so I welcomed this new opportunity for Americanization.

A few days after Anthony's birthday I received a brief letter from Katina, who was now 36. Sometime before, I had broached with her the subject of her coming to the U.S. when she was no longer needed on Imbroz, but it was understood that the care of our parents remained our primary concern. I would not forget my sister and my promise to bring her to America, but it was not to be for some years to come.

Her letter was the last one I received for some time. Neither she nor Mama and Papa wished to worry me with their needs, and they tried to discourage me from sending money. They knew I had a family to support, and with that came added financial responsibilities.

• • •

The post–World War II period continued to have a calming effect on the persecution of the Christian minority on Imbroz and throughout Turkey. The Turks were tenaciously courting the United States for aid as diplomatic relations expanded and did not want to draw attention to their poor treatment of minorities. By 1950, elected committees of Christians were allowed to participate in local government for the first time in twenty-six years.

The poor remnants of the minority population only wondered how long the gesture would last. As I enthusiastically planned my new life in America, my aspirations and attention were far away from Imbroz or Turkey. The reminders of the Old World, though, had been burned indelibly in my consciousness, as they had been in all who had endured, and brutally forged us into what we would become.

The August 15, October 22, and November 4, 1949, notices from the INS that summarized my hearing, restated the charge, and iterated that deportation had been suspended, left open the action of Congress as a final determinant of my citizenship status. I still had not received any clarity from the INS on my current status or my path toward citizenship though, merely an iteration of the recommendation to suspend. I could only wonder what the Turks had failed to do that inhibited my citizenship efforts.

That fall, with my immigration problems still not completely resolved and a small income from the Apollo, I sent Mama and Papa $50. It was the first time since leaving the Embassy that I had been able to send money home, and it felt good to be able to do so once again.

Although relieved over the formal notice of suspension, it again left ambiguity regarding my path to citizenship.

The months flew by. Between my restaurant and my night job with Blaise I was putting in over eighty hours a week, not regretting a minute. There were also my naturalization classes which, aside from greatly improving my English, taught me about my new country. I learned about George Washington, Abraham Lincoln, and how my new country had earned its freedom.

• • •

A year later my family grew. In November of 1950 Helen gave birth to our second son, Jon, named after my beloved father, Ioanni. Jon was a delight from the time he was born, and truly lived up to Papa's namesake. Within three months after Jon's birth, I had finished paying medical bills for the baby's delivery.

The early fifties, although difficult, were manageable and rewarding. Often the Apollo would not generate enough to support two families, so I would wait tables at the Place Vendôme a few days a month to make ends meet. By 1952 both my sons were walking and talking. Business at the Apollo had increased and I was successfully paying down our debts.

At the age of 34 I had developed a stoic tolerance for the unexpected. I hoped things continued to go smoothly. I was still a regular attendee at my naturalization classes. If there were no unpleasant surprises, I would finally be able to save a little money and get ahead. Yet surprises seemed to emerge from thin air and there were never enough hours to do my day's work.

"You know, Christo, some nights we hardly do any business," Taki casually observed with a shrug one evening, indicating he had no explanation for it. It was just one of those things.

As I looked at him it became clear to me that one day soon, we would sell the business and, from then on, I would buy my own. No more partners for me. Taki, too, was restless and wished to return to New York with his family, where he owned two townhouses.

• • •

In late January I received a notice from the Office of the Clerk of the Court of Alexandria, Virginia, that I was to report to the Post Office Building on February 26, 1952, and bring with me specific documents as well as two U.S. citizens who had known me personally for at least two years. I was also to bring the following documents: 1) the naturalization certificate or birth certificate of my spouse; 2) our marriage certificate; and 3) any draft registration and classification cards, if relevant. The fee was $18 for filing the petition, payable to the Clerk of the Court.

Olgalik and Blaise came as witnesses, however they weren't needed. I wore my best white shirt, Mama's silk jacket for sentimental reasons, and a nice tie. After submitting the papers and paying the fee, we were ushered into a court room before a judge where my paperwork was accepted.

Nine months later I finally completed my naturalization classes. My English had improved greatly, and the classes contributed tremendously to my knowledge of my new country. With the persistent help of family and friends, I was finally granted citizenship at the end of 1952. My wife and two young sons were present when I took the oath and became a United States citizen. That evening in District Court in Alexandria Virginia, along with a handful of others who had been in my naturalization classes, I swore allegiance to the United States of America. The odyssey that began with a ten-year-old's dream found me a quarter of a century later a citizen of America.

As I somberly stood on the steps of the courthouse, I thought of Papa's words to me on our sunny porch in Imbroz so many years before. "Go to America, Christo," he had said. It had been Papa's dream as well as mine, a goal we shared, and now I had truly fulfilled it. *Papa, we did it,* a recurring feeling of elation overcoming me as I whispered under my breath.

On the eve of my citizenship ceremony Helen approached me with an unusual request. She wanted to shorten our surname.

"What would you like it to be?" I asked, trying not to sound surprised.

"Something easier for the children to say—and everyone else, for that matter. Most people can't even say Chrisostomides, let alone spell it."

"It's hard, Daddy," little Anthony chimed in.

I looked from my son to my wife and thought about it. A moment later I had an idea.

"How about Christ, as in Christmas?" I suggested.

"That may work," Helen nodded thoughtfully.

Anthony was more enthusiastic. "Yes!" he proclaimed.

Chrisostomides is a fine old name, but if my wife and children wished, we would shorten it to Christ. "All right," I told my family, "Christ it is, then."

I received my citizenship certificate on December 10, 1952, five days before my 35th birthday. No longer was I Chrysostomos Ioanni Chrisostomides of Imbroz. I was now Chris John Christ of Falls Church, Virginia—an American citizen. I never found out what action, if anything, Congress took on my citizenship. Although the birthdate on my certificate was wrong, I wasn't about to go back to the INS to have it corrected. Yes, the whole naturalization process took five years of my life and I enjoyed every minute.

The next day I wrote Papa, Mama, Katina, and Theo Dimitris to tell them the news. I also called Sultana and Taki in New York. I was now a proud citizen of the United States of America. I could not take my eyes off the handsome certificate. It had my picture on it.

The following weekend I purchased a used DeSoto, obtained my driver's license, and proudly drove my family to church. It was almost Christmas and we drove to the Greek Orthodox cathedral, Saint Sophia. It was undergoing construction on Massachusetts Avenue in Washington. It was being built in the Byzantine style, modeled after Hagia Sophia in Constantinople.

The priest at Saint Sophia was Father Lalousis. He was a likeable man with a brilliant voice that resonated throughout the cathedral, echoing childhood memories of melodious chants from long ago on my island home. After church we introduced ourselves to him. For the next few years I brought my family to Saint Sophia when I wasn't working.

It was my duty as a father to pass this tradition to my children. The Church had stood strong for me in my youth, and I felt compelled to stand strong for her now in my prosperity.

After our first visit to Saint Sophia, we drove the DeSoto home where I made a holiday dinner, lamb and rice pilaf, while Helen fixed *spanakopita*. So began a tradition of preparing this meal for my family on Sundays and holidays. As the years passed and the generations grew, it became a favorite with my children's families, as well. That Sunday, we all ate heartily. Then, at four o'clock, I went to the Apollo to work the dinner shift, relieve Taki, and close up the restaurant for the night.

In 1953, my father-in-law sold his house and business in Cumberland and bought a piece of property in Warrenton, Virginia, where he constructed a nineteen-room motel which he named The Jefferson. As a first-generation immigrant Anton may not have known much about Thomas Jefferson, but he respected him as a symbol of America. Later that year he built a small ice cream store for his son, Gus, who had just gotten out of the Air Force.

"Chris," Gus later said to me, "I am associated with some gentlemen and may obtain the regional franchise for Tastee-Freez. That's something you should look at."

"We'll see. Maybe later, Gus," I told him.

• • •

In the summer of 1954 I found a house for sale about a mile and a half from the Apollo. It was a 1,000 square-foot rambler on a quarter-acre lot with a full basement. The asking price was $17,000, a lot of money. I was 36 years old and I had paid rent all of my life, from Constantinople to America. It was time to buy a home and pay a mortgage instead. I had finally saved enough money to make the required twenty percent down payment.

I was now a stakeholder in my new country, America. Helen, the boys, and I moved in later that summer. Anthony was four and a half and Jon was almost three. It was important to me that they grow up in a house their family owned. It was a goal, another milestone I had reached.

Most of the houses in our neighborhood were ramblers with young couples and young children like us. Helen exchanged baked goods, Christmas cards, and birthday presents for the kids with the other moms, but my busy work schedule kept my relationship with our neighbors to a few polite greetings on the rare occasions our paths crossed.

Everyone was busy raising their children, paying their bills, and earning a living. Still, most of the husbands in the neighborhood had time in the evenings and on weekends to spend with their families and to get to know their neighbors. My failure in this regard further stirred Helen's desire to have me at home more.

"Chris, why can't you work like the men in the neighborhood, like Leo or Bud Brandt? They're always home in the evenings," she would say with tears in her eyes.

"The restaurant business is my vocation and, unfortunately, it demanded long, thankless hours."

A few weeks later when Helen wanted to enroll Anthony in the Humpty Dumpty Nursery School we were able to afford the fee. Helen thought the school would be fun for Anthony.

"They have a pony there for the children to ride," she said, "and he'll learn his numbers and ABCs."

"Isn't he a little young for school?" I asked.

"He'll be five in March," Helen replied. "He's ready. He's more than ready. And he'll like it so much."

So we enrolled Anthony in the Humpty Dumpty Nursery School, and I gladly paid the tuition. Helen, Anthony, and Jon were constant sources of motivation for me. I derived a great deal of pleasure and fulfillment from giving them the things they needed and wanted. It was my hope that one day that would include college educations for the boys.

• • •

In early spring Helen received a letter from two of her great uncles, Uncle Chris and Uncle Charlie, who had come to the United States as young men in the 1890s. They had sold their place in Wheeling, West Virginia, and bought a two hundred–acre farm southwest of Winchester, Virginia, some years earlier. Neither had ever married.

Letter in hand, Helen turned to me. "You know, Chris, one of these days I'd love to visit my great uncles."

I knew what was coming. "Which "one day" would you like to go?" I asked, and made Helen laugh.

The uncles had lived alone together for all their lives, yet they were as different as night and day. Chris was short, heavy, and bald. He was extremely religious and could not stand cigarette smoke. Charlie, on the other hand, was tall and thin with a thick head of hair and a mustache. Charlie was a chain smoker and was quietly rumored to have been a gigolo in the Greek community some time before.

So one Sunday morning when Taki was opening the restaurant I took Helen and the boys to see her old uncles. When we got to their farm, we entered by a dirt road that curved through the woods for about a half-mile before ending at an old farmhouse with a sweep of lawn, a barn, and an old 1940s Plymouth parked nearby.

This property revealed a beautifully expansive view of the Blue Ridge Mountains and a portion of the Shenandoah River where Cedar Creek emptied into it. The farmhouse was a speck in the bucolic splendor of the valley, humming with birds and wildlife in a colored, seamless matting of mountains and valleys in sharp contrast to the blues and whites of an early fall sky. A couple of dogs ran up to bark at our car but fled when we opened the doors, much to the boys' dismay. Chris and Charlie stood on the front porch to greet us.

"Uncle Chris, Charlie," Helen cried out as she ran to her great uncles and embraced them warmly. She linked each of them on her arms and introduced us. The house had few modern improvements. The old gentlemen cooked and heated by wood stove and drew water from a well, but their simple lives seemed to suit them. They served us a light lunch and presented Helen with two paintings done by their mother, her great-great-aunt.

"She always wanted someone to have them who would love them. Now we pass them to you." One was of a dog and the other of men by a campfire. They would become rustic heirlooms for our growing family.

• • •

Later in the summer, as a treat for the boys and to lighten Helen's load for a few days, we drove to Warrenton to leave Anthony and Jon with their grandparents for a week. At that time, I spoke with Helen's brother Gus again about a potential Tastee-Freez franchise. "It's a small store at a resort town," he told me. "It's called Ocean City, in Maryland. I'd like to take you to see it, Chris. It's a good location and, if you like it, I can help you arrange the financing."

Taki and I were still trying to sell the Apollo. Gus mentioned three other locations that were available, but Ocean City most interested me. I was certain people would travel to the beach. One day the town, and my business, would be very popular. Although my family would have to remain in Falls Church most of the year, I was growing confident that this was the opportunity I had waited so long and worked so hard for. It was a chance to provide well for my family and to own a business that was completely mine.

Going to Ocean City was a risk, though. It was a seasonal business and I had a wife, two children, a mortgage, and a family on Imbroz to support. I also had doubts about the Tastee-Freez menu that my brother-in-law so avidly endorsed. I was 38 years old and I could not afford a misstep.

It's an opportunity for you to have your own business, Chris," Gus told me. "It would cost about $2,000 for a location. Are you interested?"

The truth was I was very interested, but something—rent, mortgage, hospital bills—always came up to deplete my savings. This added to my strong sense that I needed to go out on my own.

Gus was brimming with a salesman's excitement. "If you want, we could go see it," he suggested.

His enthusiasm was contagious. "All right," I conceded to him. "If you think it's that good, then I suppose we'd better go have a look, but not today."

That Sunday I was reading in the newspaper about Incirlik Air Base in Adana, Turkey, which we had helped the Turks build in December 1954. It had been almost ten years, yet I recalled being present at the Embassy when relations were established with America, which now had troops on a Turkish military airbase.

Two weeks later I took a whirlwind trip with Gus to Ocean City. It took a couple hours to reach the Chesapeake Bay where we drove across the new four-and-a-half-mile suspension bridge called the Chesapeake Bay Bridge. I was in awe of the magnitude of this span, which at the time was the world's longest continuous steel structure over water. After reaching the far shore, we had another two-hour drive to Ocean City. We checked into a small motel a half-mile before the bridge that crossed the bay separating Ocean City and its peninsula from the rest of the Eastern Shore.

From the time I first saw the beach town with Gus, I was captivated by its fresh air, white sand, and ocean breezes. It reminded me of my island home. Coastal Highway ran the length of the peninsula and was separated into almost one hundred and fifty blocks, yet the width from ocean to bay was no more than four blocks and sometimes less. The stretch of 17th Street where the store was located was undeveloped, but I felt certain that over time people would see what I saw and visit. I was sold. Upon returning home, Helen didn't share my enthusiasm, but she supported my decision to start a business there. I hoped she would come to love it as I did.

Further complicating matters, Helen was pregnant with our third child. In the spring of 1955, Helen gave birth to a baby girl whom we named Ianthe, the Greek word for flower. With a third child, my responsibilities had expanded yet again, but my little girl soon became the pleasure of my life. I nicknamed her *Cookie.*

I once again found myself gripping the object of my heritage, my relic coin, as I heard whispers from across the oceans I had crossed, through time, dreams, hopes, and losses. The present challenge was upon me. *I will not fail,* I whispered to my father as I kissed the sacred coin and tucked it securely in its resting place against my breast. The appeal of blue skies and sandy beaches had lured me to a new frontier, a new challenge, and I would prepare to go to Ocean City to start a new business when the building would be finished in the spring of 1956.

Luck would have it that a couple of Greek brothers subsequently agreed to buy the Apollo, and the next few weeks were spent finalizing the sale. At long last, Taki was free to return to New York. Before he left, we decided to take Helen, Sultana, and the kids to nearby Glen Echo Park for a picnic. The park overlooks Little Falls on the Potomac River, a couple of miles west of Washington. Aside from a campground, there was an amusement park with swings and an old-fashioned carousel. The children had fun reaching for the ever-elusive brass ring, hoping to win the coveted free ride. Taki's little girl, Theope, was five, about the same age as my younger son Jon, and his son Peter was about a year older than Anthony. The four of them giggled and played happily in the crisp autumn sunshine.

Taki and I tended toward excessive picnic baskets. Plentiful food at family meals was a reaction to the sparseness we grew up with. We all took our fill of food, fresh air—and probably a little too much drink for Taki and me.

"Taki, I will drive us home," Sultana insisted.

As we rode back in Taki's old Plymouth, we broke out in our favorite song, *Still one more drink, still one more song....* Even without the drinks, a picnic in America was intoxicating for two island boys from Imbroz. So ended another day of enchantment in our land of opportunity.

Taki and Sultana returned with their children to his mother's house in Brooklyn. Gus had sent the papers for my purchase of the Ocean City Tastee-Freez. He had already opened almost ten stores by himself and would have twenty-seven franchise stores in the span of the next three years. I was aware that Gus's primary motivation was to lease another Tastee-Freez store, but I couldn't forget the sunny seaside beach, so I put aside my reservations about going into business with family again. Certainly, over time, people would come to vacation there and the store would thrive. I had a good feeling about the small Ocean City carryout food store. Besides, I had grown up on an island and felt right at home.

• • •

The beach store included financing on all equipment as well as a lease from Mr. Charlie Holland, who owned the property and the building. Charlie was a man about ten years older than I was who owned a lot of property in Ocean City, property that was both inherited and accumulated over a generation. He and his wife Myrtle owned and operated Maridel Realty, as well as two motels elsewhere in town. Although Charlie's holdings far exceeded two motels and a real estate company, he never made a show of his wealth in the forty years I knew him. I nearly always saw him dressed in jeans and a plaid shirt driving around in his rusty red pickup truck with a Golden Retriever sitting next to him in the cab.

At the beginning of 1956, when I had first met with Charlie to discuss the lease he suggested, I wanted to have an attorney go over the particulars with me. "Chris, I'll lease the building to you as is for $2,500 a year, to start off," Charlie told me. "It's a five-year lease and it will go up $100 a year with a five-year option. You will be responsible for all utilities, taxes, and upkeep." He squinted at me intently—an unsettling characteristic I eventually grew accustomed to.

I finally found an attorney named Mark William who was a mild-mannered, intelligent man, reasonable in his fees. He explained the lease to me clearly and in careful detail, and I liked his way of doing business. I would see Mark for legal advice for many years to come.

Equipping the store and paying the franchise fee to Gus took all my available funds, including the proceeds from the sale of the Apollo, plus a little more. There was a certain way the people at

Tastee-Freez wanted things done, and Gus schooled me carefully in the preparation and presentation of the menu, which was very basic—hamburgers, hot dogs, french-fries, sodas, milkshakes, and, of course, soft serve ice cream. Although elementary for a person of my food background, I was polite and attentive to my brother-in-law's presentation. Handling the soft serve ice cream and sterilizing the ice cream machine, which had to be washed daily, were the only things new to me. Fries and meat were bought only through the Tastee-Freez Corporation and arrived frozen and ready to cook. The food was unimaginative and tasteless, but I followed the program to the letter, down to the white-paper hat.

I stayed in Ocean City long enough to complete all the paperwork pertaining to the lease and the franchise before returning home to Falls Church, where I filled up the refrigerator and gave Helen $100 to keep the children fed. Then I packed up some clothes and headed back to Ocean City to open up the store for the summer.

The Tastee-Freez store was bleeding my sparse resources dry, and my creditors continued to pile up. Undaunted, I managed to keep my faith, my focus, and my positive attitude, determined to stay the course. As each problem in my new home required attention and resolution, my purposeful action was empowered and renewed daily.

I felt blessed to wake up every morning with the opportunity to deal with my daily problems in America, for they were my problems and they came with blessings. I had a wife, three children, I was a citizen, I had a home and a business—all in ten years.

CHAPTER 15

A New Archbishop

I believe in Spinoza's God
who reveals himself
in the orderly harmony of what exists,
not in a God who concerns himself
with the fates and the doings of mankind.
—ALBERT EINSTEIN, 1932

TWENTIETH CENTURY CONSTANTINOPLE was decidedly hostile to its Christian minority, and by 1955 the fragile veil of religious civility that had prevailed for a decade was shattered. For a three-day period in early September Mohammedan mobs, at the encouragement of the Turkish government, once again unleashed destruction against the Christian community. The news took me back into the dark world I had struggled so long and hard to escape.

The riots were triggered by the report of a bomb that exploded outside of the Turkish consulate in Salonika, Greece—Atatürk's birth-place. The truth later came out that the bomb had broken only two windows and was detonated by a Muslim law student of the University of Thessaloniki named Oktayi. Still, the incident was used to spark riots against Christians, and the horror of Christian persecution unfolded anew.

A month later I received a call from Olgalik, who was still working at the Embassy, telling me they had received a letter for me from Constantinople. I met Olgalik at a small bar off M Street in Georgetown to pick up my mail.

"Good to see you, Christo," he said with a broad smile and a hearty slap on my back.

"It's wonderful to see you, too," I replied. "How is the Ambassador?"

"Oh, he is the same, Christo." He pushed an envelope across the bar toward me. "Here is your letter. I believe it is from the Patriarchate."

"Yes, it is." I took the letter eagerly and opened it, hungry for any news from the Old World. Jimmy wrote and explained the severity of the situation for the priests.

Dear Chrysostomos,

I am now a bishop serving Athenagoras, our new Patriarch. I understand you have married and have a family. When I left I never expected to be in Constantinople this long. I imagine you heard about the riots. The reality was much worse than the accounts reported by the western media. Chrysostomos, not a day has passed during my 45 years when I did not feel powerless to end our people's religious persecution…

I looked up at Olgalik. "It's Jimmy. He has become a bishop. He's writing about the riots last month." Olgalik nodded while handing me a drink.

"Cheers," he said, raising the glass. "To health, happiness, and children."

"Yes, thank you," I mumbled as I read on.

We estimate the destruction from the riots as follows: 4,500 shops, 1,000 homes, 110 hotels, 26 schools, and 73 churches were looted and destroyed. Countless graveyards have been defiled. A Greek Orthodox priest was murdered, along with fourteen other victims. It was officially reported that 200 Christian women were raped, though over 2,000 women were actually treated and examined for rape.

In short, the riots have been successful in uprooting most of the remaining Christians of Constantinople. A mass exodus of Christians has reduced the minority population from 300,000 to less than 100,000 and rapidly declining. Homes and businesses have been confiscated by the Turks without recompense. The riots concealed the unconscionable and illegal property transfers, violently taken during the uprooting. Those of us who remain have no choice. The Church must go on. One day, I will see you again in America. May God bless you and your family.

Your Countryman,
Bishop lakovos

"Bishop Iakovos," I sighed.

"What did you say?" asked Olgalik.

"He talks about the recent recurrence of violence in Turkey against Christians."

Olgalik nodded; it was a subject we both were quite aware of.

"Jimmy has become a bishop"

"How nice," Olgalik said, not wanting to spend more time on the violence, although we were both deeply touched by it. The rest of our time together was spent talking about my family and the Embassy. It was good to see my old friend again.

• • •

That winter I went back to full-time work waiting tables for Blaise at Place Vendôme and paying down debt. When it came time to return to open my business at the beach, I was recharged. That second season in Ocean City in 1957, I was determined to bring my family down, despite the financial strain.

A couple of blocks from where the boardwalk met Talbot Street was a rooming house called Nordica. It was owned by Gus Jones—shortened from Jonakakis—an Albanian Greek who came to America before the Iron Curtain fell. He had a bad back that resulted in an unusual, rigid walk, and prevented him from bending or lifting, as well as from looking side to side without turning his body. He gave me an apartment in the basement at a low price. There were no windows or external exit. There were two small bedrooms and a hallway with a hanging light leading to a bathroom.

We agreed to renegotiate for a larger room when Helen and the kids came down for the summer, but I couldn't afford it. I had certainly seen worse, but I wasn't happy that my family would be living there.

• • •

My first few weeks preparing for that second summer season were busy. Each morning I drove nineteen blocks north to my store. I dealt with the utility companies, cleaned and scrubbed the floors, installed equipment, and purchased supplies and food. Every cent I had was invested or spent in my venture—this white, single-story, 1,000 square-foot, cinder block building. Since my boyhood I had served many of the basic needs of others, but now the success or failure of my store would rest solely with me. I would bear the pain of failure, or endure the price of prosperity.

One Thursday at the end of April I finally opened up for business. That morning I set up the soft serve ice cream machine, turned on the grill and deep fryer, set up the stations, and waited for customers. I made $2.68. At the end of a month my revenues were minimal and insufficient. My second season was starting out no better than the first. The height of the summer season was just beginning, however, and I had high hopes that business would improve.

Running a restaurant is hard, but particularly hard when you are not making money. The hours are long and the work is tedious and taxing. To make matters worse, the three months in the summer are when vacationers visited Ocean City. The season in this beach town ran from June through August, with an uptick in business from Memorial Day through Labor Day. Business dropped off severely before and after those dates.

When school let out, I brought my family down to join me. As soon as we arrived in Ocean City we went to the Nordica. Gus's stiff posture and bald head gave him a stern, serious manner, but he was friendly with children. As soon as he saw my three kids, he exclaimed, "Here they are, here they are!" over and over until the children smiled with delight. Then he led us down one flight of stairs and a narrow hall to the apartment.

I brought our suitcases down, kissed Helen, hugged the children, and left to open the store. It was nine-thirty in the morning. The arrival of my family reenergized me and improved my outlook toward this season at the beach. Twelve hours later I would close up shop and return to our room for a few hours of sleep, the pattern of my summer routine. On weekends I kept the store open until midnight, and during the three-month summer season plus the three-month shoulder seasons my store remained open seven days a week for half the year.

Helen had brought a letter with her from Imbroz. It was a few days before I got around to opening it and reading it.

My Dear Brother and Sister,

I wanted to let you know I have followed your successes through your parents and I am so happy for you. I wish the children every success in school. I pray that God will grant them good health and anything else that they desire in life.

Everyone here is in excellent health and we wish the same for you. Don't worry about us. The weather is not cold now. I am going to save the cedar wood for next year.

My regards,
Dimitris Chrysostomides

What a pleasant surprise from my favorite uncle. For a moment I was lost in thought. I quickly snapped back into my summer routine.

Business improved during the remainder of that summer, but before it drew to a close it became apparent that sales would still fall far short of what I needed. My second year was no better than the first, but there was no turning back as my debts kept increasing. I realized that the Tastee-Freez menu was the chief problem with my sales, a problem that I could solve with my extensive knowledge of food preparation and service. I needed to improve the quality and variety of food offerings if I was to have a chance. Out of a misplaced loyalty to my brother-in-law, however, I would continue to serve the failed Tastee-Freez menu for a third year.

• • •

Late that August I packed up Helen and the kids and prepared to take them home. We left Ocean City at five o'clock in the morning on the Tuesday before Labor Day, leaving Barbara, my part time employee, to open the store. As soon as we got home to Virginia, I stocked the refrigerator with food, just as I had before I left in the spring. Although Helen could easily walk the few blocks to the store, I wanted to spare her as much trouble as I could. She would have her hands full as it was with the children. I left her money for new trousers, shirts, and school shoes for the boys, grabbed a stack of mail to take back with me, and kissed everyone goodbye. Then I turned around and headed straight back to Ocean City, arriving at Tastee-Freez by mid-afternoon to prepare for the Labor Day weekend.

That evening I flipped through the mail, sorting out bills, most of which would receive partial payment, when I came across a letter from Mama.

Dear Chrysostomos,

Papa, Katina, and I are all well and hope the same for Elenista and the children. Costa is working in Constantinople but we see him often. By next year he should have his visa completed to come to America. The Turks leave us alone but things are worsening. They have closed the Greek schools again. They close them and they re-open them depending on what Turk is in power. Thank God for Katerina, she does so much for us. Regards from your Uncle Dimitris.

With all my love,
Mama

"They have closed the Greek schools again" struck an ominous chord inside me. Immediately I wrote a response and purchased a money order for $100 to place in the letter. As pressing as my obligations remained, I knew my family in Imbroz had greater need than I did.

At the end of the season, I paid Gus for my basement apartment but I was unable to pay my full rent to Mr. Holland for the store. Fortunately, Charlie was a fair and reasonable man who trusted me to pay the balance as soon as I was able. While getting ready to close and winterize the store for the season, I got a call from Helen. I knew immediately that something was wrong.

"Chris, the children are fine," she reassured me immediately, "but I'm not well." She paused. "When can you come home?"

"Helen, what is it?"

"I'm anxious and very depressed, Chris. I saw the doctor."

"What did he say?"

"Sometimes things are just too much for me, Chris. The doctor said I need to rest."

"Honey, don't worry, everything will be fine," I tried to remain positive.

We had all been under great stress with the demands of the new business, and Helen, who worried terribly over everything, felt it keenly. I tried to console her and promised I would call every night and be home as soon as I could.

I had planned to remain open another couple of weeks, but over the next two days I rushed through closing and winterizing the store. By Wednesday I was done. After calling Helen to check in, I grabbed my bags and headed home. The boys were not yet home from school when I arrived and Helen was in bed. Moments later I was talking on the phone with her doctor.

"Mr. Christ, your wife is suffering with depression," he told me. He went on to explain that there were many ways to treat depression but that recovery would take time.

"Will she be all right?" I asked.

"I believe that with proper treatment she will recover," the doctor said carefully.

The timing of Helen's illness was difficult, but I was supportive. To my relief Helen's Aunt Anna May was coming to stay with us and help with the children. Anna May was a godsend and she managed to keep my little family running in Helen's absence.

Next I placed a call to my old friend Blaise, who had just renamed his French restaurant Rive Gauche, to see if I could start to wait tables right away. Now, with Helen's struggles and my finances so terribly extended in my new venture, I could not afford to wait. Thankfully, apparently neither could Blaise. He was short-staffed and asked if I could come into work that night.

I worked until nearly midnight. The next morning I got the boys off to school, packed up Helen and Cookie—as I affectionately called Ianthe—and drove them to the hospital, where Helen was admitted. That evening Christina Regas came over to watch the children while I worked. The next morning after Anna May arrived, I hurried to Georgetown and waited tables for lunch and dinner.

For the next several weeks my time was torn between double shifts at Rive Gauche and caring for my wife and children at home. My financial obligations compelled me to work double shifts at the restaurant, and I often remained downtown between shifts, which placed a heavy burden on Anna May and meant I saw Helen and the children less often than I wished. Still, I was there each morning when she woke up and before they left for school, and on Sunday I took the children to Sunday school and prepared a traditional Greek dinner for everyone before going to work at five.

I had regular consultations with the doctor during this time, as well, who assured me Helen was progressing with treatment. No one quite knew how to treat anxiety and depression in those days. I could not afford health insurance but we managed without it. Even though we were having some rough times, I would work through it.

• • •

The holidays of 1958 came and went. I continued to work double shifts at Rive Gauche. I had never been to Place Vendôme, Louis XIV's famous square of luxury and power in the center of Paris, or visited the Left Bank (Rive Gauche) of the Seine River, which was frequented by literary giants and expatriates. I felt as though I had, though, working at these restaurants. Much like the clientele at the Pera Palace and Park Hotel in Constantinople, only the *crème de la crème* of Washington dined there.

One of my regular customers was Jacqueline Kennedy, who would go on to become First Lady of the United States. Another of my notable customers was a gentleman dressed in a suit with an open collar shirt and a top hat that trapped his wild curly hair. When I bowed and pulled out the chair for him to sit down, he smiled and bowed back. Puzzled, I bowed in return and gestured for him to sit down. He grinned and bowed back. Again I bowed and indicated that he sit, and again he mimicked my motions.

"Please, sir," I laughed, placing my hand on his shoulder and gently guiding him into his seat. Later I learned that my playful regular—and, as it happened, my biggest tipper—was Harpo Marx.

The holidays came and went. I continued to work double shifts serving my elegant and colorful clientele. Tips were good and our finances slowly improved. We were barely treading water, though, and I knew we would never get ahead unless my small store in Ocean City became successful.

Back at home, Helen, much recovered, wanted to get a dog for the children. Although I wasn't thrilled with the idea at first, I wanted my family to be happy—so a little half-beagle, half-terrier puppy joined our family, and we named him Toby. He arrived in time for Anthony's tenth birthday in March 1959, and, on my insistence, the dog slept in the basement. Almost every evening I brought him scraps from the restaurant—usually filet mignon, a delicacy that even my own family did not enjoy. Within no time at all he was the best-fed little mutt in Northern Virginia, if not in the whole world. Come next summer in Ocean City, little Toby had a hard time readjusting to dog food.

• • •

Another memorable event occurred around that time, as well. Helen's great uncles came to visit us. They had since sold their farm to the DuPont family for a rumored $200,000—a huge sum at the time. Both men were now in their eighties and Helen had asked me if they could stay on with us for a while. It turned out to be quite a while.

They were indeed a couple of contrasting characters and kept our winter rather unpredictable. Uncle Chris was extremely religious while Uncle Charlie was still a bit of a philanderer—truly the odd couple. Uncle Chris drove his old DeSoto so slowly that one day he was given a ticket for obstruction of traffic. He still carried a crucifix in one hand and worry beads in the other, working them constantly in his palm. Uncle Charlie still chain-smoked non-filtered Camels. I think he did it mostly to irritate his brother, who fussed and nagged him about the habit constantly.

In the spring they received a letter from their niece in Greece and promptly departed overseas with barely a thanks for our extended hospitality. Before they left, I asked Chris, when God took him home, to give me a sign from Heaven.

"Don't forget," I told him.

Chris nodded in acknowledgment.

After they went to Greece, we heard they made a significant financial contribution to the building of a church, and most likely to their nieces. The next we heard was that Uncle Chris, the clean-living non-smoker, had died. Three months later, Uncle Charlie died as well. The two paintings they had given Helen would remain our only reminder of two colorful, very elderly gentlemen who lived three decades in the nineteenth century. No sign from heaven ever arrived.

• • •

Even after working the entire winter at Rive Gauche I was still not finished paying last year's rent to Charlie Holland when I returned to Ocean City in the spring of 1959. Gus Jones, knowing my difficulties, insisted I hold off in paying and gave us an apartment on the third floor with windows and a small porch facing the ocean for a few dollars more. God bless him; it was much better than the basement. All along, I shielded Helen and the children from knowledge of our financial difficulties, and I always made sure we had food on our table.

This season I was determined to deal with the chief problem of my business: the menu. My brother-in-law Gus wanted us to buy our supplies and groceries from a commissary he was establishing for the Eastern Shore Tastee-Freez franchises. I had spent the better part of twenty-five years in the restaurant business and I knew that in order to be successful the quality of our ingredients had to remain high. The commissary could not provide that quality. On top of that, the Tastee-Freez menu, with its limited offering, lacked diversity, as well as quality.

As a novice franchisee I had always thought it improper to challenge or change the menu up to that point, and therefore was saddled year in and out with the same bland fare. Now, however, it was different. The lack of a tasteful, well-rounded menu was hurting my small store's chance of success and would shortly put us out of business. I knew at that time there was no other option. I would have to change the menu if we were to survive.

I had planned all through the winter, and when I arrived in Ocean City in the spring of 1959, I was committed to changing my Tastee-Freez menu. I immediately called Dale Truitt at Swift and Company to order the best grade meats and cheeses in every category. From now on I would serve no frozen foods in my shop. If Swift didn't have them, I would use Armour and Company. Everything would be fresh and prepared with great care. I kept my focus on reasonable price, speed of service, and variety of choice. My gourmet background in food served me well, apparently, for as soon as the menu was in place my sales jumped.

All told, business that summer more than doubled. My years of experience in the best French restaurants in the world were paying off. I had made the right decision to change my menu and, had it not been for misplaced loyalty to my brother-in-law, I would have done it sooner. However, it still fell short of what I needed to stay current on our mortgage and also continue to pay down Helen's medical bills. Actually, I continued to pay my brother-in-law the franchise fee out of respect until he went out of business five years later.

• • •

In the summer of 1959, we had a big surprise: Costa, my younger brother, arrived in America. Katina, my only sibling left on Imbroz, stayed to take care of Mama and Papa. Costa stayed for most of the year with Taki and Sultana in New York where he had already found a job. His plan was to earn enough to put some savings down on a townhouse in Brooklyn.

That was also the summer I waited on a young man with a full beard who ordered a Coke and a hamburger with onions and ketchup, who approached me and asked if I needed help. The truth was that business was good enough to support more help at the time. I told him to report to work at six o'clock the next morning, and that the beard would have to go.

The young man's name was Vasili, or Bill, Moschonas. He was a 23-year-old Greek immigrant who was at that time a bit of a drifter, but he had an intensity of manner and was properly respectful. The next morning when I arrived at work, he had been standing at the back door for some time, cleanly shaven and clad in a white t-shirt and tie. He worked hard with me for over three years, becoming my first manager of sorts, before moving on to open his own store in the Maryland suburbs.

Bill was the first of many young men over a twenty-year span who worked with me and went on to start their own businesses. So it seemed, just as success had found me, others in pursuit of their success sought me out.

• • •

Costa arrived at our house in Virginia later in the fall just in time to join us for Thanksgiving dinner. When I met him at Union Station, I was surprised to see he was wearing a hat to cover his balding head. I remembered him as a small boy running down the dock to hug me farewell when I left for Constantinople, and later as a young teen arriving to greet me in the big city. When I finally held him at arm's length, I realized that, apart from his baldness, he had changed very little. With much excitement I ushered him to the car. The sight of Costa brought me, for a moment, close to Mama and Papa.

Costa had lots of affection to pass around to Helen and the children, and my family greeted him with joy. At Thanksgiving dinner that afternoon we were also joined by Helen's parents who came in from Warrenton. There was something uniquely wonderful about having my family members around me in America.

When we sat down I said a special grace in honor of the reunion with my brother. "Thank You, God, for protecting us and allowing us to be together for another year," I prayed. "We also thank You for the possessions You have given us and for the food on our table. And we offer You our greatest thanks for bringing Costa to us safely from Imbroz to share this special day. Amen."

"Amen," everyone echoed softly. Then we shared a traditional American Thanksgiving dinner of turkey served with my special rice, raisin and nut stuffing, and *tsoreki*. The tablecloth was obscured by the various savory concoctions Helen and I had prepared in honor of the holiday. Even though my debts were huge, there had always been plenty of good food for my family to eat since the day I had arrived in America.

Costa stayed the week, spending time with the children before returning to New York where he had already found a job. The brief week we spent with Costa was exciting for all of us. For me it opened the window to my past, and, through my little brother, connected me with the world I had left behind. I hoped he would be able to visit us for a longer stay before his six-month visa expired, but that was not to be. He would return to America as soon as he was able to obtain a permanent visa.

Shortly thereafter my good friend Olgalik, who was still at the Embassy, announced he was marrying a Russian Orthodox woman who was about 35 years old—thirty years his junior. Patience is often well rewarded, I guess. They would marry at the Russian Orthodox Saint Nicholas Cathedral on Massachusetts Avenue, diagonally across from Saint Sophia. The whole family was invited, and he insisted that I bring the kids. That week Helen and I went shopping for the wedding and bought white jackets and blue pants for the boys and a little white dress for Ianthe.

The wedding service, the icons, and the priest's vestments were identical to our Greek service in every respect, except it was in Russian. After the ceremony we went to Olgalik's two-bedroom apartment downtown for a small reception. Theologas and Elias and Anna Melas were there, along with a couple of his Russian friends. Olgalik and I drank a bottle of *metaxa* on top of shots of *ouzo*. It had been years since I had left the Embassy, and the four of us had much to catch up on. I introduced my family to everyone and spent the balance of the evening drinking and swapping old stories with my friends.

• • •

The fall was giving way to winter when I received a call at the store from Ted Theologos at the Turkish Embassy.

"Hello, my friend," I greeted him enthusiastically. "To what do I owe the pleasure of your call?" I asked.

Almost at once he lowered his voice. "Christo, have you heard the news that Archbishop Michael has died?" I hadn't.

"His Eminence Patriarch Athenagoras," he continued, "along with the bishops in Constantinople, have appointed a new Archbishop of the Americas." He paused dramatically.

"And that new Archbishop would be?" I prompted.

"Iakovos," he exclaimed with a laugh. "Iakovos has been chosen as our new Archbishop." The Archbishop would be the spiritual leader of all Eastern Orthodox Christians in North and South America.

"Iakovos…" I repeated, thinking of the old Bishop. "It's Jimmy."

It took a minute for me to realize that Jimmy Coucouzes, my childhood friend from Imbroz, had been chosen to be the new Archbishop of the Americas. For the rest of his life Jimmy would be addressed as Archbishop Iakovos. I thanked Ted for the call.

"God bless my old friend Jimmy," I repeated with a smile. "It's a miracle."

• • •

Later in the fall the Greek community in Washington, D.C. was preparing to welcome the new Archbishop. Preparations were underway at Saint Sophia Cathedral for the first formal visit of Iakovos, the new Archbishop of the Americas, including services followed by a reception. A week before Jimmy arrived I took the boys out and bought them new suits. Ianthe was also fitted for a new dress. Although they would outgrow them in a year, it was imperative that they look their best for the new Archbishop.

That Sunday morning Helen's parents joined us for the drive to the cathedral. I loaded everyone into the new Plymouth station wagon I had just purchased and headed off to church. The cathedral was packed with the faithful who had come to welcome their new Archbishop. I was lucky to find seats in the front for my in-laws and Helen and Ianthe, but the boys and I had to stand in the back.

It wasn't until Father Laloussis signaled for the congregation to sit down that I got a glimpse of him. Even in his imposing vestments and headdress, even with the staff of an archbishop in his hands, and even with his once dark hair and beard now a salt-and-pepper hue, I could see he was my childhood friend Jimmy Coucouzes. How far he had come since Imbroz. As for that, how far had I come, as well. I bowed my head and crossed myself three times.

Both Father Laloussis and the Archbishop had resounding voices and, backed by the marvelous choir, they filled the church with Byzantine chants. The crowded cathedral was illuminated by rays of tinted sunlight pouring through a rainbow of stained glass showering the incensed interior with a thousand glimmers. For a moment the sounds and spectacle of the service with my old friend transported me back to Imbroz.

At the end of the service we joined a long line of parishioners waiting patiently to kiss the Archbishop's hand in respect and receive the bread he blessed. When we joined the line, I arranged my family in front of me so that I was last and could assist my mother-in-law, who walked slowly with a cane. Though her legs pained her terribly from arthritis, Alexandra was not about to sit this out. She was devout in her beliefs and she wanted very much to receive His Eminence's blessing.

As we approached the head of the line Jimmy saw me immediately. His eyes lit up and he motioned to me excitedly.

"Chrysostomos," he said in a loud Greek whisper that drew the attention of the others in line. A minute later I was at his side, introducing him to my family. With a broad smile and a reverent bow, I kissed his hand, which he then placed on my shoulder.

"Come see me downstairs when I'm done," he invited. "Will you do that?"

"Of course, Your Eminence," I responded with a respectful bow.

After we had been received, I left my family and headed downstairs to the crowded auditorium to find Jimmy. When I entered the hallway, a bishop on Iakovos's staff noticed me and asked that I follow him. He led me through a suite of offices to a quiet room where Jimmy sat waiting for me. As soon as I entered, the Archbishop stood and motioned for the bishop to leave.

"Your Eminence," I said, bowing once again.

"Chrysostomos, come here, sit.

He settled me in a chair across from him and for several moments I recited the news of my family while he listened intently. "Costa, my brother, came to America a year ago on a permanent work visa and will work toward his citizenship. That only leaves Katina with my parents on Imbroz. Costa is working in New York as a tailor."

"That's good news. I saw your parents about five years ago," he told me. "I was only able to go to Imbroz twice during my years in Constantinople, but I made it a point to see your family and the old Bishop Iakovos both times. I have kept up on news about you, as well," he continued. "I heard you have your own store now, is that so? You're quite the entrepreneur."

"Yes, Your Eminence," I said, and proceeded to tell him all about Ocean City and my Tastee-Freez store.

"You are like your father, Christo."

The comparison once again pleased me, and I nodded. "And how are things in Turkey?" I asked.

Iakovos shook his head. "In many respects nothing has changed, but we make do and get by. The Church will survive and Our Lord will forge a way."

Suddenly he changed the subject. "Come see me at the Archdiocese in New York," he said warmly. "Promise me that you will." I told him I would try to visit.

"You must also promise to come as a guest to my home for dinner some time," I invited. "It would mean a lot to my family and me."

"I'd like that, Christo."

Before we parted, we embraced.

On the way home my younger son, Jon, turned to me and said, "Did you know the Archbishop, Dad?"

"Yes, I knew him, Jon." I smiled. "I knew him quite well."

From the ash of the Christian genocide, a religious leader for the Greek Orthodox Christian faithful of the Americas had risen, and it was none other than my childhood friend Jimmy.

CHAPTER 16

Ocean City Chris

My heart leaps up when I behold
a rainbow in the sky:
so was it when my life began;
so is it now I am a man;
so be it when I shall grow old,
or let me die!
The child is father to the man;
and I could wish my days to be
bound each to each by natural piety.
—WILLIAM WORDSWORTH, 1802

EVERY MORNING I ROSE AT DAWN, pinned my relic coin to my t-shirt, and said my morning prayer. I never forgot to thank God for each new day, always asking Him to watch over my family and grant me the strength to succeed in my new store. On my way to work it was my habit to stand for a moment, gazing eastward across the boardwalk and the white sandy beach to the ocean glittering in the morning sun.

It was God's grace and this tranquil sight of the sun rising over the sea that sustained me through the many years of hard work that lay ahead of me. It reminded me of my tiny seaside island, evoking emotions that I had not felt since leaving my island home twenty-five years before. The sight of dazzling ivory sand embraced by the sunlit sea, the touch of fresh ocean breezes on my face, the view of a clear, blue sky—these things refreshed and filled me with peace, placing a new perspective on the events of my life.

The chess game of violence, power, and upheaval of demagogues such as Atatürk and Hitler melted away over the waves of the timeless sea. Everything seemed insignificant when compared to the serene sounds and cool breeze over the expanse and the ancient, cosmic rhythm of the sea. These impressions would stay with me without requiring my presence, for although I worked a block from the Atlantic Ocean for nearly the rest of my life, I rarely had time to actually see it.

• • •

Early one morning I was out cleaning my asphalt parking lot with a hose when a young, black, muscular man rode up on a bicycle. The bike had two mirrors, elevated handlebars, two saddlebags, a multitude of reflectors, a large horn, tassels hanging down, a foxtail hanging on the back, and a headlight in front still shining in the early daylight. Without a doubt, it was the most unforgettable two-wheeled vehicle I had ever seen. I tried not to stare.

This was my first sight of Bernard. With slow, thoughtful speech and impeccable manners he introduced himself and told me he was 25 years old.

"Since my Mama died this winter, I don't have anyone to take care of me," he said, "and I wonder if you know where I can find a job."

Bernard lived in Berlin, a town six miles away, in the house he had once shared with his mother. Bernard was different from other people. I am not sure what Bernard's specific difficulty was, but he was a good man and he deserved the same respect as anyone else. I knew people teased and ridiculed him, maybe even feared him, but I saw his dignity and I respected him. I gave him a job, and I demanded the best from him, as well.

"Hi, Bernard. Yes, let's see what we can do." As he parked his bike behind my store, I thought how best to get him started.

"Bernard, see what I'm doing with the hose?" I was moving the hose slowly across the blacktop parking lot from left to right, pushing a line of sand, dirt, and trash in front.

"You see, Bernard?" his eyes focusing on the line of water. "Hold your thumb over the water like this, you see?" I showed him how to limit the water to force it out faster.

"Yes, sir, Mr. Christ."

"All right, you take over and I will go inside to prepare for today."

"Yes, sir. I'll take care of it," he said.

I watched Bernard for another minute. "No, no, Bernard, look down while cleaning, look down."

"Bernard," I said a few minutes later, "when you finish you can have breakfast. Afterwards, we have a lot of work to do."

"Yes sir, Mr. Christ" he said.

"You come inside and I'll fix you a sandwich." I gestured toward the back door.

"Yes sir, Mr. Christ," he repeated.

This was how Bernard's first day with me began, the start of a long relationship.

The next morning two African American women approached me. They were Bernard's sisters. "We didn't know what to do with him since Mama died," they implored. "We have been taking care of him. We were thinking to take him to the institution in Cambridge."

"Bernard will be fine helping us," I said.

"Thank you so much," came their heartfelt response.

As the season progressed Bernard became my most regular seasonal employee, arriving early every morning on his fabulous bicycle, over six miles from his mother's tiny home in Berlin, then returning in the evening. Bernard was reliable and honest and stayed with us for more than thirty-four years.

Cleaning was Bernard's primary duty, which is very important in the foodservice business. He worked hard to keep the store clean exactly as I wanted it, an increasing need as business improved. Over time, I showed him how to become a good preparations man as well, cutting and slicing vegetables, meats, and cheese. Later on he would also help me repaint the store before we opened each spring. Like Papa had done thirty-five years earlier, we painted the store white, inside and out, and, yes, the trim was blue.

My fortuitous encounter with Bernard that spring was a sign of good things to come, for my risk finally started to prove itself worth the reward. By that summer the new menu brought us a lot more business. We started serving freshly baked and fried chicken and freshly cooked sugar-cured ham. Our hamburgers were made from premium lean beef and we received ten-pound bags of premium fresh-ground beef daily. They were made into patties in our store and sold that day. Our french fries were cut from Idaho longs peeled, sliced, and fried in peanut oil. They were always served fresh and hot. Our hoagies were packed with Italian sausage, sliced ham, baloney, and provolone cheese on a bed of lettuce and sliced tomato, with a generous helping of mayonnaise—all ingredients fresh, of course.

• • •

The summer season of 1960 passed with continued success. It was that summer when I was 42 years old, some thirty-two years after I had left home the first time for Samothraki Island, that I finally felt I had made it. During that June my sales doubled again. Although the numbers were still small, my store began to thrive.

Ocean City is a barrier island one hundred and sixty miles directly east of Washington. As such we had a number of storms that caused local flooding and some near misses from hurricanes. Then, on September 12, 1960, Hurricane Donna hit Ocean City with winds over one hundred miles an hour. It put the whole barrier island under water and washed away many structures, including the iconic pier and wooden boardwalk.

During the fall, after the storm, I went down to assess the damage from Donna and start the cleanup. I was wiping off watermarks that were three feet high on the white paint of our small cinder-block structure. Even inside there were water-damage stains, but many other businesses had it much worse. I was worried that the storm might affect business that summer, as much of Ocean City had washed away. I tuned off the water, winterizing the property, then went home.

During the winter of 1960, Helen and I were approached by a group of Greek families to join them in forming a new Orthodox church in Northern Virginia—Saint Katherine's. Originally, there were thirty founding families in the congregation. For two years we held services in the Sunday school room of a small Presbyterian church. Eventually, after many successful functions and fundraisers, we were able to purchase a suitable piece of property and build a church.

• • •

I returned to the beach early to start the 1961 season because Jerry Moutzalias was coming down to show me how to prepare a steamship round of beef. Jerry was the chef at Blackie's House of Beef, a popular restaurant in Washington that was so large that it took up nearly an entire city block. The success of Blackie's roast beef sandwich was legendary among Greek restaurant entrepreneurs. I wanted to introduce the roast beef sandwich to Ocean City, and I welcomed instruction in its preparation.

"This is going to be the best sandwich you can imagine, Chris."

I watched as Jerry trimmed the beef and ran a rod through the length of the roast next to the bone. Then he added salt, pepper, and onions and cooked it at 550 degrees for three hours, pouring a little water over the beef every fifteen to twenty minutes. Finally, he lowered the heat to 375 degrees for another two hours.

"Very simple, but also very, very good," Jerry humbly boasted. I already knew how I wanted to present the new sandwich.

To showcase my new meats, I arranged three bays on a steam table with heat lamps hanging over them in the front window of my store, in plain view of my customers. On the right I displayed my specially seasoned oven-baked chicken, and on the left was our Virginia sugar-cured ham. In the center, dominating the display, was a seventy-pound steamship round, *au jus*. We thinly sliced the meat and served it on a Kaiser roll, seasoned with salt and pepper. It was important that the slices be thin, and that the top of the Kaiser roll be slightly dipped in the pure *au jus* that had been directly strained from the cooking pan without any gravy-like additives.

My concern over losing business due to the hurricane turned out to be justified as many businesses went bankrupt. However, since there were hundreds of construction workers rebuilding the island, we became very popular. Although the number of vacationers was severely down, we had an okay summer from a business point of view.

All my new sandwiches were popular, but the steamship round quickly became the most popular sandwich on the beach—let alone in my little store. People came from all over the beach to buy them and before long we were selling almost an entire seventy-pound steamship round in quarter pound portions on a seeded Kaiser roll, *au jus*, every day for sixty-five cents per sandwich.

At the end of the summer my friend Dale Truitt with Swift came by to take an order from me and to have a cup of coffee. "Hey, Chris," he said, "do you know you are buying more roast beef than any other place on the island? In fact, you're my biggest customer."

"Drink your coffee, Dale, before it gets cold," I responded, pausing for a moment to reflect on how far we had come.

I was amazed by my newfound success. I had turned a corner in my business, and we were now strongly in the black. It turned out that my idea to diversify my menu had been a gamble worth taking. I had installed sugar-cured ham, fried and baked chicken, fresh-peeled potatoes, daily fresh-ground beef patties, meatballs, spaghetti, and soon I would have fresh pizza with boiled hand-squeezed tomato sauce to add to our menu. Last year's success had carried over, and with the new steamship round added to my menu, my receipts continued to grow through the summer. The next step would be to buy the property from Charlie Holland.

Charlie Holland came by in the early morning one day that summer for his usual coffee and a ham and egg sandwich on a mildly buttered, toasted Kaiser roll. Casually dressed as usual, his southern accent gave him a disarming demeanor, but behind the slow, easy manner was a smart, shrewd businessman. I had been thinking hard about exercising my option to buy rather than just renegotiating my lease with Charlie. I ran it by him that day and we sealed the deal with a handshake. Charlie was a good man and gave me a fair deal.

One day in late summer, I exercised my option and, on a payment plan, bought my small store. My future payments would now create equity for me instead of for someone else. Along with my 1,000 square-foot rambler home, purchased for $17,000, I finally also owned my 1,000 square-foot store, purchased for $25,000. With my increased income, the revenues from my new menu would eventually pay off the mortgages.

• • •

One morning in mid-July while Bernard was busy cleaning the floors inside, I took over his usual task of cleaning the parking lot with a hose. While I was working a gentleman almost twenty years my senior walked up to me.

"Are you Chris Christ?" he asked.

"Yes, how can I help you?" I responded.

"My name is Nick Anthony," he said, extending his hand with a smile. "Someone said to come by if I needed a job."

Nick was an inch or so taller than I was and unmistakably Greek. A piece of his white hair brushed the top of his trusting eyes, which magnified through his thick spectacles. He wore a short-sleeved white t-shirt and khaki pants, which happened to be my preferred work attire. Nick was clearly down-and-out and in need of work—and no doubt a second chance.

"Do you have any experience working in a restaurant?" I asked.

"I was in the restaurant business for thirty years."

"And you're not any longer?"

Nick told me his story. It turns out he lost his restaurant in a poker game and he had a wife and two young children to support. He seemed genuinely repentant. I took a long, appraising look at him and felt that he was honest, though perhaps a little misguided.

With my growing business I could use more help. If nothing else, Nick had experience and I needed someone responsible to close the store. I decided to take a chance on a man who had gambled away his livelihood.

It was a decision I never regretted. Nick indeed proved to be reliable and honest, and before long he became my right-hand man. Nick arrived every afternoon around three thirty, and he worked until long after midnight. Within the first few months I made him my night manager, which allowed me to leave at six or seven o'clock each evening for the first time in my career.

Through Nick's white t-shirt you could often see the outline of an Orthodox crucifix on a gold chain. He always wore glasses and a smile on his good-natured face. In the afternoons as he drank his coffee I would watch him take long, quiet drags of his non-filtered Camel cigarettes. The yellow nicotine stains on the inside of his index and middle fingers revealed the only tarnish to his otherwise impeccable appearance.

Most of our conversations occurred in the few minutes after his arrival at the store, as he sat with a cigarette and a cup of coffee.

"Nick, you're going to be very busy tonight. I have a second top round in the oven."

"Okay, Chris."

I placed a steaming tray in front of him and lifted the cover.

"See these meatballs? They can't be overcooked."

Nick poked a toothpick into one and popped it into his mouth. A smile lit his face. "They're delicious," he said, reaching for another. Another successful addition to my menu.

During the thirteen years he worked for me, Nick never missed a day of work and was often visible in my store's showcase window slicing a steamship round—so much so that people often mistook him for the owner. He never allowed anyone else to prepare the sandwich. He had the hands of a surgeon. After trimming the beef, Nick would cut it in thin and regular slices around the bone parallel to the floor. He then rested each slice on the flat of his knife, supported by the serving fork, and then piled the slices onto a fresh

Kaiser roll until each serving of roast beef weighed a bit over a quarter of a pound.

Starting in the summer of 1961, the roast beef sandwich was our most popular sandwich. Within three years we would be selling more than three seventy-pound rounds a day. In later years our record was seven rounds in one day. Our distributor told us we were selling the most roast beef of any store on the east coast by 1965.

• • •

One morning in August while I was busy setting up the store I was greeted by a tall man with short-cropped hair and a handlebar mustache. It was Max, the chef at Rive Gauche, who had come down at my invitation to teach me and my boys a recipe for a fresh tomato sauce for pizza, which I also planned to add to my menu.

"Max, my sons, Anthony and Jon, will help you," I said placing a hand on each of my boys' shoulders. They grinned in agreement.

"Okay, boys, let's begin." Max moved with purpose into the kitchen and my sons both followed and listened intently, mesmerized by the chef.

Max boiled fresh tomatoes in a big, stainless steel pot, then rinsed them under cold running water, peeled them, and squeezed them into another pot. Next he added sugar, salt, pepper, bay leaves, garlic, oregano, and pure olive oil. He allowed the mixture to simmer over a slow fire for two hours, then cool for three hours before serving it up on freshly kneaded pizza dough. Although our pizza was never as popular as our sandwiches, it still contributed to the sales of our growing business.

To complement our newfound success, I decided it was time for a new name.

"Helen, let's call our store 'Anthony's Carryout.'"

I liked the idea of naming the store after my son and my father-in-law, who had given me my first chance. I finally felt like I had my own business.

• • •

The summer of 1961 proved to be even busier than that of 1960. Even with Nick, Bill, Bernard, and my sons assisting me in the kitchen we still needed more help. That was the summer Willa Mae Hobbs joined us at the restaurant. Willa Mae was a local woman with six children and a husband named Theofalos. She and her family became an invaluable asset to me. Every Sunday morning her entire family would come in to give the store and parking lot a thorough cleaning after the Saturday night rush, which often lasted until four in the morning.

It was also the summer my orders placed with Swift & Company, my food supplier, grew so large that Dale Truitt, the sales manager, offered me credit. Credit is a twin-edged sword. Dale had been coming by the shop three mornings a week to make deliveries and take the next day's order for a few years now. When money can be leveraged to a productive use, it's a blessing. When applied to consumption, however, it creates cascading debt. Thankfully, the latter did not apply in my case. No one had offered me credit of this sort before, and I viewed it as a turning point in my life. By enabling me to place a month's worth of orders before being billed, my daily receipts built up at the bank and I was able to accrue interest, making me creditworthy at the bank.

Swift & Company was not the only wholesaler I used. Our baked and fried chicken sandwiches were so popular that I also kept my chicken wholesaler, Frank Perdue—founder of the now famous Perdue Chicken in Salisbury, Maryland—well supplied with orders. In those days, before his company became famous, Frank was always hustling business himself. He often stuck his head in the back door of my store, calling out my name and leaving a wooden case of fresh chickens on ice in the kitchen with a bill tucked inside. With that small, beaked face and thin neck bobbing in at the back door, we would have to smile to ourselves. Frank not only sold chickens, he even looked like one. Later, of course, he would make Perdue Chicken a household name, but in the 1960s he was working hard to build his business, just as we were.

• • •

Another hurricane struck on September 21, 1961. Unlike Donna, Hurricane Esther was not a direct hit. Although there was flooding and some damage, it was not nearly the damage Donna had wreaked.

Then, in March of 1962, America put its first man, John Glenn, in orbit around the earth as the U.S. stepped up its race with Russia to land a man on the moon. America never ceased to amaze me with her scientific abilities.

That year was also the time Ocean City endured the Great March Storm, which became known as the "Ash Wednesday Storm." An odd confluence of events made this storm very destructive. It started on a full moon when the tides were running high, and, although the winds peaked at 65 miles per hour, which were just below hurricane level, the storm sat offshore from March 6 through March 8 and pummeled the beach and inlet with six high tides. As the water rose, it had no way to escape. By the third high tide Ocean City was underwater. By nightfall on March 7 the pier had been washed away. The wooden boardwalk had been completely erased, as well, as had the white sandy beach. The storm severed the island into three sections and washed away over forty percent of all structures.

At the storm's peak on Ash Wednesday high tide was nine and a half feet above normal. For comparison's sake, during the powerful hurricane that hit in 1933, and severed Ocean City from the mainland, tides were only seven feet above normal. Along with these high tides came continuous hard rain, 60 miles per hour winds, and twenty-five-foot waves. Ocean City was torn apart. The storm put us underwater for almost twenty hours.

On Thursday the National Guard was allowing business and property owners back on the peninsula to survey the damage. I drove over the bridge into town and down Coastal Highway with my sons. My small 1,000 square-foot carryout on 17th Street had watermarks that stained the inside and outside walls up to almost five feet, but there was no structural damage. I was one of the lucky ones. We had a lot of cleaning up to do, so we rolled up our sleeves and began what would turn out to be two days of hard labor.

Later in the week we drove to the beach. "Dad, look," Anthony exclaimed when we arrived. "There's no boardwalk."

The white sandy beaches had disappeared, torn off wooden slabs piled up at tortured angles sticking out of the ground, and the businesses closer to the beach had been severely damaged or washed away. We continued driving onwards and had to slow down to ease our way through standing water from where the ocean waves met the water from the bay.

I saw one man tearfully surveying what looked like a slab of wood. Connected to the slab horizontally was a toilet. We approached the man to ask if he needed help and he pointed to the debris. "This is my commode," he said red-eyed. It was all that he had left of his house. We got out of our car to commiserate with him for a while.

On the road in front of where the man's house used to be was a three-way intersection of Coastal Highway, Baltimore Avenue, and 33rd Street. The Ash Wednesday storm was certainly a devastating tragedy.

It would be about five years before businesses fully recovered in Ocean City. After the storm, however, I was able to reopen for the 1962 summer season and my store did very well despite the circumstances. Once again, many of our customers were the workmen who came in to replace or repair other structures.

• • •

Later that summer a man approached me as I was opening my store.

"Are you Mr. Christ?" he asked.

"Yes, sir, what can I do for you?" I was getting accustomed to people dropping by the store for me.

"My name is Jack Selby. Charlie Holland said you might need some signs."

"Yes, I do," I said enthusiastically.

My store was currently painted white with glass panes in the front and blue trim all around, and the big Tastee-Freez sign hung on the roof. Not wishing to offend my brother-in-law, I had left the sign there all these years. Nonetheless, my store had expanded past the franchise several years before and it was time that people knew we offered a lot more.

Within a week Mr. Selby submitted several sketches to me. He proposed that the main sign run the length of the store. It was to be illuminated by lights and would read "Anthony's Carryout," replacing a smaller, wooden one. With Coastal Highway now a four-lane road that ran the length of the peninsula parallel to the beach, our sign would be clearly visible to thousands of passers-by, and it still is to this day.

For the southern corner of the building, he sketched a billboard showing a tub of chicken. He also created a pizza sign featuring a little pizza man that I later used as a logo. Menu board signs were made, as well, to hang above different areas inside the store, including a giant submarine sign.

Initially I bought the internal menu signs, which Selby painted on the white block walls of the restaurant, and over time he added the others. Within three years, though, I proudly displayed them all. No one mistook my restaurant for a Tastee-Freez anymore.

This was also the summer I found an apartment on 15th Street, two blocks from the store, and ended seven years of residency at the Nordica. The apartment had a kitchen and two bedrooms and was not only a convenient walk to the store, but was spacious enough for my family.

Bill Moschonas, the Greek immigrant I had taken on three years before, was no longer with us, and in his place I hired Tony Russo, a 22-year-old Italian boy from Baltimore, Maryland.

Tony was a hard-working, responsible young man with a heavy accent. He only stayed with us two years. In 1964 he founded Tony's Pizza on Division Street and Boardwalk in Ocean City and he remains a very successful businessman to this day. His success never surprised me. In fact, at the time I hired him, he reminded me of myself as a young man.

• • •

The year 1963 was our seventh in business, and the beach was still in a state of disrepair from the storm. Mae and Bernard were still with me and were in charge of preparation and cleanup, Tony Russo made the pizzas, and Nick, of course, was in charge of the steamship round sandwiches. I supplemented this core of employees with about twelve to fourteen summer hires who were college and high school students. The cooking load had also reached a point where I hired Vito, thus marking this point of my odyssey with several chefs. My insistence that chefs stick to my formulation of each recipe so the public could experience consistency lead to a series of different chefs. Vito left after the season.

Chefs—glorified cooks—admittedly have a hard job. That said, they generally seem to have a higher opinion of their culinary ability than deserved. Some feel the need to show up on time, others don't. Some have their own ways of food preparation, and they should be avoided, too. We knew exactly how we wanted our meats prepared and just needed attendance and execution. Some generally choose a time when you're already busy and short-handed to walk out. I acquainted Vito with the carryout at the start of June, which was typically the slowest of the three summer months. One weekend after July 4th he asked me if he could take his dinner break at the Seascape to have a bowl of soup, and I told him I would wait until he returned before I left for the evening. I am still waiting for Vito to return.

For the rest of the summer, my sons were instrumental cooking and preparing foods under my supervision. I was desperate, but also proud. My older son, Anthony, now 14, was working nights and my middle child, Jon, age 12, would come with me in the mornings. Although they had been working with me very sparingly since the ages of eight and ten, they now were working full shifts during the summer. Still needing a morning cook and preparation chef in mid-season though, I found George. George was reliable and executed food preparation the way we wanted it done.

George was a big man with a thick, wide-rimmed mustache, a throwback to the World War I era. He was a heavy man in both height and weight from the old country. George only spoke a few words of English, despite having been in America for almost twenty years.

"George, I don't want to tell you again, speak English."

"Mr. Christ, it burns, it b-u-r-n-s."

"What burns George?"

"My kollo, my kollo!" He gestured toward his rear end. It aggravated me to see immigrants unwilling, or just plain too lazy, to learn English after so many years. My immediate thought was poor George had hemorrhoids.

"In English George, please."

"I have a lot of pain when I go to the bathroom."

In the old country there were no medicines and people relied on herbs to treat their ailments. My great grandmother used to wear cloves of garlic around her neck thinking it warded off disease and bad spirits.

"Okay, George, come here." I took a knife and carefully peeled a clove of garlic.

"Yes, Kyrios Christo."

"Take this," I held the garlic between my index finger and my thumb, "and put it up your rear end," I said making an upward turning motion with the fresh clove of garlic. "Far up," I added, looking George square in the eye.

"Okay, thank you, Kyrios Christo."

He took the clove of garlic and went into the bathroom. Next we heard a loud scream. My older son broke out laughing at my medieval cure and George's response. A couple moments later George emerged from the bathroom breathing hard and perspiring.

"Did it work?" I asked, looking him in the eyes.

"Oh yes, thank you Mr. Christ, thank you." I guess sometimes old cures can be just as effective in different times and places.

• • •

This was also the summer that Nick brought his family down from Baltimore to spend the season with him. He had been concerned about leaving his wife and children for weeks on end every summer, and when I suggested the obvious solution of bringing them to Ocean City, he seized on the idea immediately. I paid the cost for the larger apartment that they would need.

A week later Helen and the kids were also coming down and would spend a day at the beach with our neighbors.

"Hi, Dad," Anthony greeted me.

"What are you up to, son?"

"Mom's going to take us to the ocean again tomorrow," he told me, then added, "if that's all right with you."

"Ah, yes, that will be fun. You go and enjoy yourself."

"You don't need me to work, do you?"

"No, enjoy yourself. Take your days off before you start work." Through my children's adolescent leisure I captured glimpses of the youth I was denied.

Reassured that his day at the beach was justified, Anthony smiled and changed the subject. "What have you got there, Dad?"

"It's a letter from your aunt in Imbroz," I told him. "Now go to bed, son. You've got a big day tomorrow."

I turned back to Katina's letter, lost in thought. Papa and Mama were in their eighties and Katina was their sole caregiver. It pained me to think of them in this state on the island. Katina was right; we were beginning to grow old, too, and for Katina, who had put her entire life on hold, it was especially hard.

My thoughts were preoccupied with my family when Helen came to sit beside me. She had finished putting Jon and Ianthe to bed. I could see she had something she wanted to talk to me about. I put aside my sister's letter and smiled at her.

"Chris, it's good to be here," she said. She had been down for two weeks.

"Yes," I responded. "I have missed you all."

"And we have missed you. You are never home, and it is hard raising the children without you. Even now, when we are all here, we hardly see each other."

Our familiar disagreement had surfaced again.

"Now, Helen, we do what we must to earn a living—"

"The children hardly know you," she broke in. "It's not healthy. Anthony and Jon are always fighting, did you know that? They need their father, Chris."

I didn't know the boys were fighting. I knew it was hard on Helen to raise the children while I was working, but I also knew it was my work that would open opportunities for them that I never had.

I was too tired to argue. Instead, I squeezed her hand and rose from my chair. "Helen, it's late and I have to get up early," I told her. "We will talk, but for now let's go to bed."

The next morning I was up at four-forty five as usual. I went through my morning ritual of pinning my relic coin to my t-shirt and praying to God for strength and guidance. Then I set off to work feeling refreshed and full of energy, moving quietly so as not to awaken anyone. I knew that Helen and I would never really reconcile on the matter of my working so hard, but I also knew I was doing all I could to care for my family. I knew too well how harsh the world could be, and while I was alive and able, I would shield my family from what I had endured.

• • •

I hired a Greek man that summer—another Vasili—who spoke no English at all and had no experience in food service, but I desperately needed help. Vasili had a thyroid condition that caused his eyes to protrude in a startling manner. Small children were sometimes afraid of him, but I knew this immigrant dockworker was a good and decent man. Vasili stayed with me for three years and soon became my manager. He later went on to open Prima Pizzeria in Northern Virginia.

I still chuckle recalling the image of Vasili turning over his first English words with his heavy Greek tongue: "howt doag? hampbairgair?"

"That's right, Vasili," I replied with encouragement.

We were busier that summer than we had ever been. Many Greeks from the church communities in the Baltimore-Washington area, even if just acquaintances, would pass by the store and pay their respects to Chris from Ocean City, or "Ocean City Chris," as I was often called. We had twenty five positions open that summer, but with the season's turnover, I had to hire a total of forty employees to fill them, for most of the kids only wanted to work part-time to finance their fun in a summer resort.

The hardest part of running a restaurant, provided you know the business, is finding good people. It is an ongoing, unrelenting challenge. This was further complicated by the fact that my store was located at a seasonal resort. The beach atmosphere fostered an already high worker turnover. Nonetheless, our employees ate free and were treated well.

That season I had done so well that I paid all my seasonal obligations, had money in the bank, and was able to give Nick an extra bonus and a raise.

• • •

Eventually it came time to close up the store for the season. When I returned to Northern Virginia I finished up what would be my last winter waiting tables with Blaise. Although I was sad to leave Rive Gauche and my colorful patrons, my time that winter would soon be applied to another venture.

Dr. Koutravelas, a radiologist from Fairfax, Virginia, who frequented my store in Ocean City, asked me if I would be interested in operating a luncheonette in the newly built Seven Corners Medical Building. I accepted the invitation, obtained financing, and opened Fairfax Inn in mid-October of 1963, planning to run it during the winter. The luncheonette kept me busy, but it also meant, to my great pleasure, that I was home by seven in the evening to see my family.

One afternoon just before Thanksgiving, as I was working at Fairfax Inn, I heard news on the radio that stopped me in my tracks.

"President Kennedy has been fatally shot today in Dallas, Texas..." In an instant, all my achievements paled in the face of this great national tragedy. John F. Kennedy was my age and had my father's name. For several suffocating moments I was taken by the memories of the dreary life I had left decades ago. His loss underscored for me the fragility of life itself. I thought of his poor widow, Jacqueline, the charming young woman I had waited on some years before.

As the days following the tragedy unfolded, there was something reaffirming in the dignified way our grieving nation responded. While people wept, the government moved smoothly to install Lyndon B. Johnson as President. There was no rioting in the streets, no uprising or revolution. The mechanics of my new country's democracy had been grandly conceived and carefully thought out to enable its people to weather calamity with strength, calm, and purpose.

After the holidays, in February of 1964, I bought Helen a white Olds Cutlass Supreme. She had gotten her license the year before, and I knew the car would give her more freedom and make her feel less isolated.

Helen's parents had also joined us for the holidays. Anton was still limited in his mobility after suffering a stroke that summer. "She made me go, Christo!" Anton motioned to Alexandra as I entered his room. "I had the stroke while waiting with Alexandra to see Oral Roberts." Alexandra, who suffered from crippling arthritis, often watched Oral Roberts, a TV evangelist who claimed to have God-given powers to heal. When he announced a tent show in Cambridge, Maryland, that summer she made sure they would attend. Needless to say, Oral Roberts could do nothing for my father-in-law, and an ambulance transported him to the hospital.

Stubborn as he was, he beat back the doctor's dire prognosis and left the hospital, even though his vision was impaired, his left arm was paralyzed, and his left leg felt stiff. It saddened me that Anton, who had been active all his life, was now partially paralyzed. Yet he and Alexandra were managing pretty well on their own with the help of their maid. After such a tragic autumn, there was added meaning in having everyone gather for Christmas dinner.

• • •

That spring of 1964 I received another particularly upsetting letter from Katina. Things had worsened on Imbroz yet again.

Dear Chrysostomos,

Things have grown progressively worse since the riots in Constantinople. Boycotts of our businesses and deportations have resumed. A couple of months ago the Turks formed a penal colony here on Imvros in Schinoudi.

In March of 1964, the Turks moved another six hundred long-term convicts from the mainland to Schinoudi. They are allowed to roam free, terrorizing, destroying property and worse. We are overrun. The Christian population has been reduced to only about two hundred. A commission of elders complained to the Turkish authorities who installed an army legion between Clyky and our village. The soldiers have destroyed farmhouses and chapels, and openly stolen from the Christians, beating and terrorizing the residents. In short, they are indistinguishable from the convicts.

After forty years of occupation, the Turks are no longer subtle or covert about their agenda. They are driving us from our properties to turn them over to future Turkish settlers. Thank you for your generous gifts and God bless you.

Love,
Katerina

The Turks imposed *Eritme Programmi* in 1961 which aimed to confiscate property of the remaining Christian island residents. Imposition of economic violence began in earnest. Ninety percent of cultivated land was confiscated from island inhabitants as a result of the 1964 Law on Land Expropriation, and 6,000 ethnic Turks were brought from the mainland to live on Imbroz. All remaining Greek schools were closed. A prison was built on the island where convicts were allowed to roam freely and target locals. The island was classified as a "forbidden zone," which meant that expatriates could not visit their homes without special permission. Poor Mama, Papa, and Katina.

No sooner had I set down the letter than I took up my pen to once again plead to my parents to come to America. I felt the strength of my words as they poured from my pen. Filled with triumph and resolve I hurried to the post office and posted the letter. No sooner had the letter been posted, however, than I knew my words were useless, my efforts wasted. Papa's stubbornness had not diminished with the years. I knew he would never leave Imbroz and allow the Turks to take his home. I paused, knowing that Papa and Mama were too old to travel. Thankfully we had applied for Costa's citizenship and the paperwork was nearing completion.

Although the Christian slaughters had stopped with the Lausanne Agreement in 1923, the Christian minority on Imbroz was still experiencing horrific treatment, absent of any accountability or justice.

With the new restrictions I was not even sure I could get my family out of Turkey. I prayed that Jimmy might be strong in leading us as our new Archbishop, and thanked the Lord for allowing our paths to cross in America. I prayed that He would give us strength to face, with courage and faith, whatever the future may bring, and to watch over our people, my family—realizing more fully than ever that each moment should be savored.

CHAPTER 17

Loss and Love

Farewell to thee! But not farewell
to all my fondest thoughts of Thee;
within my heart they still shall dwell
and they shall cheer and comfort me.
Life seems more sweet that thou didst live
and men more true that thou wert one;
nothing is lost that thou didst give,
nothing destroyed that thou hast done.
—ANNE BRONTË, 1847

IN THE SPRING OF 1965 Costa had been a U.S. citizen for a few months and was now 44 years old. Shortly thereafter I received a letter from Papa, whose mind, I was pleased to see, was as sharp as ever. This would be the last letter I received from my father.

Dear Chrysostomos,

It has been since 1945, twenty years, since Mama and I last saw you yet barely a day goes by when we don't proudly reflect on you, Elenitsa and the children. Your success in America has been the light of our lives. Remember our teachings and our ways so that you may pass them to your children. And although we have been apart for so long, don't forget that Mama and I will always be with you. Please watch out for your older sister, Katerina. God will not forget the material help you have provided us over the years. All our love to our grandchildren.

God bless you,
Mama and Papa

It was so difficult for me to think that I had not seen my parents for twenty years. The fact that two decades had passed was incredibly sad. I tucked a money order for $100 into an envelope as I had done so many times before, and said a tearful prayer for them all. I didn't know what else to do since Papa refused to come to America. My success and well wishes were all I had to share with them, but it never seemed enough. I prayed for their continued good health.

Meanwhile Helen and I were still helping with her parents. We moved them into a two-bedroom garden apartment near us that spring and a caretaker moved in with them. Things were not going well between my father-in-law and his son.

"Christo," my mother-in-law implored, "what should we do? Gus has sold our house in Warrenton and we have never seen a cent from the sale." She turned and gestured to my father-in-law. "Look at Anton. All he does is sit and stare, Christo. I just don't know what to do."

"You have the apartment," I said, trying to soothe my in-laws, "and Helen is close by to care for you. Enjoy your life and perhaps the other problems will seem less important. Sometimes they even resolve themselves in unexpected ways. Just trust in God and live in happiness for today."

After his stroke, Anton had turned much of the management of his assets over to his son, and it saddened me to see that he was depressed over his mismanagement. I wished I could help Anton regain some control over his finances, but this was a private family matter. Helen adored her brother and I adored her. I didn't want to cause additional anxiety in her life by raising questions about his activities, so I remained silent. Again, I felt helpless in caring for my family.

• • •

It was now the spring of 1965 and I found a new manager for the Fairfax Inn—Mr. Merkezas, a Greek man from Cyprus—then headed off to Ocean City to open up the shop. That spring I purchased the property on 33rd Street in Ocean City and named it Anthony's Beer & Wine. I had borrowed a substantial amount of money to invest in this new property. Three years later I would also finalize plans to build and lease out six new adjacent stores in that shopping center. This was also the spring I bought a three-bedroom townhouse, ten blocks north of my store at the beach. We had come a long way from our little room at the Nordica.

We expected a strong summer, God willing. The vacation crowd at Ocean City seemed to increase each year. My pizza chef, Tony Russo, had left us the year before and I had a hard time filling the position. I finally hired a young man from California with long hair who arrived in Ocean City with a surfboard in need of a job. His name was Brian Tara, and he stayed with me for five years, never once missing a single day of work. He was a very good pizza man.

That fall I think I began to feel my age creeping up on me for the first time. After closing up the store in Ocean City I headed to Fairfax Inn. The kids returned to school, and I began to realize how much they had grown. At this time Anthony was 17, Jon just turned 16 and Ianthe was ten. I rarely spoke to my children about my life in Imbroz, or the events of my past. I always believed in living for today, not dwelling on the past. As a result, though, I realized that my children were being deprived of knowing their grandparents, and the courage and spirit they had.

I thought about my children more and more, perhaps because I was watching them grow up and become young adults, working beside me as I had with my father and Uncle Russo so many years before. My sons and daughter had taught me much and I suppose the realization struck me that time was running out for me to give them everything I wanted to give them. I had given them financial security, but was that enough?

• • •

During Thanksgiving week, I received a letter from Katina. For some reason—perhaps I was busy working at Fairfax Inn—I put it aside unopened and did not remember it until the Sunday morning after Thanksgiving. In the back of my mind I guess I expected to receive this letter someday. Nonetheless, my sister's words hit me hard. There is a chasm between expectation and acceptance. My knees gave way, and I sat heavily on the edge of my bed. I read the letter through twice as if I could not comprehend her words, as if by rereading it I could find the "catch," the words I had missed that would make it not so.

Dear Chrysostomos,

It is with a heavy heart that I bring you news of our parents. On October 5 Mama grew ill. She could not keep anything down. During the night of October 6, our Mama passed away. I only became aware of it in the early morning when Papa called. She was still warm and I ran to get the doctor, but nothing could be done. When we buried Mama, Uncle Dimitris, Uncle Russo, and Aunt Cleo attended with Papa and me as well as some old-time residents. At Papa's request, Bishop Iakovos performed the service. Yes, he is still alive but retired.

A month later on November 8 I fixed Papa dinner and we sat down to eat. After dinner he went to bed early. About midnight he called out for me and when I went to him, he was sitting up in bed. As soon as he saw me, he sighed and went limp. I ran out into the street screaming for help, but it was too late. Papa was gone.

Uncle Dimitris and I buried Papa, and some of his few old remaining living friends came to the funeral. I am sorry to bring you such sad news. God bless and protect you and your family.

With all my love,
Katerina

When Helen walked in my tears were streaming. She had never seen me crying and didn't know what to do. Yet she tried to console me as I sobbed openly for my parents—poor Mama and Papa—who had endured such difficult lives.

They had been my inspiration. I had carried them with me to America in my mind, knowing they would never come, and now they were gone. I had not seen them for over two decades, and now the words on this sheet of paper had robbed me of them forever.

Poor stubborn Papa, I thought as I fought back my tears. He lived under Turkish rule for forty years and refused to leave his beloved island, and now a few cruel strokes of ink pronounced him dead. I wept uncontrollably with grief. Never had I been in such pain.

"There, there, Chris, it will be alright."

Her words reconnected me and dried my tears. My tears had brought my children into the bedroom, filled with worry and concern. "Your Dad has received some bad news," Helen told them as she tried to usher them out, but Anthony wouldn't budge. "What news?" he demanded.

"Your Papou and Yiayia in the old country have passed away," she said, steering Anthony toward the door. "Now please give your Father some privacy. That's how you can help him. You can give him a little time to himself, okay?"

When Anthony had gone, Helen turned to me. "They have never seen you cry," she said gently. "In fact, neither have I." It was the only time in all my adult life that I had ever cried.

Life is an uneven administrator, apportioning grief and joy disproportionately in time. The same is true of loss and love. Although death is part of life, I don't believe anyone ever entirely gets over the death of his parents.

I do not harbor regrets, but my remorse at not having seen Mama and Papa before they died has never left me. It also saddens me to think how little I spoke of my parents to my children. Mama and Papa were strangers to their American grandchildren. Even Katina was little more than a holiday mention to my children. They simply had no understanding of her sacrifice for their grandparents. How could they? They had been sheltered from my past.

The next day I rang Sultana in New York, who had yet to receive the news. We cried together, as only siblings could, over the passing of our dear parents. During the next few weeks I turned my attention even more intensely toward family and work. It was also time for me to make good one final promise. I would help Katina, now 49, to finally come to America. The only thing I asked is that she bring from our home the tapestry that hung by our front door that Papa had written and Mama had sewn.

• • •

I found solace during this time by watching my older son, Anthony, wrestle. Anthony was a contender for the state wrestling championship. In 1966, during his junior year in high school, I planned to attend a regional tournament. Prior to the event I hosted a training meal at Fairfax Inn. Anthony coached me on the time and particulars.

"The weigh-in is at two thirty and the team will get to the restaurant around four," he said. "There will be fourteen of us. It's a training meal, Dad, so don't fix too much."

I nodded in acknowledgment of his directions. "And the match?" I asked. "When does that start?"

"At seven," Anthony told me, then added, "the coach is dressing two extra guys, but I'm sure I'll be wrestling tonight."

A few minutes after four the team arrived to a dinner of seven-ounce Delmonico steaks, mashed potatoes, peas, rolls, and iced tea. For dessert I served some of my homemade rice pudding. The boys descended on the meal, weary of various food restrictions required for "keeping weight" in the sport. They were nice boys, polite and disciplined. One by one, they thanked me for the meal. I was pleased Anthony was on the team, and it was my pleasure to prepare the meal for them.

The match that night surprised me. I began the evening sitting quietly on the front corner of the bleachers, but when Mrs. Godfrey, the mother of Anthony's friend Dennis, began to cheer, I was immediately caught up in the excitement. Spectators all around me were shouting and jumping out of their seats. It was exhilarating and infectious, made even more intense because they were cheering for Anthony. I had never in my life experienced anything like it.

To most of the spectators these matches were probably much the same as any other, but my pride in my son's performance was beyond words. By his senior year Anthony was the top-seeded wrestler in his weight division in the state. The joy in my heart was from the satisfaction of seeing my sacrifices pay off to give Anthony this opportunity I had never had. The price was high and I knew it; Helen knew it too. It had come at the cost of great pain, from the ashes of a world destroyed. I had a tough life, but I had no regrets.

The Sunday after that first match, I made a special dinner: shish kebab with beef tenderloin and rice pilaf. It was not often I could have dinner with my family. My meticulous food preparation was one way I demonstrated my love for my family, and it gave me great pleasure to prepare special treats.

I was still fussing with Helen over the *spanakopita* when they all began teasing me.

"Dad, get in here and eat with us. You're so busy cooking, you won't even know how good it is," Anthony called out.

Everyone was in good spirits, all of us together sharing a good meal. After dinner that night I played *tavoli* with the boys while a Redskins football game played on the television. For that day we were the family Helen had always wanted us to be. As my family dined merrily that evening, I glanced around at some empty chairs and imagined Katina, Mama, and Papa dining with us.

• • •

That winter President Lyndon B. Johnson talked about a "Great Society," a world where all people would work only thirty hours a week. For much of my life I had worked seventeen hours a *day.* I couldn't help but laugh. Only now, after years of labor, was I able to cut back a bit on my hours. During the winter at Fairfax Inn I only worked twelve hours a day during the week, and a mere nine hours on Saturday.

It was just before the holidays in 1965 that I sent Katina and Uncle Dimitris, who was now living with her, a long letter and some money. I made all the arrangements for her journey to America. Uncle Dimitris would be left alone, our last relation on Imbroz.

At about the same time, my brother Costa returned with his new wife from Imbroz, Afrodite. No longer just travelling on a visa, my little brother had married a younger woman on Imbroz and now at age 44 was ready to settle down in his adopted country. My family's migration to America was nearly complete. Only Katina remained.

"Costa," I said, embracing him for what seemed like an eternity.

"Big brother," he responded, just as he had years before.

It was comforting now, more than ever, to have my brother here. He turned to introduce me to his new wife, Afrodite. Afrodite grew up a few years after us on Imbroz. I vaguely remembered her as a little girl.

"It is so good to meet you, Christo," she said. "I have heard many good things about you from Costa and others back home. Your parents were fine and wonderful people, and I am very sorry for your loss."

Her words touched me. I thanked her and welcomed her to our home and family. I felt immediately comforted by Afrodite's warm, inviting demeanor and I was happy for Costa.

When they first arrived in Virginia, Costa and Afrodite stayed in a room in our basement for a month or so, then they rented a garden apartment not far from Helen's parents. Later, I loaned Costa money for a down payment to buy a small house within two miles of mine.

Costa found a job as a tailor for the Lord & Taylor department store. Afrodite was also an accomplished seamstress in her own right who worked for twenty-four years at Loehmann's, the discount designer clothes store. Within eight years, he and Afrodite would have four beautiful and very talented children.

• • •

Earlier that year, Harry Jagoda, a friend of mine from the Apollo, visited me with his friend, Lincoln Vance. The two were partners in a development where they were building large, spacious colonial homes on half-acre lots, and they urged me to buy one. I had been thinking of moving my family to a larger house for some time, and Harry and Lincoln's advice intrigued me.

A month later I took them up on their suggestion and picked out a lot on a hillside cul-de-sac. It amazed me to think that I could trade my 1,000 square-foot rambler for a 3,600 square-foot, center-hall colonial. My dream home would cost $66,000. I was so proud of my home. I would put down twenty percent plus closing costs as required and borrow $52,800 at four-and-a-half percent interest for thirty years.

By the end of the year we were happily settled in our new house. That Christmas was especially festive. Helen's parents were with us and Costa and Afrodite were at our Christmas meal when Costa announced that they were expecting their first child. The prospect of a new baby in the family was exciting, and Helen was delighting in helping Afrodite.

I marveled how my little brother, whose hair had receded and whose voice was the level of a raspy baritone, was the instant center of attention for my two sons. I recalled our childhood as I spent the evening watching them play *tavoli*. I had taught the boys the game on our Sunday dinner get-togethers, years earlier, much like Papa had taught Costa and me.

Indeed we had a lot to be thankful for, and my prayer was an old one, though no less heartfelt, as we sat down to Christmas dinner in our new home. "God bless and watch over us. Thank You for the food You have given us. Thank You for allowing us to be together and for bringing Costa and Afrodite to us. Please deliver Katina safely to America and allow Mama and Papa to rest in peace. Amen."

"Amen," my family replied.

After spending nearly thirty-nine years of our lives apart, except for a few brief visits, I finally had my little brother close to me. It wasn't that I expected to see him every day, but the thought of him living nearby was pleasing. It was a bridge of continuity connecting my past life with the present. I knew Mama and Papa would be happy to know we were all in America, or soon would be.

• • •

After the holidays I sold the Fairfax Inn to Mr. Merkezas for about the same price it had cost me to open it a few years earlier. The sale freed me up to oversee my Ocean City businesses, which consumed all my time. A few months later I was at the beach readying my stores for the 1967 season.

The procession of cooks through Anthony's Carryout continued that summer. One cook named Phil picked the peak hour to show his dissatisfaction by leaving without a word to anyone. Thankfully I had the skills to fill in for him after he left. Then came Jean Pierre. He was a good man and actually stayed with us for two years.

Business steadily increased, but otherwise that summer was unremarkable except for the day a call came from my sister Sultana in New York. "Christo," she said gaily, "I have someone with me who wants to speak to you." A moment later I heard another voice, tentative and soft.

"Chrysostomos?"

"Katina!" I exclaimed. Even after all these years I knew her voice. "I cannot believe you are here already. Was it a good trip?"

"Yes, it was, very good—"

"You must come to see us," I interrupted.

"Of course, I will," she said. "I'll wait for your call and then I'll—"

"And Uncle Dimitris," I asked, interrupting her. "What of him?"

"His goddaughter found him a room in a nursing home in Constantinople. We must send him money, Christo. He has no one."

"Don't worry, we will, I promise," I replied, a tinge of regret clouding my joy.

"I can't believe I'm here, in America," she said.

"Me neither," I told her, laughing in return.

• • •

In mid-June Helen and the kids had arrived in Ocean City for the summer. With the store fully staffed, and Monday business being slow, I was able to resume what I had come to relish—my joyous sunrise fishing expeditions. They were food for my soul: almost mystical experiences that soothed and calmed the frenetic pace of serving summer tourists.

I returned around noon one day with wisps of misty thoughts still clinging to me. As I walked into my store, I saw rising before me what appeared to be an apparition walking in the back door. I must have dropped the cooler full of sea bass and trout, for I heard a loud crash beside me. I rubbed my eyes to shake off the spirits and bring me back to the present, but then I saw her as clear as day—Katina.

Her arrival was an unexpected surprise and we rushed into a long, joyful embrace without a word. "As a child on Imbroz you would go fishing—and now, after so many years, what do I find you doing? Still fishing. Nothing has changed," she teased me happily.

"You are truly a man of your word, Christo. You have brought us all here." It was now more than twenty years since I had left, but I guess Katina was right—I had successfully brought my brother and sisters to America.

"Christo, before I left Imbroz, I was forced to sell Papa's property to the Turks for practically nothing." Papa and Mama had been the last stronghold, and that was difficult for me to accept. Our home, the store, the fields, their toil, all are gone now. Although I was angry and saddened to learn of the so-called "sale," I realized she had little choice.

"Did you bring the tapestry?" I asked. It was the only thing I had asked Katina to bring.

"Of course." Her eyes moved over to a frame leaning against the wall, and I walked over and picked it up. It was wrapped in brown paper, and I gently placed it aside to open later.

"Thank you, Katina."

She nodded in acknowledgment. "How could I ever forget such an important thing as that?" she responded.

"Papa was so proud of you," she told me. "A day hardly passed that he would not boast of your accomplishments as if they were his own. We all lived your successes. Even though we have been separated by distance, we have all gained strength from you, Christo."

"Katina, it is you who has shown the true strength. You sacrificed so much." We embraced and spent the evening talking long into the night, too excited to sleep.

Katina did not stay with us long in Ocean City. She revealed to me that she had met a man who wanted to marry her—a widower named Nikos Pananis. Katina was 50 years old, but she had wasted little time after arriving in New York to begin living her new life.

I heartily encouraged her to marry and have a home of her own. She was anxious to return to her fiancé, but before she left, she smiled and kissed my forehead. "May God bless you and always be with you," she said, and departed for the bus to New York.

• • •

When John F. Kennedy was assassinated, it deeply scarred the heart and soul of our nation, yet the country picked up the pieces and continued on. We would not be so lucky during the spring of 1968 when Martin Luther King, Jr., was gunned down by an assassin as he stood on a hotel balcony. Dr. King had argued for reasonable yet revolutionary change, and cities erupted into a contagious violence that spread from coast to coast with the news of his death.

In Washington, D.C., whole blocks of the city burned, and looting was widespread. Smoke rising from the nation's capital stirred unpleasant memories of the old world I had left so long ago. I was swept by overwhelming sadness for my adopted country, the land of freedom. In the wrong hands, boundless freedom leads to chaos. In Turkey these actions would have provoked gendarmes to fire on the crowds and many would have died. In America we tolerated the riots hoping the anger would subside.

Only a few weeks later, just as suddenly and dramatically, Robert Kennedy was also assassinated in a hotel kitchen in Los Angeles, California. The country, stunned by the violence that had followed King's death, was crushed by grief. As I watched the events of the summer unfold, I realized that America had lost a part of her innocence and seemed to be drifting without a rudder. I wondered if we would ever recover, but just as strong individuals survive devastating tragedies, so do great nations.

In November of 1968 Richard Nixon was elected President and the problems of the Vietnam War had also increased. The prospect of my son or anyone else's son fighting a war so far from home saddened me, but freedom costs dearly. To my great relief, Anthony returned to school at William & Mary College, and Jon, who was managing Anthony's Beer & Wine, began attending the University of Virginia.

Then on July 20, 1969, two Americans landed on the Moon—Neil Armstrong and Buzz Aldrin. The tragedies of the three assassinations and a war were mitigated by the accomplishment of landing men on the moon that showed American excellence. It instantly became a source of pride in our country for all Americans.

CHAPTER 18

The Archbishop's Dinner

Two roads diverged in a yellow wood,
and sorry I could not travel both
and be one traveler, long I stood
and looked down one as far as I could…
Then took the other, as just as fair
and having perhaps the better claim,
because it was grassy and wanted wear;
though as for that the passing there
had worn them really about the same…
—ROBERT FROST, 1916

IN JANUARY 1969 Nikos and Katina were married in New York by Archbishop Iakavos. No matter how long it had taken, I could not have been happier for her. It was a small wedding. Taki and Sultana were present, of course, as were Nikos's daughter and son by his first marriage. Before the service, Iakovos called Katina and me to join him behind the altar. A moment of silence passed as we all looked at each other. It had been over forty years since the three of us had played as children in our little village. Each of us had travelled very different roads, but eventually we found our way back together.

As we stood together for that moment before Katina's wedding, the years melted away from us as our memories travelled back together to those moments of our youth, our innocence. Yes, our bodies had aged, but our eyes saw the silent, still frames of our youth.

Finally, Iakovos spoke. "Katina, you look as beautiful as ever," he said. "And Christo, my friend, we are growing old in America." Then he addressed us both. "I prayed for your parents this morning as I have so many times over the years. Let us go out now and join the others. We have a wedding to celebrate."

Katina may have sacrificed her youth to care for our parents, but during the ceremony she beamed with youthful happiness. Katina was 52, but that day it was as if she had recaptured time. As Iakovos performed the marriage ceremony, I wished my older sister every happiness. She had given much, and now she deserved that and more in return. Her sacrifice seemed to have been rewarded abundantly.

After the wedding I wrote to thank my old friend Jimmy for performing the ceremony and to remind him of my earlier request for him to join us for dinner sometime after the summer season. One evening after Labor Day, Helen called to say she had received a letter from the archdiocese in New York stating that the Archbishop would be in Washington in mid-October and wanted to know if that would be a good time to take me up on my dinner invitation. I replied by letter to Jimmy immediately confirming the date.

• • •

Two weeks before Jimmy's visit we began receiving requests from various priests in the Washington-Baltimore area, most of whom we did not even know, to attend the dinner I was hosting. In the end we found room for three priests to join us. I spent the entire day before the Archbishop's visit cooking and preparing. Helen assisted me.

Promptly at four o'clock on the afternoon of the dinner, a long black limousine pulled up in front of our home. Instantly, there was pandemonium inside the house. Our visiting priests jumped to their feet and rushed into the hall, carefully collecting themselves in ecclesiastical pecking order to form a receiving line. Meanwhile, Ianthe bounced excitedly in front of the window.

"He's here, Daddy, he's here!" she squealed.

"Oh, my goodness," Helen gasped, her hands smoothing the front of her dress.

Katina, who had come from New York for the event, gathered Anthony and Jon.

"Okay, okay," I said, trying to calm everyone, myself included. "Everything's ready, I'll get the door. Everyone relax, please."

Before I went to the door I paused at our bay window that looked out onto the street. There, surrounded by the golds, reds, and greens of the autumn foliage, I saw two bishops clad in black helping Jimmy from the limousine. A black headdress covered his salt-and-pepper colored hair, and he carried a staff in his left hand. I watched as he moved slowly up the walkway, then I went to the door and opened it.

"Welcome to my home, Your Eminence," I said, bowing deeply with a broad smile.

The Archbishop smiled and gave a sidewise glance to the bishops flanking him on his right and left. Instantly they bowed and retreated to the limousine, which drove off quietly, leaving the Archbishop with us for the evening.

"You have done quite well for yourself in America, Chris Christ," he said, placing heavy emphasis on the shortened, American version of my name.

"Thank you, your Eminence." As soon as he entered the foyer, the three priests who had been waiting inside snapped to attention and descended upon him like excited children, falling all over themselves in their eagerness to show respect.

It is traditional in the Orthodox Christian Church for lay people to bow and kiss the hand of their priest, and the same custom is practiced by priests to show respect to their superiors. This custom might explain why many Orthodox priests of all levels walk with their hands folded before them—to discourage kisses from the faithful. The day Archbishop Iakovos came to dinner at my house was no different.

The three priests mingled briefly in the living room with Jimmy, chatting politely and sipping drinks, while I was busy working in the kitchen. When dinner was ready, I placed the Archbishop at the head of the table and my son Anthony to his right. Father Ted, our local priest, sat on Jimmy's left.

I sat at the opposite end with Helen and Katina on either side of me, and Fathers John and George were seated next to them. I had delegated Ianthe and Jon to act as servers since there was not enough room at the table. They had place settings at the small kitchen table next to the dining room.

Besides the plates and silverware, every inch of the dining room table was covered with food. There was a tray of *spanakopita*, a large bowl of rice pilaf, Greek salad, *kalamata* olives, feta cheese—and, of course a leg of lamb, sliced on a big platter. There was even a small table next to the dining room table also covered with food. All my special dinners had an abundance of leftovers that were distributed after the meal.

Conversation ceased as we were all seated. Looking straight over my left shoulder on the adjacent wall, Jimmy noticed the tapestry.

"Is that your father's tapestry from Imbroz?" He pointed to the wall.

"Yes, it is the only thing I asked Katina to bring me from our home."

"You know your father wrote it in *Koine* Greek. *Koine* was the language of the Greek translation of the Old Testament, or the Hebrew Bible, in about 200 B.C., and centuries later the New Testament of the early Christians." The Archbishop stated this in a matter-of-fact manner.

"I did not know, Your Eminence."

With his eyes lingering on the tapestry Iakovos lifted his clasped hands and lowered his forehead, offering up a nearly inaudible prayer followed by a melodious "Amen." Dinner had begun, and Ianthe and Jon began serving us from the various plates on the two tables.

The Archbishop, appearing famished, reached to his left for a basket of bread and as he extended his hand, Father Ted—either intending to show respect or mistaking Iakovos's intention—greeted it with a kiss. Abruptly, the Archbishop pulled his hand back, fixing his eyes on the poor priest with a cold, disapproving stare.

"I am sorry, Your Eminence." Mortified, Father Ted repeated his apologies over and over, accompanied by equally ineffective head bows. Iakovos responded with silence and focused his attention on the bread tray again. My children fought back laughter as they continued to serve dinner.

Apart from that episode, dinner went well. I received much praise from all the guests regarding my food preparation. Afterwards I invited the Archbishop to move to the living room for after-dinner drinks and dessert. As we stood to exit the dining room his eyes went once again to Papa's tapestry and he paused to study it.

"Tell me, Christo, how have you found life in America?"

"Very busy, Your Eminence," I replied honestly. "As long as a man is not afraid of work, there is more to do than time to do it in America."

"I guess that is so," he laughed out loud.

I excused myself to assist Helen in clearing the table. When I returned, Anthony was engaged in conversation with the Archbishop.

"The war in Vietnam doesn't have a clear purpose," my son was saying. "I doubt very much that our country should even be involved in this conflict."

I stood quietly watching my son, who was six feet tall, as he sat next to the Archbishop of the Americas and discussed one controversial subject after another. Both my son and the Archbishop had full beards.

"And what about the poor people in America?" Anthony asked when the topic moved from war to world poverty. "What has the Church done to help them?"

"Let me tell you a story," the Archbishop said. "When the Patriarch first dispatched me to America I found a building for the leadership's use in New York City. It had electricity, indoor plumbing, and running water, but no air conditioning. The building was five stories high and made of stone and mortar. I thanked God for helping me to find it. It was not until some years later that I learned that the building was located next to Harlem, which is considered one of the poorest areas of the city. To many, it was a ghetto. To us, it was a godsend."

His story was simple, but the point was profound. In the eyes of much of the world, poverty in America wasn't poverty at all. Much of the perception was in the eyes of the beholder.

An instant later Helen and I began serving pastries, including the Archbishop's favorite, *loucomades.* Pastry in hand, the Archbishop strolled over to the dining room wall and I joined him, both of us gazing at the tapestry. A series of thirty-six boxes each with a single word in a large box stood on a corner. Papa's tapestry was embroidered by my mother on pale white cloth and framed behind glass in a standard thirty by thirty-inch frame.

"Papa used to read this to us when we were children. It hung on the wall inside the door of our home on Imbroz for as long as I can remember."

"Want me to read it?" Jimmy asked.

"Yes, of course, please." It had hung on the wall in our dining room since Katina had brought it from Imbroz two years earlier. That day Jimmy would give us the precise translation from *Koine* Greek.

"Tapestries like this were an accepted method to pass wisdom from one generation to the next for hundreds of years. To read it you must start with the diamond in the top left-hand quadrant, then you read the first row with the second, third, fourth, and so on." I nodded as Jimmy began, pointing to the contents of each diamond as he read it aloud.

1. *Don't judge what you see, for he who judges what he sees often judges what doesn't exist.*
2. *Don't spend what you have, for he who spends what he has often spends what he doesn't have.*
3. *Don't believe what you hear, for he who believes what he hears often believes what is not true.*
4. *Don't do what you can, for he who does what he can often does what he's not allowed to.*
5. *Don't say what you know, for he who says what he knows often says what's inappropriate.*

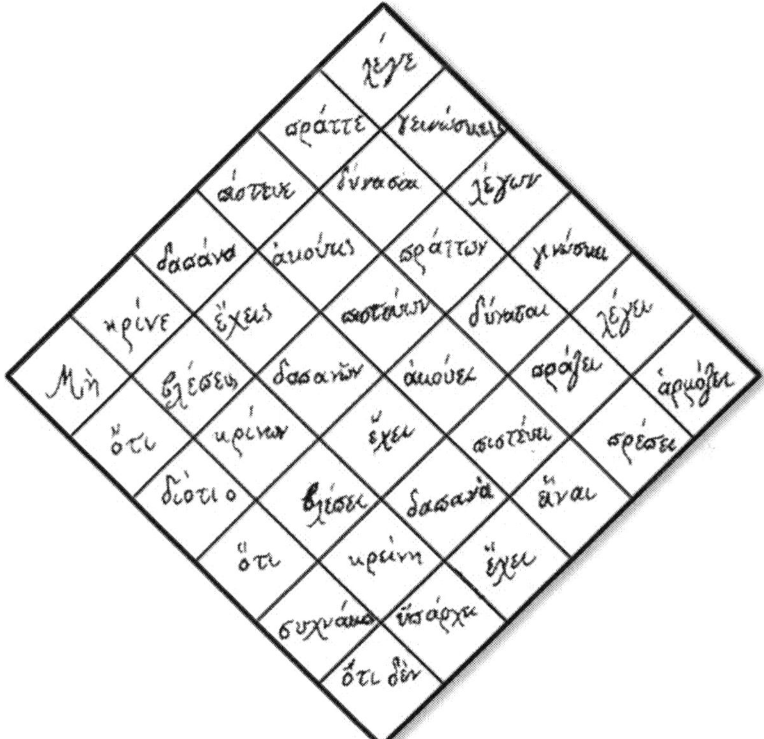

A tear swelled in my eye, and as Jimmy and I stood for a moment we became two little boys on Imbroz again listening to Papa read us his ancient tapestry. They say time passes quickly for old men, yet there we both stood clinging to our memories, and for that moment stubbornly refusing to let go, as time stood still. Two childhood friends whose paths had been so different, for that brief moment they crossed one more time.

"Your Eminence, the car is waiting outside, we must go," one of the priests finally said. The limousine had returned and sat at the bottom of the cul-de-sac awaiting the Archbishop.

The mood had lightened and everyone was relaxed. I reached for my camera and tried to capture the moment, but, to my great disappointment on this once-in-a-lifetime occasion, my camera wouldn't work. In a moment, my old friend was at the door bidding us goodbye and descending my steps to get into his limousine.

The next day I took Helen, Katina, and Ianthe to church where the Archbishop was the centerpiece of the service. When we advanced in a line to accept the blessed bread from him after the service, he called us to join him, then signaled for someone on his staff to take a photograph. Remembering my disappointment with the camera the night before, this was his gift to us. I was touched. We all travelled home and enjoyed a much lighter dinner and some well-deserved rest.

CHAPTER 19

Changes

Footfalls echo in the memory
down the passage which we did not take
towards the door we never opened
into the rose-garden....
There is only the fight to recover what has been lost
and found and lost again and again: under conditions
that seem unpropitious. But perhaps neither gain nor loss.
For us, there is only the trying. The rest is not our business.
—T. S. ELLIOT, 1936–1942

THE TURKISH PRESENCE on Imbroz had assumed many forms over the years. Since the year before the death of my parents in 1965 the Turks had established a penal colony in the once cheerful and bustling village of Schinoudi, one of the seven villages on Imbroz, just south of our village of Panayia. The convicts unleashed one horror after another on my little island's inhabitants. Violent criminals roamed freely and terrorized towns and villages. That day I received a letter from Istanbul Turkey.

Dearest Chrysostomos,

I left Imbroz a week ago and now reside in a nursing home in Istanbul. No one is left on the island. I love you, Eleni, and the children very much. I love you all very much.

God bless you always,
Your Uncle Dimitris

It was so sad. Poor Uncle Dimitris was all alone. I thought of the remaining Greek villagers and of Uncle Dimitris's relegation at age 96 to a Turkish nursing home.

Yet still, if I closed my eyes, I could still see the windmills of Castro turning in the breeze, just as I remembered them from my childhood. Castro, the island's oldest village, dated back well before Christ. Much of our cultural heritage was rapidly vanishing. Like my favorite Uncle Dimitris, my memories were becoming artifacts lost in time. It was a loss of people and a way of life, surviving only in the memories of a few sad tales told by a few old souls.

• • •

At the post office one day in January, I purchased four sheets of the 1970 commemorative stamps. The collection I had started in Constantinople had continued to grow through the years.

Helen often said there were four things that gave me pleasure: helping my children, watching my azaleas in bloom, fishing, and collecting my stamps. Perhaps she was right.

I spent many evenings with my stamp albums open in my lap and a magnifying glass in my hand. This was what I was doing one evening in January when Helen's brother, Gus, called.

"You think you and Helen can make it to a Tastee-Freez convention in March? The president's going to present you with an award."

"Really?" I said with surprise. "Where's it being held?"

"Acapulco," he replied, "beautiful, sunny Acapulco." I had heard of Acapulco, a beautiful beach resort town on Mexico's Pacific Coast.

"Well, we'll have to see, Gus. Maybe we will."

After I hung up, Helen called to me from the kitchen. "Who was on the phone, Chris?"

"Your brother," I said. "He sends his regards."

Helen came out of the kitchen, wiping her hands on a towel. "He didn't want to speak with me?"

"He wants us to go to Acapulco," I told her casually. "I'm supposed to get some sort of an award." I had continued to pay the franchise fee to Tastee-Freez directly, even after my brother-in-law had declared bankruptcy. I felt my store was doing so well that I didn't want to change anything except the menu—a bit of superstition on my part.

Helen's smile widened. "Chris, let's go," she said without hesitation. "We've never had a real vacation. I would love to go to Acapulco. Wouldn't you?"

"Yes, we can go," I said slowly, remembering the many years Helen endured my long work hours. Perhaps it was time to relax a little and dip our toes in another ocean. The thought of arranging the responsibilities of all the stores in my absence was unsettling to say the least, yet life was passing us by.

"Yes," I repeated, much to Helen's delight. "Yes, we will go."

Late in March we departed for four sunny days in Acapulco to enjoy our first real vacation in twenty-two years. We spent much of our time wandering happily around like the tourists that we were, buying t-shirts for the kids, some jewelry for Helen, and, for me, a three-foot detailed replica of a pirate ship complete with orange sails. When we weren't shopping, we lay on the beach under the warm sun, and in the evenings we drank daiquiris and listened to Calypso bands.

The last evening in Acapulco was the night of the formal Tastee-Freez banquet where the founder, Mr. Leo Morany, would address the audience. I had been daydreaming when Helen tapped my shoulder and I heard Mr. Morany say, "And now it's time to announce the Eastern Region Production Leader. I would like to present this award to Chris Christ of Ocean City, Maryland, for selling more ice cream during the past summer than anyone else in his region," he went on. The applause began.

Smiling, I walked up to the podium, received my award, bowed, then returned to my seat next to Helen, who squeezed my hand. She was proud of me, but I was a little embarrassed. As the applause subsided, I leaned over to Helen and said, "I had no idea I was selling so much ice cream." I placed the plaque between us on the table and during the evening I would steal a glance at it from time to time.

• • •

A few weeks later our vacation was a distant dream as I opened my small carryout for the 1970 summer season. Nick came down to join me a couple of days later. He was 71 years old now and I was 52, nineteen years younger, yet we both were beginning to feel our age. I asked about his health and he asked about my vacation.

"Well, Nick," I said after a thoughtful pause, "we are getting old. Nothing under the sun stays the same." He looked up as if to say he knew, but he didn't have to say a word. "We have a lot of work to do," I added. Drink your cup of coffee and let's get going."

"Okay, Chris," he responded.

With that the summer of 1970 began. The vibrant economy of the sixties left a legacy of excess. Little did we know the extended post–World War II growth cycle was about to come to an end. Our reliance on the gold standard was attacked and reversed by President Johnson in 1968 and, under President Nixon in 1971, the United States began for the first time to issue money with nothing backing it up. The Byzantine Empire survived for eleven centuries on the gold standard, but I guess from now on we would rely on PhDs and politicians to determine how much money we have.

During that spring and summer the cultural revolution erupting among the youth of the country began to hit me too close to home. Shortly after I opened the store, Anthony, who was now 21 years old and wrestling at William & Mary College, drove up with his friend Charlie in Charlie's MG Midget. "Dad, I'm going with Charlie to play in a chess tournament in California," he told me. "We're plotting a course out to the West Coast." Charlie, a graduate math student who was in the Army, was the Armed Services' chess champion. I could only wonder if Anthony's studies were progressing along with his chess skills.

"You'll need some money," I said, reaching for my wallet.

Anthony accepted the cash with appreciation, then headed off to the townhouse to get his belongings and say goodbye to his mother. "Take care of yourself," I said.

Around the same time, Nick started having difficulty breathing, and it would only be a matter of time before his coughing would develop into deadly emphysema—the result of smoking two packs of unfiltered Camels every day for decades. During the eleven years Nick worked for me, he had never missed a single day of work, but I knew this could not continue.

Anthony returned from his trip out west later that summer and worked for two weeks before heading back to school. With Jon working full time at Anthony's Beer & Wine and returning to the University of Virginia in the fall, as well, I found myself shorthanded all summer. I had always encouraged my children to go to college, yet I still occasionally needed their help. At this point, though, it was becoming more and more clear that neither of my sons would work in Anthony's Carryout in the future.

The intense pace of the summer of 1971 soon withered with the leaves of fall as the sun-bleached sand cooled under the autumn sky. That winter when I returned home to Virginia I ordered a stamp book called *United States First Day Covers* from the Postal Commemorative Society, and subscribed to the series. The commemoratives were beautiful, but twenty of these little covers cost nearly $50. I would not be so extravagant in the future.

• • •

Two men past our prime, Nick and I made it through another difficult season in Ocean City in 1972. Meanwhile, though, my own health began to worry me. That winter, as I was shoveling snow from the porch and steps that descended down to the cul-de-sac, I felt a warm pressure in my chest. Even after I finished shoveling, the pressure persisted. When I went inside I discovered I was perspiring, and a minute or two later my stomach was upset.

"Chris, are you okay?" Helen asked.

"I think I have a little cold," I said, waving her off, but for five days I had a chronic low-grade fever and couldn't hold any food down. The numbness in my chest persisted.

"Chris, please call the doctor," Helen repeated almost daily. "This could be something serious." I didn't have time, with so much left to do.

"It's the flu," I told her. "I'll be fine." It took two weeks, though, for the fever to subside, and a month later I still wasn't feeling myself.

Finally, at Helen's insistence, I went to see a doctor. After an examination and a number of tests, the doctor sat down to talk with me. "You've had a bad heart attack," he said, staring at me gravely. "A large part of your heart muscle has been damaged. Why did you take so long to come see me?"

I had always avoided doctors, but this time I had pushed myself too hard. Now there was damage that would never completely heal, damage that couldn't be fixed.

"It is critical," he added, "that you learn to take it easy. You've simply got to reduce your workload and eat lighter."

I had made work a lifetime habit, and old habits are hard to break. Nonetheless, I would discipline myself to a new diet and shortly thereafter to a substantial reduction in my workload. There were too many things to do and it was not yet my time to go.

Because of my heart problems I ate extravagant meals no more than half a dozen times a year, sustaining myself mostly on lentils, beans, and fish, which I caught in Ocean City. To relieve the monotony, I also baked a chicken recipe I particularly liked with carrots, garlic, onion, and a touch of tomato.

Helen urged me to retire. Although I was only 54, she was concerned that the work that I loved so much might kill me. I agreed with Helen and the doctors. I had led a hard life and I was worn out, and Helen knew it. Work that normally invigorated me left me tired and drained, and for the first time in my life, I knew I could not continue to work at my accustomed pace. I also came to respect the fact that my sons appeared to be following different paths than I had.

• • •

By the summertime I was feeling slightly better, but the nation had plunged into recession. It was the first year the store sales had not grown. This was my nineteenth year of business in Ocean City and Nick's thirteenth year with me. Late in the summer of 1973, not only had Nick and I had slowed and worn down, but the economy had begun to sputter as well. For the first season in nineteen years, sales remained flat. As the season wound to a close, I finally made a decision. This would be my last summer in Ocean City.

When I told Nick, he gave me a solemn smile.

"Chris, I will soon be 78. If this is to be my last year with you, I take nothing but gratitude with me." The words of my loyal employee and friend meant a great deal to me.

The last day Nick and I were at the store, we shared a cup of coffee together. Fall was upon us and a cool, constant breeze had swept over the sun-soaked island resort once again. I thanked Nick for all his years of service and friendship, gave him a large bonus, then called a cab to take him fifteen blocks up to the Trailways station where he would catch a bus home to Baltimore for the last time.

"Nick, if you need me for anything, just call," I told him.

Nick nodded his thanks and shook my hand. He looked old and frail standing there on the sidewalk. I sometimes think it was the carnival atmosphere of the friendly beach crowds that partially sustained him all that time, and I wondered how well he would fare in retirement in Baltimore.

As I watched the bus drive off, I realized it was the end of an era for us. I never had a desire to retire and only prayed for the energy to perform the daily tasks in front of me. If retiring meant an end to old routines, it also meant an end to over forty years of grinding, unending workdays, and an end to solving the problems they presented. I finally realized it was time to move on, to turn my energies to other things.

That same fall, a full-blown extended recession plagued the economy because of obligations from recent political reform and the Vietnam War. Though perhaps not the best time to retire, I had already set that course in motion. A man named John Simms, in partnership with two other men, agreed to lease Anthony's Carryout beginning the following summer.

• • •

Early in the spring of 1974 I returned to Ocean City, not to open the store, but to meet with the group who wished to buy the business and lease the property. I had store vacancies and owed money to the banks. Although it would be difficult on me during the ensuing economic recession, I never regretted my decision to rent my store to John Simms. He took the lease over the following year. He had a wife and small children and was just starting out in business. Most importantly, he had an enthusiasm and energy I respected. It would take high energy and a positive attitude to run the store. I liked him at once.

I spent a few weeks with him and his partners acquainting them with the business, and then in April I left for Baltimore. When I walked out of the store that last time, I felt a tremendous sense of sadness mixed with a surprisingly deep relief, as I knew I had found the right man to take over my business. Although over time John made numerous small changes in the operation, some of which I didn't agree with, he kept the menu that had served the public so well—and he has continued to do so every year.

The point of my trip to Baltimore was to visit Nick who had recently been admitted to Baltimore General Hospital. When I entered the room, I greeted Nick's wife and then moved to his bedside. I noticed that his breathing was labored, but he was conscious and lucid.

"Nick," I said. "It's me, Christo."

Nick raised his hand in acknowledgement, then moved it to the small side table, fumbling for his glasses. Then he removed the oxygen mask so that he was able to speak.

"Christo," he greeted me in Greek, his voice raspy. "How are you? How is your health?"

"Improving," I replied in Greek. "And you?"

"I am having a hard time breathing, but don't worry, Christo—in a month I will be fine," he reassured me. "In June I will come to the store and be ready to work."

"Nick," I said with a quiet laugh. "I leased the store, remember? We can relax now."

"Ah," Nick shook his head sadly. "So, you really did it, eh? I had thought that over the winter you might talk yourself out of it."

"I would have, my friend, but my family would not allow it."

I smiled, hoping my words would give him some closure. "No, the store is leased, and now you have plenty of time to rest and get well again."

Nick closed his eyes, and for a moment I thought he was asleep. "Chris, my time with you was the best. You are a good man, Chris Christ, the best I ever worked for. The work was hard, but the store was my joy. My every moment feeding the crowds was my paradise."

"I know, Nick," I said.

A few moments later, Nick smiled and closed his eyes tightly.

I turned to his wife and pressed a check for $500 in her hand.

"No, Chris," she protested, "I can't take this…"

"Take it for Nick," I urged. "He earned it. And there will be more as you need it."

"I don't know what to say," she stammered, turning so that I wouldn't see the tears welling in her proud eyes.

"You don't need to say a word," I smiled. "Just please take care of my friend."

• • •

In August of 1974 Richard Nixon resigned from the presidency under threat of impeachment. That fall the nation faced a gasoline shortage, the economy was in the throes of a recession, bankruptcies were on the rise, and we were evacuating our troops from Vietnam. It seemed as if the social and economic fabric of our nation was being torn to pieces. The legacy of Johnson's Great Society had smothered the economy like a wet blanket.

Late in September I returned to Baltimore one last time to attend the funeral of my longtime friend. Nick was sadly now a part of my past, a memory as precious to me as Mama and Papa. He would be sorely missed, but his time had come. Through his final illness I had sent money to his family, and on this visit I pressed a final, generous check into his widow's hand after the funeral. Nick had always been loyal to me and had worked hard. He was always there when I needed him, and I would be there for him now. Easing his family's loss seemed the least I could do.

Although I was no longer operating Anthony's Carryout, Helen and I still spent summers at our Ocean City townhouse. That summer of 1974, I managed my rental stores and helped my son Jon daily for six to eight hours at Anthony's Beer & Wine each morning, making the macaroni, potato salad, shrimp salad, coleslaw, and rice pudding. I also attended bank board meetings and fished. I was retired, after all, and so I tried my best to act like it. Counting my time with Uncle Russo, I had worked almost forty-five years straight.

I also enjoyed visits from a seven-year-old neighbor that summer. In the evenings he used to nudge open the sliding screen door to our townhouse and play with the toys my children had long outgrown. His name was John and he was the youngest of Dr. and Mrs. Carrol's five kids. The Carrols owned the townhouse next door. I would lecture John on philosophy and life in general, much as I might have my own children when they were his age.

• • •

It was not because of politics, economic opportunity, or lack of comradeship; nor, more importantly, was it due to any reversal in my motivation or drive. I was simply succumbing to old age and I needed to retire. I felt privileged to be allowed to work my long days preparing and serving food to vacationers and locals in America in my own little 1,000 square-foot carryout restaurant. I would not allow myself the thought that it would not go on forever. It was my own grueling and gleeful paradise which life had uniquely equipped me for. Self-deception can often be selfish. Retirement for me would mean cutting back to a thirty- to forty-hour week.

Nothing could stop the march of time. Each and every one of us is imbued with life, yet there is not a cell in our composition that is not finite. Up until that moment, each day in Ocean City had been a joyous paradise that would not end. That was my self-deception. From now on, I was forced to admit that every moment, every day, is in constant change. No, there is no stopping the clock of time.

CHAPTER 20

Lost at Sea

I never saw a moor,
I never saw the sea;
yet know I how the heather looks,
and what a wave must be.
I never spoke with God,
nor visited in heaven;
yet certain am I of the spot
as if the chart were given.
—EMILY DICKINSON, 1886

AFTER NICK'S DEATH, the fall and winter of 1974–1975 were uneventful for me, but the nation was still reeling from a severe economic slowdown, compounded by a significant increase in oil prices and interest rates.

Helen's parents were living with us again. We had fixed up a downstairs room for them and Anton, who at 88 was ten years older than Alexandra, sat in a chair most of the day ceaselessly fingering his worry beads. One January evening after dinner I sat with him a while and showed him my new stamps. Anton's eyesight was nearly gone, and so I described each stamp to him in detail.

"They are beautiful, Christo," he said smiling, "just beautiful." "Thank you, Christo, for your help." His dim eyes locked onto mine, and in the silent moment that passed between us a mutual understanding was expressed.

"You once helped me, a young man with few prospects," I told him. "You loaned me money and believed in me. If it had not been for you, I may not be where I am today. It is only right that I do what I can for you now."

At the end of February Anton had a blackout and, worried about his health, we moved him to a nursing home nearby. Anthony, his name sake, visited his grandfather a few weeks after he was settled in and introduced him to his new girlfriend, Lee Ann.

Later that evening Anton lay in bed clutching his crucifix and cursing his son, Gus, for taking his money. Just a few hours later, he passed away.

My father-in-law was a remarkable man who had been active all his life. In many ways he had a successful life, but it saddened me to think that his last ten years were marred by a paralyzing stroke. After Anton's death, Alexandra continued to live with us. Her health was very poor and, crippled by severe and painful arthritis, she was confined to a wheelchair.

• • •

In late 1977 Ianthe, a recent graduate of Lynchburg College, became a public school teacher in Fredericksburg, Virginia, some fifty miles south of us. Jon had graduated from the University of Virginia in 1972 and continued to manage Anthony's Beer & Wine, and Anthony began work as a bricklayer's apprentice while taking college classes at night. I was so proud of all my children.

The following summer my brother Costa came to Ocean City with Afrodite and their four children. His children had all learned Greek before they learned English, and I found them delightful. They called me Theo Christo, and would kiss my hand and offer me respectful bows.

Some years before, Afrodite methodically and patiently had worked on arithmetic with each child during their pre-school years, thus largely explaining their impressive academic success. By the time they began formal schooling, her children were not only bilingual, but their mathematical skills were quite advanced for their age.

The morning Costa arrived I excused myself from my obligations with Jon and took my little brother fishing in the ocean on my small, twenty-foot runabout.

"Big brother," Costa said, using his life-long nickname for me, "perhaps you should slow down a little." He sat clutching the rail of my boat with a white-knuckled grip, his feet firmly planted against the bulkhead, as we rounded a point and hit the whitewater in the inlet where the ocean met the bay.

Finally we stopped to drop our lines. My mind drifted back to the difficulties of our past, then propelled me forward to blessings of the present. We were indeed two fortunate men. God's light had shone on our lives.

Costa must have been thinking along the same lines as he idly fingered the reel in his hand. "And so, from Greece to America," he continued at last, "from an old life to a new one, and we are still fishing." We both laughed.

Suddenly his line snapped taut. "I think I have something, Chris."

"Yes, I think you do," I exclaimed. "Bring it in slowly, Costa, slow and steady."

Minutes later we had a four-pound sea trout onboard and a very pleased Costa.

"Here, Costa, have a beer," I said as I snapped a pop tab on a can of Budweiser.

Costa grinned, showing his thanks.

During the afternoon we pulled in more fish, and that evening everyone dined on our catch.

"Costa, eat the head, too," I said, pointing at the trout on his plate. "It's very tasty."

"Ah, so it is," Costa announced, his mouth full of fish, and all the kids followed suit.

Although we hadn't seen each other that frequently before, the thirteen years I spent with Costa in America seemed to almost make up for all the time we had spent apart. Yet life as I knew it was never fair. It had been a great fishing day with my little brother, and the children had the time of their lives visiting their older cousins.

The following year, in mid-March 1978, without any warning, Costa suffered a massive heart attack. He died in the ambulance on the way to the hospital, leaving behind Afrodite and his four children, ages six through 12. It was a tragedy every bit as sudden, unexpected, and severe as any I had witnessed. When everything was going so well, without rhyme or reason I had lost my little brother. Costa was only 55 years old.

That morning when I arrived at the house, Costa's children surrounded me crying out, "Theo Christo! Theo Christo!" I reached out my arms and drew them close to me, then released them to embrace their mother.

"I've lost Costa," Afrodite sobbed. "I've lost Costa."

I shared Afrodite's shock and sense of sudden loss. It was as incomprehensible to me as it was to her. We had survived so much together, Costa and I. How could he be gone—just like that, without a warning, without a word or a goodbye?

Costa was still my little brother, the small boy who had followed me around our island home, the youth I had brought to Constantinople, the man I had helped come to America. It underscored in the sharpest of ways how fragile and precious our lives are.

The days that followed were a blur. Lord & Taylor sent a note of sympathy and a check for $500 to Afrodite. I helped her arrange for Costa's burial, and then I handled his estate. I immediately sold his second home and used the proceeds to pay off the mortgage on his first home. What remained was about $10,000, which we put into a certificate of deposit. Without a mortgage to pay, Afrodite was essentially debt-free, but she and the children would have to live on Costa's social security.

Costa was gone, but the gentle love he felt and gave so freely to his family would live on. In years to come all of his children would flourish and reflect positively on him through their every accomplishment. Three of the four would attend Harvard—quite a legacy for my little brother and an honor for our whole family.

• • •

That fall Katina called, compounding the year's tragedy with news that Uncle Dimitris had died in the nursing home in Constantinople. He had outlived his wife. His only remaining family members were his nieces and nephews thousands of miles away in America. Apart from visits from his goddaughter, he had lived these fifteen years alone, and his only support was the money and small gifts we sent him.

My favorite uncle was very knowledgeable. I had so many vivid memories of Uncle Dimitris from my childhood. He was Papa's younger brother and, although we weren't entirely certain of his age, we believed he was 101 when he passed. The pain of not having shared his company and wisdom with my family in America struck me the same as it had upon my parents' demise.

"Christo," Katina said, "Uncle Dimitris was a good man and his mind remained sharp up to the end. He last wrote me six months ago and he always asked about you and your family."

"Yes," I agreed soberly. "He was the last of our family and of a generation lost in that part of the world."

"That is true," Katina acknowledged.

"God rest his soul." Our parents' generation had now all but disappeared.

The fragility of life was only overshadowed by the quickened passage of time. The death of all these important people shook me. First my parents, then Nick, Anton, Costa, and finally Uncle Dimitris.

Though quite a year of loss, it gave me an increased desire to spend more time with my family. My life was passing before me with greater speed. I would not waste one precious moment of my remaining time. My days from a very young age had been filled with countless hours of work, but now that would change.

• • •

Finally, in 1979 Helen and I received some long-awaited good news. As the decade drew to a close, Anthony, who was still working in construction and attending night school, became engaged to Lee Ann, a nurse whom he had been dating for quite some time. I liked Lee Ann and felt from the beginning of their relationship that she was good for my son. I welcomed their engagement with an open heart.

At a dinner Helen and I held for them in early December 1979, I turned to Lee Ann and said, "You can't continue calling me Mr. Christ anymore."

Lee Ann smiled. "What would you like me to call you?" she asked.

"You are marrying my son," I told her. "That makes you my daughter, so I think you had better call me 'Dad.'"

"And me 'Mother,'" chimed in Helen.

Anthony and Lee Ann married in April 1980. As I watched him exchange vows with Lee Ann, I offered God a prayer of thanks. Anthony's dark eyes and hair belonged to his mother, but his smiling expression was the same as my own. For a brief moment I saw myself in his eyes. I looked at my oldest son with satisfaction and affection.

• • •

Late in August 1980 I also arranged a fishing excursion on my new boat with my friend and first mate Paul Yeonas, a successful homebuilder in Northern Virginia. I was up at the crack of dawn, readied the boat, then came in for coffee and a toasted muffin while waiting for Paul.

Paul was a tall man, about six feet two inches, and like me he was in his mid-sixties. He wore thick glasses and had a full head of white hair. There was a rugged quality about his appearance that was confirmed by his hands, which were worn and rough from his years in construction. His rugged exterior contrasted sharply with his personality, which, though firm, was kind and gentle.

There was a heavy fog over the bay that morning that reduced visibility to thirty feet. I never carried a compass or a two-way radio with me, relying instead on the sun and stars and my own experience and judgment to navigate. Paul thought the fog would lift as the morning unfolded so we weren't too concerned.

"Good morning, hello?" An earthy, somewhat nasal voice greeted me through the crack in my front sliding door.

"Come on, Paul," I exclaimed, motioning him towards the dock.

"What can I do to help get ready, Captain Christ?" he asked with enthusiasm.

"Relax, Paul. Sit down and have your coffee." I gestured him inside the boat with a nod while pouring him a freshly brewed cup and refilling mine.

Within a few minutes we had embarked and were in the channel headed south toward the inlet at twelve knots, enveloped in the heavy fog. I somehow managed to find the boating lane through the bay despite the poor visibility, and we hit the inlet in fifteen minutes.

"Paul, keep an eye peeled for the jetties."

"Aye, aye, Captain. Have you ever seen anything like this?"

The blanket of white mist enveloped the calm sea with no signs it would turn to chop. Within minutes though, swirling three-foot swells of tepid bay water abutted the ocean brine. We were in the crosscurrents of the Ocean City inlet. Whitecaps sprayed us as my small twenty-two-foot vessel rode the jagged swish of choppy water.

"Captain Christ, I can't see the jetty."

The inlet was about six hundred feet-wide and cut through the rock jetty of Ocean City to the north and a sister jetty off Assateague Island to the south.

"Don't worry, Paul. We will be in the ocean soon," I said as we both strained to see through the white curtain.

"What do you make of it?" he asked as we motored from the inlet's tempest.

"It's early yet, only seven thirty. Let's see if it lifts in an hour," I responded as I turned northeast, heading for the ten-mile buoy. We arrived about forty-five minutes later and fished for an hour.

We only managed to catch a single three-pound hardhead, and the fog had not lifted a bit.

"Paul, pull up the anchor. We're heading out to the fifteen-mile buoy."

"Okay, Captain," Paul promptly responded. About thirty minutes later we were at the second fishing marker. Over the last five years I had frequented these fishing spots so often that I could literally navigate them blindfolded.

When we reached the bobbing buoy bell, though, our engine sputtered, then failed. Neither Paul, the builder, nor I, the waiter, knew much of anything about engines. After a few minutes of vain attempts, we dropped our anchor and began to fish the becalmed sea again.

"Here, Paul, have a beer," I said, popping open a can.

"Thanks, Captain, believe I will," he responded. Within an hour we had eaten the cold cuts I had prepared and drank all but two of the beers we had brought. By mid-afternoon we had caught three more fish and had intermittently attempted to restart the engine, to no avail.

Gradually the weather had begun to change for the worse again. The small, slow rhythmic swells were hastening and losing cadence. The chill of early evening air roused a breeze that rocked the little boat, ushering in the specter of worsening weather. The rocking of an anchored boat in harsh weather follows no rhythmic movement or pattern and is quite unsettling.

Paul was the first to voice concern. "Captain, we have some weather coming in."

"I know, Paul. Get some rest. It will be dark soon."

I spent a restless night seated in my captain's chair, jacket zipped up to my chin, while we tossed and turned on inclement seas. Paul lay in the back quadrant of the deck, crouched in the corner.

"Captain Christ, what are we going to do?" he asked.

"We are going to wait, Paul. I'm sure they are looking for us. We are going to wait. Good night."

"Good night, Captain Christ," he echoed.

As the boat violently rocked, I dozed from exhaustion, my mind cascading back to my first trip in a rocking boat with Captain Koutris as a child going to Samothraki. A whitecap splashed over the bow and slapped me back to the present with cold sea spray. I wondered if this is how it might end, in the cold churning waters of the Atlantic.

The next morning, the weather worsened, intensifying our fears. The cloudy cover remained and the wind quickened with intermittent gusts. A weather front was definitely moving in again. The fog, still pervasively thick, obscured all vision. We were without food or water and out of beers. Vulnerable and subdued, we sat on our boat fighting the spray of increasingly savage seas that refused to subside.

My hand found its way to my sacred keepsake as I silently prayed. Paul put our fears into spoken words. "Captain, it looks like a squall is moving in—as the weather worsens, they won't be able to rescue us."

"When the weather worsens, rescue will be the least of our problems." Although I knew they were looking for us, since we failed to return the evening before, the fog obscured visibility by air, and rescue by boat would be limited should the seas continue to worsen. "Don't worry, Paul, Captain Reed will find us... he must be on the way."

Captain Reed, my longtime friend, owned the townhouse next door to mine. He was a judge from Baltimore, and a meticulous, consummate fishing chum. We had shared the same fishing haunts for years. He owned a powerful twenty-six-foot vessel, often sporting a crew of three. With a pipe usually clamped in his jaws, his worn countenance presented a potent profile that brought memories of Captain Koutris.

By late afternoon, the weather had significantly worsened, and I was really beginning to fear our small craft would succumb to the battering waves. We began bucketing water out of the bottom of our small vessel caused by the overwash. I knew that any search expeditions would quit at nightfall, and I dreaded the prospect of another night in the storm.

We had hoped that the increased wind and tide would push off the fog, but visibility had only improved to fifty feet, not much on the open sea. There was nothing to do but peer into the fog, desperately seeking a glimpse of another boat hopefully in search of two desperate fishermen.

Suddenly from somewhere in the fog came a faint voice, "Captain Christ? Captain Christ?" It was Judge Reed on his bullhorn!

We looked at each other with joy and relief. "Over here!" I screamed in the direction of the barely audible voice.

"Over here!" Paul repeated.

"Ship ahoy." It was the voice of Hawk O'Brien, Captain Reed's brother-in-law. Within moments, we were under tow toward safe harbor.

When we had safely docked, our families and extended families gave us a resounding chorus of applause in excited relief. It was at that time that Captain Reed shared his rescue story.

"Chris, when I left the inlet, my boat held unalterably on a course of thirty-six degrees directly to your boat. I have been on the water for over thirty years now, and I have never had anything like that happen. When you're steering at sea, you know how hard it is to hold a course. Yet, every time I turned the wheel, it would return to 36 degrees and hold on a north-northeast course. Even when I tried to get more easterly it veered north-northeast. It was the hand of God guiding my vessel to you both. You realize you were nine miles off the coast of Bethany Beach? If you had not dropped anchor, you would have been off the Jersey Coast."

I nodded my acknowledgement with a broad smile of gratitude. It was divine intervention, I guess. At that moment the weather worsened, lightning cracked nearby, and torrents of rain angled through the slicing gusts, chasing us from our dock to the shelter of our townhouses. A nor'easter unleashed its fury, pummeling the beach and closing the port throughout the night, as well as the entire next day.

The following week, largely due to my family's insistence—they had not slept nor stopped worrying during our nearly three-day seafaring absence—I bought a two-way radio. Neither Paul nor I was a world-class boatman, but we were avid fishermen. What I never admitted was that if we had known how to flip on the backup gas, we could have avoided all the dramatics. Chalk that one up to experience. After all, I knew there were worse places to be than lost at sea.

CHAPTER 21

Fishermen

Everything about him was old
except his eyes, and they were
the same color as the sea
and were cheerful and undefeated.
—ERNEST HEMINGWAY, 1951

RECESSION CONTINUED to plague the new decade. With the economy at a standstill, I had a number of vacancies among my rental stores and my income was sharply curtailed. If I had worked a few more years, when the recession lifted I could have cleared off my debt. Instead, with the explosion of interest rates in 1981, the economy recessed once again, and I found it necessary to borrow to cover the gap between income and my family's expenses. Nevertheless, I was thankful for my family's health and welfare and for the assets I had built over time.

By the end of 1982 President Reagan had reduced taxes, and interest rates began to subside from their previous record high. This stimulated the economy and rekindled productive growth. It seemed that the mood of the country brightened in response after nearly a decade of stagnation. In September of that year, Anthony and Lee Ann also welcomed their first child, a little boy they named Brian Anthony. To become a grandfather is a momentous occasion for any man. A grandson gives a feeling of extension beyond our own lives, a gateway into the future, a glowing light after we have gone.

Anthony had received his bachelor's degree the year before, and by the end of 1982 he also received his master's degree in economics with high honors. The fact that it was a decade late did not diminish his accomplishment. He was the first person in our family to obtain a master's degree and we were tremendously proud of him. In fact, Anthony was subsequently accepted into a PhD program, but left his studies later to begin work as a stockbroker.

Jon had now settled in Ocean City where, besides running Anthony's Beer & Wine during the season, he worked part-time in real estate during the offseason. Jon would receive and forward my mail from Ocean City when I was back in Virginia. He maintained this routine throughout the seventies and into the eighties. Although I encouraged him to find a wife and get married, I was more concerned with my daughter Ianthe.

Since becoming a kindergarten teacher in Fredericksburg, Ianthe had achieved teaching awards and seemed very content, but she was approaching 30 and remained unmarried. She had always had scores of boys interested in her since high school, but nothing ever seemed to develop into anything serious. It was difficult for me to understand why a young woman was not more interested in settling down and marrying. This was neither the old country nor the old days, and I had a certain awareness that American women held different attitudes, but I still could not understand such behavior.

• • •

Nearly every day in the spring and fall when weather permitted—after finishing my chores at Anthony's Beer & Wine—I would routinely start my boat and round the southern tip of Ocean City where the bay met the sea. The inlet was always choppy and often downright dangerous—as I had learned a few years before—with squalls blowing in at a moment's notice and swells reaching six feet or more.

Most of the vessels that cruised the channel were larger pleasure boats and commercial fishing vessels, but my little runabout always made it safely out to and back from sea, with that one notable exception. Traversing the inlet and weathering the elements was always exhilarating to me, although sometimes my guests couldn't quite stomach the excitement, proving themselves a little unseaworthy.

One day in early June 1983 a neighbor in Falls Church, Mike Pappas, called and said he and Father Theodore Chelpon, the priest at Saint Katherine's and a New York Yankees fan educated in Brookline, Massachusetts, were coming to Ocean City, so I invited them to go fishing with me. I included on this fishing outing two other friends of mine: Dr. Economous, a surgical internist, and Paul Yeonas, my first mate. Dr. Economous sounded interested in the invitation, but admitted he had no boating experience. Aside from Paul, I was uncertain if anyone in the group had deep-sea fishing experience.

The next evening after work I readied the boat for a dawn departure. Early the following morning Paul and Dr. Economous arrived promptly at the dock.

Paul and I were dressed in shorts, knit short-sleeved shirts, baseball caps, and tennis shoes. Dr. Economous, on the other hand, looked as if he had stepped from the pages of a fashion magazine. In his early sixties and bespectacled, the doctor was perhaps my height—five feet nine—but that's where the similarities ended. From his stylish, tan fisherman's cap to his handsome, tan deck shoes, he was color coordinated and expensively dressed in "fishing attire" that no experienced fisherman, mindful of the effects of baiting hooks and cleaning fish—let alone the turbulent tides—would ever wear.

While we waited for Mike and Father Ted to arrive, Paul barked out in his raspy voice, "What can we do to help, Cap'n?"

"Finish your coffee, then let's load up the supplies," I responded, nodding toward the coolers lined up on the dock. One contained squid for bait, a second one sodas and beer, and the third was packed with sandwiches and chips. Paul and the doctor dutifully hefted the coolers and placed them aboard while I carefully lifted the fishing gear propped against a deck railing—three deep-sea fishing rods and two spin reels, each with two hooks threaded into cork for safety—and stowed them away in the stern.

By this time Mike and Father Ted had arrived. Father Ted was a sturdy-looking man with a receding hairline. He had a broad face and a short neck that made his head appear as if it were set directly atop his thick broad shoulders. He was about the same height as I was, and almost as wide as he was tall. Though three inches taller, Mike carried sixty pounds more than the stately priest, bearing no resemblance whatever to the reconnaissance paratrooper he had been during World War II. Both men were about ten years younger than the rest of us. With curly black hair running down their arms and forearms, they resembled two sizes of the same stout black bear.

Mike was dressed in long pants and a white shirt, which he wore with the tails out so that it stretched over his extended middle and rear, the tails covering his ample thighs. Father Ted was dressed in traditional black priest's garb complete with his white clerical collar. Both men wore black dress shoes, which were highly unsuitable for boating. We were a rather comical group of "fishermen."

"Hello, Father, Mike," I greeted them. "You sure you'll be comfortable dressed like that?"

"I don't plan on getting wet, Chris," Father Ted responded.

"Oh really?" I chided.

I nodded, thinking how unsuspecting they both were. Looking up, I caught Paul shaking his head in disbelief. Then, as was my habit, I spelled out the rules of the boat for everyone before I allowed them to board.

"Keep your hands and feet inside the boat," I instructed them, "and remain seated while the boat is moving. As we pass through the inlet, you may want to hang on tightly—there's a stiff, intermittent breeze and I expect the ride may be a little bumpy. We will cruise out to the ten-mile buoy where we will drop our anchor to fish, and we should return by one o'clock." I paused to survey my passengers, and then added, "And we're not coming back early for anyone—for any reason."

"Aye, aye, Captain," Mike laughed.

Having survived the rigors of paratrooping in World War II, he thought my admonishment was highly amusing.

When we boarded, the boat was full. I took the seat behind the wheel and Paul sat next to me. Mike and Father Ted, both large men, could not be seated on the same side of the boat, so I assigned Father Ted the seat behind me and seated Dr. Economous behind Paul. Mike sat on the backbench in front of the outboard motor. It was the only place I could seat a man of his size and, even so, his weight made the stern of the boat ride noticeably low, angling the bow up out of the water.

When my passengers were settled, I slipped the boat from its mooring and headed into the channel. While cruising down the bay toward the inlet I noticed that the wind-driven chop had intensified. About twenty minutes later, as we rounded the corner to the inlet where the bay and ocean met, the breeze intensified and I noticed that the waves were significantly higher than usual. With every swell, spray broke over the bow and hit the windshield.

A stiff, swirling headwind whipped up three-to-five-foot seas, and the pitch and roll of the boat were worsened by the full load of my passengers. Although it served as ballast, their collective weight lowered the plane of the stern, allowing spray and splash to wash aboard.

For several long minutes my attention was focused on navigating the treacherous inlet. Finally, I risked a glance toward the stern.

"Mike, you okay?" I called out.

In reply Mike offered me a fisheye stare. His usual smiling, ruddy face looked clammy and nearly colorless, and his shirt and trousers were drenched with water. With white knuckles he clutched at the boat rails on either side. Then suddenly, and without warning, we all heard a loud, unpleasant belch and saw a spray of vomit splatter across the deck. Poor Mike, who had been so amused at the idea of seasickness, found himself seasick.

After I navigated a series of swells I turned and saw that Mike had slithered off his seat and was lying on his side in a fetal position, crumpled on the deck of my boat, his back propped against the bench and his face blanched white with misery and vertigo. He vomited again, this time less dramatically, staining his shirt and pants. "Easy there, Mike," I tried to reassure him.

"It's a little rough out today, Captain Chris," Paul commented nonchalantly.

"A bit," I agreed.

My eyes then travelled from Mike to Father Ted, who, I noticed, had the same fisheye stare and had turned the same suspicious shade of pale white. With his index finger firmly pressed against his thumb, he reverently crossed himself. "Holy Father, please watch over and protect us in our time of need," he muttered over and over.

"We're almost through the inlet," I announced cheerfully to my passengers as a swell slapped up against the bow, drenching us with spray once again.

A minute later, as we rode out the last of the inlet swells and broke into the open ocean, I heard a groan over my right shoulder. It was Father Ted. Grasping the wheel firmly I leaned hard to the left to avoid what I knew was coming, but I wasn't quite quick enough. My right hand became the victim of Father Ted's unseemly eruption. Having traversed the inlet, our fishing trip had just begun.

A half-dozen episodes later the priest had slipped from his seat to the wet floor, his forehead resting against the railing behind me. Poor Father Ted. He was so stricken he was incapable of either crossing himself or praying, but rather lay panting and listless on the deck.

"We may be through the inlet, Captain," Paul observed, "but the seas are still running high. The fish won't be biting in these conditions. It looks like rough seas all day."

"Let's see what we find at the ten-mile marker," I responded.

When we reached the buoy about nine forty-five, the sea had calmed somewhat, but we were still buffeted by a stiff breeze that whipped the swells into whitecaps.

Paul and I readied the poles with bait, our windbreakers zipped to the neckline, while Mike and Father Ted sat on the deck, where the salty wash had thankfully swept away most of the vomit. I gave each of them a beach towel. Father Ted buried his face in his, while Mike tied his like a bib around his neck to catch the salty drool from his chin. Mercifully for the rest of us their stomachs were practically empty, but the persistent rocking of the small vessel did nothing to alleviate their misery, as their intermittent dry heaves continued.

I handed the doctor a baited pole. "How are you doing?" I asked.

"Not bad compared to those two, Christo," he said unconvincingly.

"Cast your line over to the left," I instructed. He took the pole hesitantly, and I helped him cast his line. "If we don't get any bites here, we will troll for a while."

"Right," he said, swinging the rod back for a cast. Dr. Economous was thrilled to be doing something so as to take his mind off the rocking, repetitive vertigo of the sea. It took about an hour, but when he had a strike on the line his face lit up.

"What do I do, Chris?" he called excitedly.

"First you set the hook," I told him, grinning. 'Then you reel it in, like this." I demonstrated the motions.

A moment later he reeled a three-pound sea bass into the boat. I helped him land it and removed the hook. A few minutes later Paul caught a somewhat larger bass and I caught a small sea trout.

By this time Father Ted had recovered sufficiently enough to hold a pole weakly over the side of the boat, but poor Mike could barely hold up his head. He lay sprawled in the stern, clutching at the deck for support with one hand while the other rested across his distended abdomen.

"Hey, Chris, how about a beer?" Paul asked.

"A little early, isn't it?"

"Nah, it's eleven o'clock—almost noon," he protested, and we both laughed.

"So what do you think of this surf, Captain Chris?" Paul asked as I handed him a beer.

"It's starting to kick up again," I told him, keeping my voice low. "And there are some dark clouds to the northeast. I don't like the looks of it. Let's hook up the two-way radio and see what we can find out." Wiser from our experience a few years back, we knew the dark clouds confirmed that the weather could worsen.

I cut the engine and stopped trolling, then channeled on an open frequency for a few minutes until I heard a Coast Guard officer issuing a warning. "Storm approaching from the north," a distant voice crackled across the airways through a buzz of static. "All small craft head immediately for port. Larger vessels head to sea. Possible gale force winds, landfall within less than an hour…"

The message was repeated several times, but I didn't need to be told twice. "Paul," I said quickly, "let's pull in the lines." The storm was coming from the north and we were southeast of the inlet. We had to travel toward the storm to make it to port. "We've drifted about a mile beyond the buoy, I would guess, so it's going to take at least an hour to reach the inlet."

"Aye, Aye, Captain," Paul said as he pulled up the lines.

I ordered our passengers into life jackets. Mike groaned and the doctor paled, showing the same fisheye stare. Father Ted once again began moaning and praying. "Protect and guide us back to port, O Holy Father," he intoned over and over, until the increasing speed of the boat upset his stomach again and silenced him.

As soon as the poles were reeled in and secured and my passengers were safely seated, I turned northwest, toward the dark clouds, and headed full steam for the inlet. Gusts were reaching thirty-five knots, whitecaps broke and smacked the sides of our small craft, water rushing over the low gunwales of the boat.

Because the winds were coming in a north-northeasterly direction I had to turn the boat into the wind, travelling to the northwest instead of directly westward. Although the narrow inlet joining ocean with bay was almost due west the winds were pushing our small craft south forcing me to go northeast into the wind. Gusts had risen to forty knots. A dark wall of storm clouds was rapidly closing in on us as we cut through the wind and waves, with the inlet in sight.

Father Ted had sunk back to the deck where he muttered intermittent prayers. Mike lay moribund in the stern, and Dr. Economous gripped the rails, all color drained from his face, appearing like a potential third victim. Beside me, Paul calmly watched the sea with interest.

"Cap'n, this is really something."

The sea rumbled about us in fury and the sky hung low with angry black clouds. We cut doggedly through the heavy swells, drenched by spray. Ahead of us a bolt of lightning lit the horizon.

My small craft was full throttle to prevent from being pushed south by the gnarly seas.

"Paul, how are the passengers doing?" I yelled into the wind.

"Not too good, Captain," Paul replied, grinning. "We have two hugging the floor, and the doctor and his elegant attire look a little worse for wear."

"Is everybody in lifejackets, Paul?"

"Aye, aye, Cap'n Chris," he paused. "You think we'll be able to make it through the inlet?"

As he spoke, the rain finally caught us and a huge swell smashed into the bow.

"This is pretty bad, Paul," I told him. The squall was intensifying as we neared the inlet. "We've got to turn to the southwest to make the inlet."

Actually, I couldn't see that we had much choice. As I held on course, a call came over the radio from the Coast Guard, instructing small craft to tune to a certain frequency immediately. As both my hands were on the wheel, Paul tuned our dial. Through wind and static we heard the same voice saying, "Small craft needing assistance entering the inlet should contact the Coast Guard cutter at the head of the inlet upon approach." The alert was repeated several times.

Finally, after fighting wind and sea for over an hour, we reached the inlet. The inlet's swirling seas showed white-capped swells that were large and non-directional, more so than I expected. Paul surveyed the churning waters and turned to me. "I don't think we can make it, Captain."

"Yes, we can," I told him, "God willing."

The truth was that although I had navigated my way through several storms in the past I had never encountered anything this intense.

"Paul, check that their life vests are securely fastened." I had to scream over the whistling wind.

"Aye, aye, Captain."

"We have to return through the inlet, no choice. Everyone hang on."

As Paul checked our passengers, the Coast Guard cutter hailed me. "Small skiff, this is Coast Guard cutter four-four-three-five. Do you require a tow through the inlet?"

"No, thank you," I radioed back, "no tow needed."

"Small vessel, follow our wake and keep your bow to the swells," the cutter instructed me. Moments later it had pulled about fifty yards in front of us, its wake lost in the pounding sea.

The inlet between Assateague Island to the south and Ocean City to the north was a tempest of swells and whitecaps about three hundred yards wide. Jetties extending into the sea abutted both landmasses from each side of the inlet, arresting the shifting sands to keep the inlet open.

I braced myself against the wheel and watched as the cutter, now in the middle of the channel, tossed about on the waves. Winds were gusting to forty knots and sheets of hard rain pelted down, making visibility difficult, but following the cutter's wake allowed us to negotiate the inlet. We edged farther into the inlet, swells breaking all around us and washing over our bow. Suddenly, the two-way radio crackled to life. "Small vessel, you are clear ahead to safe harbor."

"Aye, Aye," I responded, "and thank you, four-four-three-five."

A moment later in the relative calm of the sheltered bay I turned to my passengers just in time to see Dr. Economous, white-faced and purple-lipped, vomit on Paul and promptly wilt to the deck where he joined Mike and Father Ted.

"Three down," Paul laughed, stripping off his soaked shirt.

Once safely through the inlet we slipped carefully through the whitecaps of the bay, and twenty minutes later, in wind and rain, we tied up at my dock.

"Paul," I called out, "leave some slack in those lines."

"Yes sir, Captain Chris," Paul replied cheerily. "That was a hell of a ride, Captain. I've never been through anything like it."

"It was a little rough, wasn't it?" I said with a weak laugh and a smile.

"A little?" Paul laughed at my understatement. "Nothing gets you in a flap, does it?"

As I grinned back at Paul, I touched the relic coin pinned to my t-shirt and offered up a silent prayer of thanksgiving to God.

"Give me a hand with the good Father, will you, Paul? Grab his right arm, I'll take his left."

With a little effort we dragged Father Ted from the boat and put him on the dock where he collapsed all over again muttering, "Praise the Lord, Praise the Lord...." Then we hauled the doctor out and put him down beside the priest.

Mike posed more difficulties. When we got his upper half on the dock he managed to pull the rest of himself out. Groaning, he crawled on all fours past the inert bodies of Father Ted and Dr. Economous, and eventually stood to walk down the dock to the sidewalk and onto the porch of my townhouse, leaving Paul and me to unload the gear.

Watching his friend's slow progress down the dock, Paul turned to me and said, "Cap'n, today was something I'll never forget."

"Yes," I agreed, heaving a cooler onto the dock, "and I don't care to repeat it, either."

Paul tipped his head toward the dock. "I don't guess those three will be going fishing again any time soon."

I paused, looking at the bodies lying on the dock and at Mike's wet retreating backside.

"You know, Paul, I think you're probably right."

We broke out in hearty laughter.

CHAPTER 22

Dinner with the Patriarch

The tattered outlaw of the earth,
of ancient crooked will;
starve, scourge, deride me: I am dumb,
I keep my secret still.
Fools! For I also had my hour;
one far fierce hour and sweet:
there was a shout about my ears,
and palms before my feet.
—G. K. CHESTERTON, 1936

THE EXCITEMENT of a stormy fishing trip would prove to be a precursor of a more distant trip, a return to the Old World. That September of 1983, Helen and I would travel with a group from Saint Sophia's to the Holy Land in Israel.

When I made my pilgrimage to the Holy Land I was 65 years old, a retired man travelling with a church group to learn more about my Christian roots. Yet for me the trip was more than that, for it brought me back to the world of my youth, after thirty-eight years in America. Although Jerusalem was neither Constantinople nor my island home of Imbroz, the cultural and architectural similarities were striking. It stirred feelings I had not experienced for a long time.

Oddly, the presence of religious tension in Jerusalem was hardly noticed by most of our party, but for me the images of the young Uzi-armed Jewish boys stirred memories of the Turkish gendarmes of my youth. I was sensitive to what I saw there and to the violence that lay so near the surface because I had known violence in a similar context. I, too, had witnessed uprisings and bloody repressions and knew the signs only too well. These stark images, like ghosts revisiting from the distant past, were no less menacing than the soldiers of my youth.

• • •

It was the summer of 1985. I continued to help Jon by making the deli salads and desserts and working the register in the gourmet deli at Anthony's Beer & Wine. As part of my morning routine in Ocean City I would first visit my old carryout some sixteen blocks away to have a cup of coffee with John Simms, who had purchased my old business and leased my 1,000 square-foot building. Each time I walked into my small store, a feeling that I should start working would overcome me. I enjoyed a comfortable, pleasant relationship with John, and I enjoyed my morning visits with him. He still maintained the store pretty much as I had, which I found gratifying, and his family helped him run it.

When I arrived at Anthony's Beer & Wine, Bernard was in the parking lot sweeping, just as he had done countless mornings at my store.

"Bernard, good morning," I called out.

"Morning, Mr. Christ. I'll be through here in just a bit."

I smiled and headed toward the kitchen in back of the store where I began to cook. I boiled potatoes and macaroni, cooked chickens, and prepared fresh tuna fish.

A moment later Bernard came in and we set about cleaning up the kitchen. "We miss you, Mr. Christ." When I sold the carryout business, Bernard started working with Jon.

"Thanks, Bernard, I miss you too. I'm just too old to stay here and work all day." He laughed.

"I know, Mr. Christ. Don't worry, I'm here."

My chores in the deli were somewhat relaxed. I was now sixty-eight years of age and could still outwork younger people, but the deli was something I did to pass my time and help my younger son, who was running the business. A day of work at the deli was a breeze, and I simply enjoyed the work and being with Jon.

One morning when Jon was gone, the day manager, Mike Herr, reported that the air conditioner was out. He fussed with the equipment to no avail, then poked his head in the kitchen.

"It's hot," he announced irritably.

These kids had not known a day's work without air conditioning.

"Really?" I raised an eyebrow at him then busied myself with a knife and a cucumber. A minute later I emerged from the kitchen with a slice of cucumber on my forehead.

"You see, boys," I announced to the staff, "put a slice of cucumber on your forehead, like this, and it will cool you off." Within moments, all five of us had a cool slice of cucumber stuck to our foreheads.

For much of my life I didn't even know what air conditioning was, let alone have it where I worked or lived. Even in all the years I ran Anthony's Carryout—all those long, hot Ocean City summers—I never had air conditioning. Yet today in Jon's deli, paralysis set in when the air conditioner stopped. I couldn't help but think of all the creature comforts that had made America go as soft as my ice cream. When Jon finally arrived he thanked me for dropping by. "I'll take care of the air conditioning right away boys," he told his workers.

I jumped into my station wagon and drove down past the bridge to Tony's Fruit Stand. I particularly enjoyed sweet, cool, fresh fruit on a summer day. Tony was an Italian, and I had frequented his fruit stand every week for more than two decades. Tony was about five years older than I was. He was a stickler for the quality of his fruit, which was unfailingly fragrant and always fresh. Often I would haggle with him over cost and quality, but I think we were fond of each other and enjoyed the bicker and babble over the fruit.

My varied interests in life also helped me to stay physically active. I loved to garden and I did all my own yard work with the exception of cleaning gutters and trimming trees. In fact, my yard work was medicinal, and later in the autumn when I had returned home I spent hours trimming my azaleas and tying up my rhododendrons. I worked hard to winterize my plants, so that in the spring they would reward me with their lovely blossoms. It was something I always looked forward to. Each spring, my garden was reborn in beauty.

Time marched on. Late in January 1986, I received my thirteenth set of commemorative stamps. There within the first two pages was the commemorative stamp for the lady who had greeted me when I first arrived on these shores thirty-two years earlier. It was the hundred-year commemorative for the Statue of Liberty that caused me to recall with some emotion my entry into New York Harbor almost forty-one years ago.

• • •

During the 1980s a few miles off Ocean City's shore Russian trawlers would deplete the enormous bounty of fish by extensive trolling with nets, but I still returned with some fine catches that I cleaned and froze. Trout, sea bass, croakers, and blues were always plentiful and I enjoyed them all.

My love of seafood came with a cost, though—a bout or two of gout—and late in February 1986 I made an appointment with Dr. Mandes. It was not my first attack of gout, and Dr. Mandes prescribed the usual medication. On this occasion, however, it gave me little relief. For a week I took the medication religiously, yet I grew increasingly uncomfortable. Although I did not notice, something else was happening.

"Dad, you're jaundiced." My daughter-in-law, Lee Ann, who had just stopped by for a quick visit, noticed something wasn't right. I greeted her with pleasure and gave her a fatherly hug.

"I have a bit of a cold," I told her.

Lee Ann, a nurse, shook her head. "No, Dad, you're yellow," she exclaimed. "You need to get this checked out right away."

It was true. My skin had turned a pasty yellow. Lee Ann was persistent, and eventually I called Dr. Mandes again who sent me to the hospital, where other doctors determined that my gall bladder had to be removed.

After the surgery my fever shot up to a hundred and two degrees and the area surrounding the incision was infected. I was in the hospital for two more weeks. I'd had a reaction to the gout medicine.

"Dad, how are you feeling tonight?"

I opened my eyes and saw Anthony bending over me.

"Okay, thank you, Anthony."

"Hello, Dad," came another voice.

I turned my head slightly and saw Lee Ann.

"Do you feel better since they stopped the gout medicine?" she asked.

"Yes, a little," I said, nodding.

"Dad, did you know Dr. Mandes was restricted from practicing at Fairfax Hospital?" Anthony asked me. "I think you should get another doctor before he kills you."

Anthony's bluntness made me smile. Still, Tom Mandes was my doctor. I liked him, and I was loyal. Anthony could chide me all he wanted, but I wouldn't change doctors, and he knew it.

"We'll see, Anthony," I said to placate him.

Despite surgery and medication I still felt pressure in my side. I still had gout, and no one seemed to know why my condition was lingering. The experience validated my life-long conviction: Except for social occasions you should stay away from doctors. Helen was just the opposite, she couldn't go a month without seeing a doctor. We were so different. I guess that's why we fit together so well after all these years.

I watched as Dr. Mandes bustled into my room, herding my family out into the hall. We exchanged pleasantries as he examined my chart, and then we got down to business.

"Chris," he said, probing and examining me, "you still have a low- grade fever and a little redness around the drainage tubes at the site of your incision." I had been in the hospital for almost two weeks.

"Hmmm," I commented noncommittally.

"So we'll need to keep you through the weekend," he went on. "Then next week, we'll see about you going home."

It was only Thursday. I knew I'd never survive another weekend in this place. At that moment I made a decision. I had to get out of this place. If I stayed any longer, the combination of this doctor and the bland hospital food might really kill me.

"You're the doctor," I said with deceptive complaisance.

Dr. Mandes smiled and retreated to the hall where he fell into a muffled conversation with my family. A moment later, the doctor departed and my family returned. Momentarily, everyone began making motions to leave. Ianthe leaned over to give me a kiss and Lee Ann patted my shoulder.

"Goodbye, girls," I told them.

"Bye, Granddad," Brian said in his sweet, childhood voice, while little Katelyn Elaine, Anthony's eight-month-old daughter, fixed me with an innocent wide-eyed stare.

"Goodbye, kids." I watched as my family began to file out.

"Good night, Dad."

"Good night, Anthony."

"G'nite, Dad," Jon said as he headed toward the door. "See you tomorrow."

"Oh, Jon, before you go," I said casually.

Jon stuck his head back into the room. "Dad?"

I waited a minute until everyone was safely down the hall, then I cleared my throat. "Jon, would you get my clothes for me please?"

Jon looked puzzled. "Do you need something?"

"What I need is to get out of here," I told him calmly.

"What about the tube?"

"Just get the clothes," I told him firmly. "I'll take care of the tube."

"But, Dad."

"No arguments," I said.

"You need more rest, you need medicine, you need…"

"To go home!" I cut him off. "I *need* to leave this place and *you* need to get my clothes. Now don't argue with me, please."

For a moment Jon hesitated, then moved reluctantly to the closet. The instant his back was turned I slipped my hand to my right side. Just below where my gall bladder used to be was a plastic tube that exited from the surgical site. It was taped to my side and descended to a container on the floor that collected fluid draining from my wound. Suddenly I grasped the tube, said a quick prayer, and yanked, pulling the tubing out of my side.

I paused to survey the damage. Surprisingly the only discomfort I felt was a mild burning around the opening. I took a breath in relief, then I held the end of the tube aloft and looked at it.

"Dad!"

I looked up to see my son gazing at me in horror.

"You shouldn't have done that," he gasped, looking a little pale and weak-kneed.

I shrugged, holding the gown to my side where the tube had exited.

"This simply isn't wise," he admonished me as he placed my clothes into my outstretched hands. "The site could get infected. You could end up back in the hospital, you could—"

"Go to the Safeway—" interrupting his objections.

"What?"

"I want you to go to the Safeway down the street," I repeated carefully, "and get me some chicken legs and lemons. Then go home and start preparing them. I'll be there shortly."

Knowing he was defeated, Jon departed without another word, and a minute later I was out of bed. I peeled off the adhesive that held the tube to my side and replaced it with a few Band-Aids from the bathroom cabinet. Then I dressed, found my keys, and walked cheerfully past the nursing station and out the door. No one noticed.

Since I had driven myself to the hospital, my car was exactly where I had left it in the parking lot. The mild breeze contrasted by the warmth of the setting sun invigorated me. I climbed in my car, unsure for a moment if it would start, turned the key, and headed home where, in a few minutes, the familiar aroma of chicken baking with lemon and oregano greeted me from the kitchen. For the first time in almost three weeks I had an appetite.

Helen, of course, was waiting for me, her hands on her hips.

"Chris!" she said sharply. "The hospital called. They want to know where you are."

"I'm here, that's where I am," I told her, stating the obvious, patting her arm, and giving her a peck on the cheek.

Helen stared at me in exasperation. "You know, you're being very foolish."

"I've already told him that," Jon said as he turned the chicken baking in the oven. "But he didn't pay any attention."

Helen's eyes went from our son and back to me. "Are you crazy? What possible reason could you have for not listening to the doctors?"

"My reason is my health," I said mildly, opening the refrigerator door and taking out a cold beer. "If I had stayed there any longer I would have died."

"You must go back," she demanded. "Go back this minute."

I eyed the chicken in the oven, grabbed my beer, and sat contentedly at my kitchen table taking in the comforting, familiar smells that surrounded me. I was famished. For several long minutes I sat quietly, eyes closed, and basked in the pleasures of my kitchen—until I felt Helen's disapproving gaze upon me. I blinked my eyes open.

"Chris," she said, pointing a finger emphatically at my chest. "For the last time, call Dr. Mandes." The oven-baked chicken legs were delicious.

In a brief week I fully recovered from the damage I had sustained from doctors and hospitals.

• • •

Later that year a tragedy struck my friends and neighbors from Ocean City, the Carrols. Their youngest son, Johnny, now a young man, was injured in a serious motorcycle accident. He was paralyzed from the waist down, struck severely in the prime of his youth.

My heart ached for him, but I never let him feel pitied. I treated him as if nothing had changed. His life lay in front of him and he had to carry on and live it, independent of his handicap. It would be tough, I knew, but what Johnny needed most was not sympathy, but strength. Strength derived from people who believed he was the same as anyone else. Johnny's accident put into perspective my little brush with hospitals and doctors.

Time continued to march on. Then, in March of 1988, my good friend and first mate, Paul Yeonas, died. I saw him shortly before his death and was deeply saddened by how ill he looked. A big man all his life, cancer had reduced Paul to a shadow of his former self. Although in much pain, he never complained.

"Hello, Paul," I greeted him that day.

"Hello, Cap'n," he replied.

"How are you feeling, old friend?"

"It's rough, Cap'n. Rough."

I put my arm on his shoulder, and we said nothing further. Those peaceful dawns and exhilarating ocean excursions that comprised our fishing adventures were behind us. His passing was a loss to all his family and friends, but he had been released from his lingering suffering and pain.

• • •

That summer Anthony left his stockbrokerage firm to straighten out a deli he had acquired with a partner in downtown Washington. His partner had poorly managed the business and had now left it in debt. Bookkeeping was a mess and bills were unpaid, including a bank note that bore both their signatures. I told him that if he walked into the restaurant he might have to stay, and he did for three years.

Helen and I preferred that he use his education—but there he was, back in the restaurant business. Nonetheless, I was a little proud of him. Whenever a cashier or kitchen helper failed to show up I would get a call to help—and I did. I couldn't complain, though. I enjoyed work, always had, and I liked to help my kids, even at 73.

"That'll be $3.95, please."

Money changed hands as I placed a sandwich in a plastic bag, along with napkins and plastic fork. Anthony's detour back into the food business gave me plenty to do off and on through the winters for the next few years.

Early in 1989 I also received a special treat. I had ordered a full set of *Encyclopedia Britannica* for the house. Owning a set of the *Britannica* had been a secret desire of mine since the late fifties when I had sold *World Book Encyclopedia* part-time door-to-door. *Britannicas* were the finest, in my opinion, and all my life I had wanted a set for our house.

That evening I sat down with the first volume and started reviewing each page. So beautiful, I was struck with the depth and detail of the content. Over the next three or four years hardly a winter evening went by that I didn't read an *Encyclopedia Britannica* from my collection. My readings were so enjoyable and informative, particularly for an island boy who had only completed the fourth grade.

Anthony was working long hours to keep his restaurant afloat and filling in for absent employees. He and Lee Ann now had a third child, Ashley Elisabeth, and Helen felt they needed a vacation. So I decided to look after the deli that week while Anthony and Lee Ann drove the kids to Walt Disney World in Orlando, Florida, during Christmas break that winter.

"Dad, you only need to prepare the deposit. Don't make that trip to the bank. Just give it to Jose and he'll take it over after lunch. Oh, and here are the catering orders we have for the week. Alex and Janie will prepare them, and Miguel will make the deliveries."

"We'll manage fine," I told him. "Don't you worry."

"And here's a list of our suppliers," Anthony went on as if he hadn't heard me. "The deliveries are all set, but if you find you need—"

"I will be okay, Anthony," I said, interrupting him. "I know what to do. Go, enjoy yourself."

Eventually I managed to get Anthony out of the deli and off on his vacation. The deli was a busy place with long lines at lunch and at least five different daily specials, but I had the right background to handle it, and even though I was seventy-three the experience hardly ruffled a feather. The week went very fast.

The truth is, as long as I had the time and health, helping my children was what I lived for. It seemed to me the full essence of life.

• • •

That spring my azaleas were especially lovely. Oftentimes I awoke long before Helen to see them. With the kids grown and moved away, the house was quiet and empty, except for holidays. The blossoms, heavy with dew, glittered jewel-like in the morning sun. Mornings like these, with my flowers in bloom and alive with light and color, were truly a gift from God.

Depending on the ferocity and duration of winter, my azaleas usually began blooming in March or April, a feat they repeated faithfully every year. Their blossoms heralded the arrival and warmth of spring and to me symbolized renewal and life. The buds and blossoms of my garden became my own springtime Byzantine temple.

By 1990 Ianthe, who was now 34, began dating a Greek man, Steve Yeatras, and I became a big and enthusiastic supporter of this relationship. Perhaps I was overly occupied with seeing that Ianthe was married as a result of some guilt I may have felt over my sister Katina's own sacrifices. I don't know. For my peace of mind if not hers, though, Ianthe needed to be married and have a family of her own, and that was that. To me, Steve was an excellent candidate.

• • •

The summer of 1990, a special dinner was held in Washington. For the first time in America's history, the leader of over 300,000,000 Orthodox Christians—the Patriarch of the Orthodox Christian Church—would visit America. The Patriarch would be honored at a dinner downtown and accompanied by his bishops and archbishops, including my friend Iakovos, Archbishop of the Americas. Imbroz would come to America.

I had not seen Jimmy since he had visited my house for dinner over twenty years before, though I had followed his career with interest. He had prayed at Presidential inaugurations, marched hand in hand with Martin Luther King, Jr., in Selma, Alabama, in March 1965 in defiance of segregation, and was credited for building up the Orthodox Church in America. I could not let pass this opportunity to see him—who knew when our paths would cross again?

I bought tickets to the Patriarch's dinner for my entire family—including Ianthe and Steve. Time was racing by, and I made every effort to get all my children and grandkids there for what I knew would be a special night.

As we arrived at the Sheraton in Washington, an entourage of bishops passed directly in front of us dressed in black gowns and impressive headdresses. A moment later Ecumenical Patriarch Demetrius I of Constantinople appeared. An old man in his late-seventies, he was of slight stature with a beard that extended to his waist. Although he was born on Imbroz he was ten years older than I was and I never knew him. To think that my tiny island produced so many of my faith's religious leaders was a coincidence not lost on me. As he passed me I bowed my head and crossed myself in respect.

The ballroom at the Sheraton was packed with dignitaries and the faithful. Since this was the first trip by an Ecumenical Patriarch to the United States, many of the Orthodox faithful had travelled far to attend. Even President George H. W. Bush was there to give the keynote address, although he departed with his security detail shortly afterward, leaving the head table and the black-garbed, bearded bishops.

When the Patriarch rose from his seat to address the crowd I wondered if he would say anything about the problems, past or present, that the Church encountered at the hands of the Turks. It was a longstanding habit, for reasons I did not fully appreciate, to keep the mistreatment of the Church by the Turks out of public attention. The Patriarch's speech was conciliatory, appreciative, and short, failing to mention, even in passing, the lengthy persecution of Christians of Asia Minor. It was not lost on me that the Patriarch and his bishop would have to return to Turkey after the function.

After dinner the Patriarch, Archbishop, and bishops remained seated at the head table while the guests moved about and mingled. I signaled to Anthony and began moving from the back of the ballroom to the head table of bishops. As we approached, Archbishop Iakovos caught my eye and motioned to me.

"Chrysostomos, my friend," he exclaimed. "Come!" He gestured for us to go around the table and join him, and a minute later he welcomed us with open arms.

"Chrysostomos, it has been years since I've seen you."

His affectionate smile and warm facade seemed immediately familiar as I approached him, while his eyes surveyed me in a slow, nostalgic stare. Yes, it had been a long time. Our keen memories allowed us to embrace with childlike excitement.

"Too long, your Eminence," I replied, bowing. Then I brought Anthony forward and added, "Do you remember my son?"

Anthony bowed as the Archbishop replied, "Yes, Anthony—of course I remember him. When last I saw you, Anthony, you were a young man full of ideas and a little righteous anger."

"I remember all too well, Your Eminence," Anthony smiled, blushing.

In that moment of conversation I surveyed the Archbishop. Though the color of his hair and beard had faded to pure white, the glow in his eyes had not faded. We were two old men now, reunited for a brief moment in the twilight of our lives.

"Chrysostomos," the Archbishop said, turning his attention back to me, "allow me to present you to our Patriarch." With that he placed a hand on my shoulder and moved me toward Dimitris.

"Your All Holiness," he addressed the Patriarch, "may I present Chrysostomos Chrisostomides. He is from Imbroz. His father was Ioanni Chrisostomides."

"Ioanni Chrisostomides from Panayia? Yes, I knew your father, Chrysostomos. He was a good man. Come closer," he beckoned.

"Yes, Your All Holiness. My pleasure," I said, bowing deeply and kissing his hand.

The Patriarch placed his hands gently on my shoulders and righted me. "Let me see you," he said as I rose. "Yes, it has been many years, but you look like your father. May God be with you, Chrysostomos."

Deeply gratified by this small reference to my father, I murmured my thanks. Then the Patriarch turned to a bishop behind him. "May I introduce Bishop Demetrius Arhondonis. He is also from Imbroz. Demetrius, this is Chrysostomos Chrisostomides from Imbroz."

"My pleasure," the bishop responded. "Where on Imbroz are you from?"

"Panayia," I replied.

"I am from Agios Theodoros," he smiled. "And your last name is Chrisostomides?" I nodded in response. "Your sisters babysat me when I was small." I nodded again my surprise and acknowledgement.

Little did I know that when Patriarch Demetrius died, Demetrius Arhondonis would take the name Bartholomew I of Constantinople and become the next Patriarch of the Orthodox Christian faith, yet another Patriarch from Imbroz—and babysat by my sister Katina to boot.

As I moved to leave the table Jimmy turned to me. The light was shining on him in a way that seemed to create a halo on his snow-white hair and beard that flowed beneath the large, impressive headdress, and sparkled off his jewel-studded gold cross and staff. He looked dignified in his ethereal splendor. He seemed almost otherworldly, but when our eyes met again, I saw for a brief moment the boy I had befriended on Imbroz over sixty years earlier.

"Chrysostomos, my friend, it is so good to see you."

"The pleasure, Your Eminence, is all mine."

At that moment, the thought occurred to me that this might well be our last meeting. I think he sensed it, too, and our eyes exchanged this knowledge with a simple, poignant acceptance. For a moment he placed his arm on my shoulder, then our eyes disengaged.

I turned and left the table. That brief interlude with the bishops returned me to my past and my childhood and refreshed me. On this special evening, I gave something of my ancient Greek heritage to my children and their families. It was a proud night for me, mingling, as it did, my past, present, and future with the leadership of our Church. Imagine, three bishops, the leaders of our faith, all from the tiny island of Imbroz. When the Patriarch gave the closing prayer marking the end of the evening, all present felt they had been touched by the hand of God.

CHAPTER 23

Grandson's Interview

Do you think, O blue-eyed banditti,
because you have scaled the wall,
such an old mustache as I am
is not a match for you all!
I have you fast in my fortress,
and will not let you depart,
but put you down into the dungeon
in the round-tower of my heart.
And there will I keep you forever,
yes, forever and a day,
till the walls shall crumble to ruin,
and moulder in dust away!

—HENRY WADSWORTH LONGFELLOW, 1841

THAT FALL THE COUNTRY was also in the midst of a crisis. Saddam Hussein had attacked Kuwait in August 1990, and American troops were deployed to the Gulf region. The military expense coupled with our weakened banking system was enough to plunge the country into a recession. The causes were numerous, and the effects were predictably painful. I was suffering from vacancies, bank notes, and a leaking flat roof in need of repair.

It was September 1990. I had worked all summer for Jon at Anthony's Beer & Wine, making salads and rice pudding daily. In Ocean City there were no missiles, no troops, no war. The summer vacationers had gone home. Now, it was fishing season and, recession or not, I had a freezer to restock for winter.

In the morning I was readying my fishing gear when Dr. Bill Greco knocked at my door.

"Chris, I'm ready."

"Come on in, Bill," I called. Ever since Paul's illness and death, Bill and I often fished together. He knew exactly what to do and required very little supervision, which is more than I can say about some of my other companions.

"They're calling for fair weather," Bill said by way of greeting. "It should be a good one."

For a brief burst of time we were casting out one line as we were reeling in another. Over and over we performed this ballet of casting and reeling, laughing with exhilaration and excitement. Eventually the torrid pace began to subside, but our catch remained steady until, by early afternoon, we had hauled aboard nearly ninety fish: some croakers, but mostly trout.

"Chris," Bill said finally with happy exhaustion, "we've got to knock off. It's going to take us hours to clean this catch."

I popped open two beers and we both sat and sipped in silence, contemplating the beauty of God's creation.

"Bill," I mused a little later, "what more could life give? A beautiful day and two old men having the time of their lives outwitting these beautiful sea creatures. Fresh air, calm water, a gentle breeze, and the bounty of the sea: It is by God's grace we've been allowed to enjoy these things."

"We're lucky men, Captain." Bill smiled.

"Yes, we are, very lucky," I agreed.

We made our way toward port and home on the perfect Indian summer day, cutting through a mesmerizing, luminous sea that had kindly yielded two old fishermen a most generous bounty.

• • •

Operation Desert Storm wasn't the nation's only concern in 1991. The country also suffered through savings and loan closures and the near-failure of the American banking system. This in turn triggered a recession the following year. In 1992, with the country still in the grip of an economic downturn, voters ushered in a new president: the young Democrat and ex-governor of Arkansas, William Jefferson Clinton. If it is true that leaders reflect the societies they oversee, then we should question our own social and moral conditions before condemning the foibles of our elected leaders, I thought.

It is noteworthy that a young Greek Senator from Massachusetts died of cancer at this time as well. He had cautioned the nation on the dangers of an unbridled feeling of entitlement that he predicted would fracture our democracy one day. His name was Paul Tsongas.

The recession and the Gulf War would end, but a silent moral shift from traditional Christian beliefs to political definitions of what was socially correct was undermining traditional norms in America. The term "politically correct" was creeping into the American jargon, and "cultural diversity" became another phrase for strange and unprincipled behavior. For a culturally diverse person who spent his life trying to be American, I couldn't understand.

The working population remained apathetic as it was led deeper and deeper into the soothing political rhetoric of equality and notional fairness. After all, who would argue with these principles? No one said anything that might be considered "insensitive." Instead of individuals taking responsibility for their own beliefs, the government was going to make sure we all had the same one—for the good of all, of course.

The loss of any individual's human rights under any pretext is unscrupulous and fosters corruption. The diminution of God-given freedoms and rights would most certainly be followed in lockstep by lost welfare and opportunity. This social impairment would not be easily reversed. The precursors for a future crisis were in place.

Ironically, the genocide of the early twentieth century that annihilated almost three-quarters of the Christian population from Asia Minor had begun under the guise of a politically correct doctrine professing equality for all minorities, a democratic constitution, and the lessening of religious influence over the state. As then, this new group that had gained prominence over the political scene had intellectualized away the very chairs in which we sit. I was left wondering how my children and their children would face a future crisis, as we were becoming a nation of "entitled citizens" thoughtlessly granting government our responsibilities and ceding to government the corresponding liberties attached to those responsibilities.

At the turn of the prior century, the Young Turks had issued the same mumbo jumbo and after gaining power they passed gun control. Makes one wonder what the future for America holds.

• • •

Back in my own personal world the recession left me with many vacancies in my rental stores and a serious reduction in my income. I was in need of a loan. My son Jon had also borrowed a large sum of money to renovate Anthony's Beer & Wine two years earlier and, although the carryout was busy, Jon seemed unable to get the kind of return on his investment I would have expected.

In the summer of 1991, we had a blessing: Steve Yeatras asked my Ianthe to marry him. At 36, my little Cookie was finally getting married. I was ecstatic. Steve, who was a year older than Ianthe, treated her well and she seemed very happy. I felt marriage and a family would be the sobering ingredient needed to help them fashion a good future together.

"Chris, I want to invite Father John Travis, Ianthe's godparents, and of course their children, too," Helen told me one evening. "And Ianthe wants Father George Alexon to perform the service at Saint Katherine's, and you wanted to invite Father George Papaiouniou. Oh, and our friends Christina Regis, Stan and Stacia Mastaracus, Terry and Gus Decalas, Mary and Gus Bochanos, Elenitsa and George Karambelos, and..." The list went on and on.

It would be a proper Greek wedding for my little girl. I borrowed money and rented the ballroom at the Radisson in Alexandria in the fall of 1992 and planned all seven courses of the meal with the *maître d* myself. We had an open bar with *hors d'oeuvres* for two hours in the lounge. Over three hundred friends and relatives attended Ianthe and Steve's wedding and the formal dinner reception that followed. I was not an extravagant person, but when Greek fathers marry off their daughters, excess is the norm. At long last, my beautiful little girl was married.

• • •

I had interests other than stamps and fishing. A couple of years earlier my friend John Delta had involved me in the Hellenic Society of Constantinopolitans, and eventually I became its treasurer. The society was composed of a handful of Orthodox Christians of Greek descent who had survived the holocaust in Turkey seventy years before, and a couple of others who were younger, yet had immigrated from that part of the world.

The Hellenic Society of Constantinopolitans had about twenty members in the Washington area. Nine of us were actual survivors of the Christian holocaust in Anatolia from 1909 to 1923, and all of us actively attended the meetings. We survivors averaged in age from 75 to 89 and we were glad to be alive. We understood the fragility of life and wished only to share each other's company at these monthly meetings.

Like the Nazi Holocaust survivors, all of us were quiet about our survivor's guilt. Many of our families did not even know. Yet at our meetings, amongst ourselves, we spoke freely about the horrors so long ago which were branded in our memories. We were a small organization of professional working people—business owners, teachers, doctors, and the like—and, despite our age, we were still in awe of America and the freedoms she gave us. Our respect made us particularly sensitive to her change, no matter how small.

It was an interesting group and I enjoyed hearing the stories of the members very much. Their experiences as survivors of the Christian holocaust were often compelling. After church service on a Sunday near the holidays in 1992, I noticed a member of our group telling a familiar story of the 1922 Smyrna slaughter to a few members. I approached with interest, listening to the old man, in his eighties, recounting his family's story to a small crowd.

"When the slaughter started we were at home. The soldiers broke in and looted our house.... By the time they were done, they had seized all our valuables except for a few gold coins that Mama had sewn into our clothes the day before." I edged closer standing behind the man to hear more.

"Then the fires came. Papa and Mama packed our belongings and we joined the throngs in the streets.... We finally escaped the crowds and hid in a foundry by the docks. All around us were billowing clouds of black smoke, the stench of fires and charred flesh, and the screams of dying people. My two brothers, my parents, and I made our way to the docks where a Greek merchant ship flying an American flag took us aboard. This is how we escaped."

I had heard this story before but when? I tried not to stare but suddenly I realized who he was.

"Thomas Vasil?" I asked when there was a break in his story.

"Yes, who are you?" He was a slender man with a few white hairs combed back over a balding head, and as he looked my way he pushed his thick glasses higher on the bridge of his nose, which magnified his eyes to appear as large as the frames themselves.

"It's Christo Chrisostomides. Do you remember me?"

He came closer to me as the crowd moved on to other conversations. "Thomas, do you remember making a brief stop on the island of Imbroz after your family escaped Smyrna?"

"Yes," he nodded absently.

"That was my family. You came with your father and Bishop Iavakos to visit us."

"Chrysostomos," he stared back at me wide-eyed. The sheer coincidence left us speechless and smiling to be in each other's company. An improbable chance meeting.

Although Thomas was a member of the Hellenic Society of Constantantinopolitans, he rarely attended our meetings and I had never associated him with the boy I met so long ago.

The years and the sites we had seen flashed across our minds. Alive and in old age, our paths had crossed again in America. From that moment forward at the coffee socials following church, Thomas would always find his way to my side.

• • •

Hearing Thomas's story that day troubled me. I found myself thinking of the past more often than I wished. For the first time in many years I felt bitterness toward the Turks over what they had done to my family. In the coming weeks I even began to quarrel with Katina for signing over Papa's small house and store to the Turks when she left the island in the 1960s.

It wasn't the material loss that offended me most—the fields and other properties had gone to the Turks long before. Rather, it was that Papa's house was a symbol of his lifelong toil, a possession that dated back for generations. The loss seemed to disrespect Papa. Our small home was lost, yet it still represented to me Papa's unyielding protest to the conquest that surrounded it and now, after all these years, all we had left was a memory.

It struck me that the Jewish people had thankfully gotten some measure of justice in prosecuting their Nazi war criminals. They received public attention and even some reparation for loss of property, but very few people were informed enough to even acknowledge that a Christian genocide had occurred twenty years earlier in Turkey. Debates in Congress still rage on about whether it was even genocide. The world seems to prefer to view what happened with a blind and often ignorant eye. Powerful interests have worked long and hard to conceal the truth, keeping it hidden from public opinion, and soon, no one will be left to remember.

• • •

As Easter approached that year, I made a quick trip to Ocean City. I had ordered two legs of spring lamb, which I picked up along with other supplies for Easter dinner. I also went to see my old friend and creditor, Fred Parker, the president of Home Bank. I had an interest payment due on April 15th, but that wasn't what was on my mind. As soon as Fred and I had exchanged pleasantries I got straight to the point.

"Fred, I need to borrow another $10,000."

"You want me to put it against the stores?"

"Yes. You know that our business is in the summer, Fred. I'll take care of it then."

"I know you will," he nodded. "I'll defer the interest on the present balance until then. I'll have the papers ready for you to sign by Friday. Will that work for you?"

"Thanks, Fred. That will be fine."

• • •

One evening shortly after this, Sultana called. We went through the usual greetings, asking about everyone's health, but when we got to Taki, Sultana's voice broke.

"I am worried, Chrysostomos. Taki is not well. There is something wrong with his intestines. He should have surgery, but he won't go. . . ."

I had no idea Taki was not well, and the news was unpleasant. I spoke a few words to soothe my sister, then asked to speak with Taki. A few seconds later I heard his voice.

"Hello, Chrysostomos. Long time since I speak with you," he said in English, his familiar, heavy Greek accent ringing in my ears. As I had with Sultana, Taki and I went through the familiar ritual of inquiring how everyone was doing. "How are you and Helen, the children and grandchildren?" he asked.

"Everyone is fine, Taki. And your kids and grandkids?"

"Very fine, Chrysostomos, very fine."

"And you, Taki, how are you?"

"I'm all right, Chrysostomos," Taki told me, then paused.

"To tell you the truth, a few months ago I passed some blood in my urine. The doctor did a test and thought he saw something, then they did the test again and the results were not conclusive."

"I see… and how do you feel?"

"I'm better, Chrysostomos. It's nothing, really."

In that moment I knew what Taki already knew: that his illness was something very serious.

"Can I do anything?"

"No, no, Chrysostomos, nothing, thank you. Nothing at all."

"Take care of yourself, Taki," I said. "Please take care of yourself."

"Don't worry about me, Chrysostomos. I thank you for your concern, but please don't worry, I am fine. God willing, I am fine."

"Goodbye, my friend," I told him.

"Goodbye, Chrysostomos, my good friend."

Taki and I were Greek Christians from Imbroz. We believed that when it was our time, we would go with God, and yet we would be the last to admit that time was approaching. For a moment I felt my own mortality and I realized how little time there was left to accomplish all I wanted to do.

Within a month, Taki had been hospitalized. A week later his condition became grave. Peter, Taki and Sultana's son, took his family up to New York to be with his father. It turns out he had abdominal cancer. Taki was in a lot of pain, then he was gone.

I gathered my family, and we drove to New York for the funeral. It was quite a trip. The children thought highly of their Uncle Taki. I remembered Taki in his sailor's uniform, cap in hand, asking permission to marry Sultana, our time as newlyweds in northern Virginia, drinking and singing, our picnics in Great Falls with the kids.

Taki's passing was another link in the chain of my life now broken, and I spent the next few days contemplating our shared past. I was carrying forward, and he had moved on in a different direction.

• • •

The following autumn my grandson Brian asked me if he could interview me for a school project. I was amused at the idea of being interviewed—even if it was by my nine-year-old grandson—and interested to know what his questions would be.

Brian arrived with a sheet of paper and a small tape recorder and, in a solemn voice, he hit the record button and began, matter-of-factly.

"What country are you from?"

Easy so far. "Greece," I replied into the tape recorder.

"What was your school like?"

"Well, the school we had on our island was an elementary school. It went up through sixth grade, and I attended through fourth."

"How far away was the school?"

"The school, from our house, was more than a mile.... We used to walk. We didn't have any transportation like here."

"Were the teachers very strict?"

"I'd say so. They were very strict if you did something wrong. You'd get spanked in school, which of course you don't have here."

"What was your childhood like?" Brian asked.

This question was more difficult, and I hesitated a minute.

"Ah, my childhood was not exactly what you all have here. You know, we had to work harder, had to do a lot of chores, help the family, because we were not as rich as in this country."

I paused again, thinking for a moment of the many difficulties we had under the Turks, yet it was nothing for a school project. How could I tell Brian about the purging of the Christians, the terrible deprivation and loss? How could I tell him that our language was banned, our records stolen, and our property confiscated? The fact was that I couldn't tell him. There was no point in dredging all that up for a child who would not yet understand.

Sensing that I had more to say, Brian looked at me expectantly, but I shook my head. 'That's it," I said.

"Okay." he fumbled a bit with his paper.

"What were your houses like?"

"They were not exactly what you have here. They were very small. We did not have the facilities we have in this country, of course, like running water. Most of the houses had no toilets. Toilets, they were outside, you know. In our little house we had only two rooms, and in one room I used to sleep with my three siblings, and my father and mother used to sleep in the other room."

"What traditional food did you eat?"

"Well, the foods we had there... we didn't have the beef that's here. It was more olives, vegetables, cheese, fruit, and occasionally fish or lamb."

"Did you go fishing or hunting?"

"Yes, we used to fish, of course, and hunt, too."

"Where did you go to get your food?" Brian asked.

"We grew most of our food, but we had a market and if you needed anything you went there."

"What kind of games did you play?"

"We didn't have too many games like you have here, believe me," I told him. "All this... forget about electronics and everything else. I had one ball which we threw and kicked around."

"Okay." Brian nodded in agreement. "What sports did you play?"

I shook my head. "We didn't have sports. You're talking a few years back. We had soccer... and just chasing each other around the field."

Brian nodded his understanding, a mature nine-year-old ready to press on with his interview. "What kind of money did you have?"

"It was Greek currency... drachmas, and, later, the Turkish lira."

"What kind of technology did you have?"

"Oh, technology." I paused. "We didn't have much technology," I smiled. "The typical transportation we had was donkeys and, ah, stage coaches—you know, something like that—and no electricity when I left."

"What age were you when you left your country?"

"When I left it was during the war. I was almost 28 years old when I left to come to America." I glossed over the years in Constantinople and the years prior to that on my uncle's island.

"What did you do after you left your island?"

"I came to the Turkish Embassy and I worked at the Embassy for three years. Then I got my papers and stayed here."

"Do you have any other interesting facts you can tell me?"

That was a good question, I thought, but I wasn't sure how to answer. "The interesting facts, really…" I paused, then began again. "There is no comparison with what we have here… and especially when I was a child many years ago. There is no comparison with this country. You can't know or even imagine how lucky we are here. Remember that."

"Where in Greece were you born?"

"On an island in the Aegean Sea. The name was Imbroz Island."

My grandson smiled and lowered his eyes to the tape recorder. "This is Brian Christ's interview" he intoned, "October 14, 1991."

CHAPTER 24

Hauntings of My Youth

Then doth thy sweet and quiet eye
look through its fringes to the sky,
blue—blue—as if that sky let fall
a flower from its cerulean wall.
I would that thus, when I shall see
the hour of death draw near to me,
hope, blossoming within my heart,
may look to heaven as I depart.
—WILLIAM CULLEN BRYANT, 1832

IN THE BLINK OF AN EYE it seemed that the summer of 1993 passed. Helen and I went home to Virginia where I caught up on things that needed doing. Later in the fall I returned briefly to Ocean City to take care of some business at the bank and, of course, to fish one last time. When I returned to Ocean City I had many thoughts on my mind and much to do.

The recession was lifting but I still had not leased my vacant stores, and one of my tenants was trying to sell his restaurant. I had managed to pay interest on the money I had borrowed from the bank once for Ianthe's wedding and a second time to help her and Steve buy a house. I was treading water on both sides of the balance sheet, yet I was too busy that summer to worry.

At the end of the season I drove down to the southern edge of town. Four blocks beyond 1st Street on the right-hand side was Tony's Fruit Stand, the old landmark that I had frequented for decades.

"Hello," I said, climbing out of the car.

"Hi," an unfamiliar voice replied.

"What do you need?" a young man arranging the fruit asked.

Tony's absence overshadowed the fresh fruit arrangements and hung heavily in the air. Seeing the familiar flies feasting on the fruit served as a reminder of the shortness of time and the fragility of life.

The young man told me Tony had passed away. I wish I had heard sooner so I could have paid my respects, but how would I have known? Our paths only crossed during the brief summer seasons, yet we were good friends for brief moments over many years. Our camaraderie was forged among honeydews and cantaloupes. I knew him as "Tony the Fruit Man" and he knew me as "Ocean City Chris."

The bounty of fruit stood starkly against the decades of summers past. Years of memories compressed to fleeting moments of time. For that instant, nothing was the same. The smell of fresh fruit was bittersweet. I lifted one ripe apple and then another, making my selection, breathing the scent of old times, of memories past. What was happening?

I was 76 years old. The friends I made in my new life were beginning to pass on as well. My routine through the summer and fall that year were the same, yet I felt almost detached from my life, as if I were viewing frames of still-life photos in a kaleidoscopic manner.

The next day I awoke to clear blue October skies and warm breezes—a perfect fishing day. I couldn't overlook the allure of a warm, calm Indian Summer day. I packed my gear and, dressed in sneakers, a windbreaker, and my fishing cap, I headed out to sea alone to soak up the solitude of sun and sea one more time, a solitary fisherman awed by the calm.

Within thirty minutes I rounded the point and faced the inlet. With my twin-engine outboard I cut through crystal reflections on water set against a clear blue sky and broke out into the ocean, heading for the ten-mile buoy and some trout. At the buoy I cut the engine, dropped two lines with double hooks, and waited for a bite.

I left all of life's problems at the shore when I fished. An unnatural calm had quieted the void. While the sun warmed me, the sea gently rocked me in my little boat. A long time ago I was a poor island boy whose family had lost everything, and now, half a world and a lifetime away, I was a man with plenty, but short on time. At that moment I felt detached from the scene, as if the water around me, although just inches away, was as distant as the Aegean Sea.

While I fished I touched the relic coin my father had given me the better part of a century before, and which I still kept pinned close to my heart every day. My fingers played over the ancient surface of the coin, this relic from my past, this generational hand-me-down from Papa, and I prayed. I felt in my heart that this coin had always been my source of inner strength, my inspiration, and my connection.

As I returned through the inlet later that afternoon with my catch of two fish, there was an uncanny calm where the bay met the ocean—the place where tempests had often raged in the past. The mild fall breeze whispered of serenity, unable to stir either water or sound. The bay was a pristine glass lake reflecting the warm late-summer sun as my small vessel cut a path to carry me home.

I cleaned the fish I'd caught on my dock and enjoyed a glorious dinner of trout that night, then prepared my things to leave the next morning and went to bed.

My car meandered down a vacant Coastal Highway the next morning as I headed out west, back home to Virginia for the winter. It had been thirty-eight years, half of my life, since I first crossed the Chesapeake Bay to set foot on this sunny seaside city, a world so far removed from my beloved Imbroz, yet a place I had come to love just as much. Ocean City was the shining paradise of my second life. I raised a family and built a business there, and much of what I loved, much of what I had achieved, was reflected in my narrow, sandy, sunlit home.

I slowed the car over the Division Street bridge leading out of town, stretching out those few fleeting minutes as long as I could, breathing in the salty air. As I watched the seagulls spin and soar over the blue waters of the sea, a drizzle began to fall. I know nothing is perfect and that each day serves up a new challenge, but that is part of the song of life, the high notes and the low. I took momentary survey of my work-worn body, then, with an uncharacteristic sigh, surveyed the sea. As I continued over the bridge westward toward Virginia that day, images of sea and sand were slowly swept away by the rhythmic pulsing wipers.

• • •

"Are you coming for Thanksgiving?" I asked my son Jon during a routine phone call one afternoon.

"Yes, Dad. I'll be there Wednesday, for sure."

"Did the beauty salon give you a check?"

"No, they didn't, Dad."

"How about the photo shop?"

"No, nothing there, either."

"Well, if you get anything from them, deposit it and let me know."

"Okay, Dad. See you Wednesday."

To my great regret, he was 43 and still had not married. On the other hand, though, it was his life and I knew I could do little about it. Funny, how different my attitude was towards my unwed daughter as compared to my son.

The family life I was deprived of in my youth was something I never got enough of now with my children and recently my grandchildren, no matter what their ages. My elder years had finally afforded me the opportunity to spend time with my family and I wished to give them every free moment of my time.

On Thanksgiving Day Anthony and Lee Ann arrived first with their children. I greeted them warmly, with kisses for Lee Ann and the children, who threw their arms around me and gave me hugs. Each moment with them was a godsend.

For a while they chatted, sipped their drinks, and munched on shrimp appetizers while I shuffled back and forth preparing to serve various foods. Then I ushered my family into the dining room and seated everyone around the table. This year Katelyn, now seven, offered to say grace.

"Thank You, God, for the food Granddad made," she said. "Amen."

I'd anticipated that the moment would be fleeting. Jon offered some more solemn words of prayer.

"Thank You, God, for allowing us to celebrate another year together and for looking over us. Thank you for the beautiful food you have provided. Please protect us and grant us good health for another year if it is Your will. Amen."

"Amen," my family chorused.

Then I felt inspired. "I will offer a toast," I said, lifting my wineglass. "To all my children and grandchildren: to your health and happiness, and may your future successes be many."

The older children raised their wineglasses to mine in acknowledgement, the younger ones their milk and Sprite cans, toasting each other, and me, and the festive occasion of being together that Thanksgiving Day.

• • •

One evening that winter I attended a meeting of the Hellenic Society of Constantinopolitans in Washington. Dr. Delta brought the meeting to order and asked me to make my report as treasurer. I kept my update brief and to the point.

"We have $584 in our treasury," I said, glancing at my notes, "and we plan to hold our New Year's dinner dance this year at the Westpark Marriott. Any proceeds after expenses will be donated to reopen the Constantinople Orphanage," one of the charities to which we donated.

Dr. Delta, as secretary, asked if there were any other business and then adjourned the meeting, ushering in a social hour of the members who gathered that evening. The group buzzed for several moments, exchanging gossip and news of the day. It was only a matter of time before someone regressed to discuss the past.

Basil Assakopoulos, a research engineer and academic in his early sixties, described a story I knew all too well. "During the two days of terror in Constantinople in September of 1955, we lost everything. Many Christians were killed. Graves were desecrated, businesses were destroyed, and many women were raped. The newspapers at the time reported the mobs were out of control, but it was common knowledge that Turkey incited and even organized the mobs.

It was Sedat Semavi, a Turkish Jew, who, along with his relatives, published the two dominant newspapers in Constantinople in the fifties," he explained. "In September of 1955 the *Hürriyet Daily News* published a fake news story that stirred the mob concerning an alleged bombing of the Turkish consulate in Thessaloniki, Greece, where Atatürk was born. With the government's tacit support, two days of violence erupted and Christians were attacked and killed. Dozens of Christians were killed, some 200 were raped, and just over 3,000 Christian businesses were destroyed."

Hurriyat Daily is widely read to this day, I thought.

Basil turned to me and asked, "Chrysostomos, weren't you a child during the holocaust?"

"Yes, I was very young. It was a long time ago, Basil."

"Do you remember much of it?"

"No not much." The truth was, when I chose to, I remembered more than I would admit. Mama and Papa, our tiny island of Imbroz, or Gökçeada as they call it now, a lost relic of Byzantium—they are all lost to religious persecution and the passage of time. Eleven centuries of Christian culture was extinguished. 4,000,000 poor souls were erased.

Basil captured the attention of a small group that evening. Though Basil was too young to have known the horrors of the genocide firsthand, he described them as if he were there.

"In 1908 the Turks put forth a supposed democratic constitution and proclaimed that all Christian minorities throughout the Ottoman Empire would have equal rights. After the Balkan Wars of 1912–1913, when Thrace was taken back by Greece, some people of Jewish ancestry left Salonika and migrated to Turkey. They were the masterminds of the Christian genocide. Within this group of Salonika Jews were certain Young Turks who became the new leaders of Turkey. They first passed gun control laws and disarmed the Christians, then initiated the Christian holocaust," he paused. "Later Salonika became known as the 'Mother of Israel.'" For a moment he reminded me of Uncle Dimitris.

"Yes," I interrupted, "although that may be true, the Jewish people have been widely persecuted and suffered a horrific genocide themselves." Not sure whether it was a question or a statement, I let my words hang. Basil continued undeterred.

"Parading as secular reformers, the Young Turks gave assurances to the rest of the world that they were separating government from religion and civilizing Turkey, but, as you all know, nothing could have been further from the truth. They were engaging in ethnic cleansing, and the rest of the world was too busy or too preöccupied to care. 4,000,000 unarmed Christians were murdered by the Young Turks. By 1923 ninety-three percent of the 5,500,000 Christians in Turkey had been erased, exiled, fled, or exchanged. Only 400,000 Christians were left."

I noticed a gentle tap of my shoulder. It was Thomas Vasil, who had joined the meeting late. "Hi, Thomas, how do you feel?" I asked in a hushed tone. He was over 80 now and I had heard he was having health problems.

"I am fine, Christo, thank you." Thomas sat by my side and we both listened as Basil recounted the horrors of our youth.

"There have been many genocides during the century that have followed ours," Basil offered, and continued to detail a chronology of genocides. "There were 7,000,000 who perished in Stalin's genocidal starvation, the Holodomer, in Russia from 1932–1933, followed by 1,200,000 executions during the Great Terror or Great Purge of 1937–1938. Then came Hitler's Holocaust in Germany from 1933 through World War II when nearly 6,000,000 Jews perished. From 1958–1962, during Mao Zedong's Great Leap Forward, 45,000,000 Chinese perished. Genocides continued during the century: Bangladesh in 1971, Cambodia from 1975–1979, East Timor from 1975–1999, Bosnia from 1991–1995, and Rwanda in 1994."

"Hopefully people in power in the next century will learn from these senseless murders by evil players in evil governments. Why can't we learn to live in peace with each other?" Thomas asked Basil.

Neither he nor anyone had an answer.

"Sometimes people go awry and pure evil manifests itself in genocides. Some of us experienced this in Turkey and then we saw the cycle repeat itself, later in Russia and Germany with Stalin and Hitler, then in China with Mao Tse-tung. All were irrational and pure evil. These were all times when the sanctity of and respect for life was forgotten." I said.

"Governments exterminating groups of their own citizens under any pretext is pure evil. There is nothing more uncivilized," Thomas said. "Shadows in my memory, all the poor lost souls. Will they ever be remembered? Will people ever know?"

"The day will come, Thomas. People will know," I responded.

"I only hope one day the world will know what happened in Turkey and who was at fault," Thomas lamented.

"Although we may not be there to see it, I am certain one day the world will know," I said.

"Nothing under the sun is perfect. God in His infinite wisdom has made mankind a very twisted puzzle. All of us—Jews, Christians, and Muslims alike—fall prey to the pursuit of senseless power. Power when unbounded equals pure evil. Sometimes even basic kindness eludes us. We must remember the golden rule: do unto others as you would have them do unto you. Our efforts confirm our civility," I offered those words, which brought our digression into the past to an end.

Later when I was alone Basil took me aside. "Chris, here's a book on the genocide that I'd like you to read," he said, pressing the thick volume into my hands. "Today although the Patriarchate stubbornly remains in Constantinople there are less than 300,000 Christians left in Turkey."

"Let the ghosts of the past rest in peace." I thanked him for the book and information. Exhausted from the familiar conversation, I decided to go home for the night.

For the ten-odd years I was a member of the Hellenic Society of Constantinopolitans, I don't know of one of our survivors who talked of the Christian genocide in Anatolia to our families or friends in America. Except for an occasional question from my older son who would pester me or my sister Katina, the genocide was certainly not discussed within my family. We all felt privileged to have lived our lives in America as citizens and for that matter to be alive.

That was the last time I saw Thomas, who passed away shortly thereafter at 82. The survivor of Smyrna I had met as a boy and reunited with so many years later was called home.

• • •

The Hellenic Society of Constantinopolitans New Year's dinner dance was approaching, and I began to round up my family for the event. I called Ianthe and told her I had tickets if she could make it.

"I wish we could, Daddy, but Steve has to work late and—" Abruptly she switched topics. "Daddy, what's wrong with you?"

"Wrong?"

"Mother said you have been sick."

"Oh, I have a cold."

"Take care of yourself. Please, Daddy."

"I will, Cookie. Don't worry."

After I talked with her, I called Anthony, who promised to come.

"I'm glad Anthony is coming with us, Helen. I want to introduce him to more of the members."

She nodded. "Yes, it's more fun when the children come."

That evening Helen and I met Anthony, Lee Ann, and the kids at the nearby Westpark Marriott for the New Year's dance. We didn't discuss the past much at this year's dance, but we did have fun. The turnout was pretty good—over seventy people attended the event, including about ten kids. I took Anthony around and introduced him to a number of other Society members.

I had been thinking quite a lot about Anthony's growing family. A neighbor had pointed out a house to me that was in a different development, but just one block away from mine. It was a split-level, about 2,400 square feet. I thought it would be perfect for his growing family and I had mentioned it to Anthony before Christmas. His attendance that evening reminded me to ask him about it.

"I drove by the house the other day," he said casually. "It seems pretty nice."

"Pursue it, Anthony," I urged him. "The old lady who lived there died, so maybe her heirs will sell for a reasonable price."

"Okay, Dad," he said. "I'll check it out." Suddenly, he smiled.

The dance was too small to merit a live band, but we had taped music and, before I knew it, I was holding hands with my two beautiful granddaughters who had joined the circle and were dancing to the music of a Greek mandolin. "One, two, kick… one, two, kick," I repeated along with them laughing.

Here I was, an old man dancing with his two lovely granddaughters. What more fun could I imagine?

The dance was a bit more exhausting for me than usual. That night Helen and I stayed up late to watch the ball drop in Times Square.

"I'm tired," Helen yawned.

"Only ten more minutes," I told her, handing her a glass of champagne.

"Shouldn't we wait until midnight?"

"Well, it's almost midnight. In fact, it's already midnight in other parts of the world."

"Well, that's a thought," Helen smiled and took my hand in hers.

"Helen, remember when we were first starting out? Remember the boarding house?"

"And how we used to leave the milk on the window sill to keep it cold?" she added.

"Ah, yes," I chuckled. "The good old days. We were so happy to get an apartment with a kitchen. Do you remember the Tyler Garden Apartments?"

"Oh yes, with the paper-thin walls you could hear your neighbors through," she added.

"And the rambler," I added. "Our first home."

Helen nodded. "I miss that house, except..."

"Except what?"

"Except, you were never there. I felt like a single parent, raising the children alone," she said, beginning a replay of old complaints, but lacking the conviction of a current battle.

"My gosh, still talking about that. We've had a good life, Helen," I told her. "God has been good to us. We have our children and grandchildren, and we have our health. My life has by some measures been more difficult than most, but I feel nothing but proud and blessed."

"Oh, Chris."

In Times Square the crowd counted off the last ten seconds of the old year as the ball descended. At the stroke of midnight, I raised my glass to Helen.

"Happy 1994, Helen."

After forty-six years, she was still my Elenitsa, once my burning passion, and now my life's companion and confidant. I took her small, careworn face in my hands and looked deeply into her familiar eyes as I kissed her with the warm emotions of past and present.

"Happy New Year, Chris," she said.

• • •

One day in the new year my old friend Lincoln Vance called. For years he had been caring for his wife, Kitty, and was now mourning her recent death. Helen answered the phone and talked to him first, so by the time she gave the phone to me Lincoln knew I was not exactly well.

"How are you feeling?" he asked right away. "Helen sounded worried."

"Well, I have the flu," I told him.

"It's not anything more serious, is it?"

"No, just a bad cold. Listen, Lincoln," I said briskly, changing the subject, "as soon as the weather improves, we must go out for coffee and talk."

"You bet, Chris. It will be my pleasure." Lincoln paused, then added, "I have a lot of respect for you, Chris, and I always enjoy your company. Take care of yourself and I'll see you soon."

Not long after my conversation with Lincoln, a second ice storm swept the area, and for the first two weeks of February a weather pattern of extremely cold temperatures kept everything frozen. My flu seemed to parallel the weather—the colder it got, the worse I felt. Just climbing the stairs of my home left me weak and out of breath. I began to wonder if I would ever see the bloom of my azaleas again.

The freezing rain weighed down the power lines, toppled trees, and left a glaze of ice on the hill surrounding my home, making it impossible to come and go until the weather broke. At least we still had electricity. Many families were without power.

After a week of being frozen in, Anthony came to see if we needed anything, driving carefully over the ice-covered streets into our cul-de-sac. As soon as he saw me, a frown creased his forehead.

"How are you feeling, Dad? You don't look so good," he added, sounding concerned.

I shrugged. "I'm okay. I still have that cold."

"He hasn't felt good for over two weeks," Helen interjected. Anthony looked at me in concern.

"You need to go to the doctor," he said.

"I've been to the doctor," I told him. "I'll be fine. Look, I want to take you and Lee Ann and Ianthe and Steve and all the kids out for your mother's birthday. She's going to be seventy-two, you know."

"Dad, no, you don't have the money to do that right now."

My son was right, although I didn't like to admit it. "Well then, would you prefer to come over here for dinner?"

"Yes, we'd like that, but I don't want you to wear yourself out."

"I'm not about to do that. I'll prepare something easy, nothing special, so don't worry."

I could see Anthony was not convinced. "Where's your snow shovel, Dad? I want to clear your walk and driveway."

"I'll get to it later…"

"No, Dad, you don't need to do that. Is it out in the garage?"

I told him where to find the shovel, and then I stood at the window and watched as he scraped my driveway free of ice. When he left that afternoon, I reminded him about his mother's birthday and told him to arrive at two o'clock on Sunday. Then I called Jon in Ocean City.

"I want you to come up next Sunday for your mother's birthday."

"I don't think I can make it."

"Yes, you can," I said firmly. "It's your mother's birthday."

Actually, this was an unusual request. Normally, I did not make such a big deal over our birthdays—Helen's or mine—especially when it came to Jon, who had a long way to come.

"Is there any special reason why I need to come?" he asked finally.

"Yes," I told him sharply, "because I *want* you to come."

The truth was I did not completely understand why this was so important to me. We had been together for Christmas and our usual protocol called for a gathering at Easter in the spring. It was only late February, but for some reason I felt an urgency to bring everyone together for Helen's birthday, and if that meant arguing with Jon, so be it.

"Okay, Dad," he sighed. "I'll be there."

Relieved that all the children and grandchildren would come, I retired to my office to put some bills in order. That evening as I went through my bills, I realized that for the first time in twenty-two years I had not sent in my monthly check or order form for my 1994 commemorative stamps.

I wondered for a moment what would happen to my stamps after I was gone. No one in my family had shown an interest in them. Well, that was okay, I decided. The repetitive ice storms and my recent sickness had distracted me. Besides, money was a little tight. I would have to take a pass on my stamps this year.

The frigid weather and my weakened condition had brought on a temperamental introspection that was uncharacteristic for me. The foreboding insistence with which I had made Helen's birthday a family gathering in spite of the inclement weather gave the event an air of unintended urgency, the urgency of a tired old man short on time.

CHAPTER 25

Twilight

O Captain! my Captain!
Our fearful trip is done;
The ship has weather'd every rack,
The prize we sought is won;
The port is near, the bells I hear…
—WALT WHITMAN, 1865

WHEN THE ICE FINALLY MELTED, a cold, foggy drizzle shrouded the streets. The inclement drear made me wonder whether I would see the bud and bloom of my flowery little friends again. My symptoms had improved enough to allow everyone to arrive for their mother's birthday celebration in late February.

Helen made the same lemon pound cake she always made for my birthday, and I prepared a simple meal with what was on hand—baked chicken, broccoli, pita bread, and *kasari* cheese. I was a bit embarrassed by the ordinary meal. The simplicity was out of character for me, and I found myself apologizing for the sparse spread.

"Ianthe, I'm sorry I don't have much."

"Oh, Daddy, don't be silly," she said. "This is fine. We came to see you and Mom anyway."

When we sat down at the table, I took a long lingering look at all the faces around me. The prayer I offered was simple.

"Thank You, God, for bringing us together. Thank you for this food. Please grant us health throughout the year and watch over us. Amen."

"Amen," my family chorused.

I sat my beautiful granddaughters on either side of me. Brian sat next to his sister Katelyn, and Ianthe and Steve's baby Krislyn sat in her high chair beside her mother, but near enough so I could see her. Much of dinner I spent in humorous discourse with little Ashley, showing her how to hold her fingers to make the sign of the cross, and then teasing her until she squealed with laughter.

"I'm going to squeeze the juice out of you," I joked, hugging her tightly in a big bear hug.

"No, Granddad," she protested between giggles. "No, no, no."

Eventually we cleared the table and I brought the cake, complete with a single lit candle, to the dining room.

"Happy birthday to you…" I sang, and soon the rest of the family joined me, singing and honoring Helen on her 72nd birthday.

That evening when Ianthe bundled up Krislyn and prepared to leave, I held her close for an unusually long time.

"Good night, Daddy," she said a little quizzically, kissing my cheek.

"Good night, Cookie. You and Steve take good care of Krislyn."

"We will, Daddy," she smiled, and a minute later they were gone.

By now Anthony and Lee Ann were getting ready to go. I watched as Anthony snugged a cap over Brian's head, then I touched his arm and took him aside.

"Anthony, what have you done about the house?" referring to the one around the corner.

"I spoke with the people who own the house," Anthony told me, "and this week I'm going to see it."

"You need a bigger house to raise your children," I told him.

"I'm looking into it, Dad," Anthony smiled. "I promise."

Before I could reply, the children came up to hug me goodbye. Lee Ann kissed Helen and then embraced me. I loved her as if she were my own daughter, and returned her hug with one of my own. Then I turned to embrace my son. Even though he towered over me, I sometimes felt like he was still my little boy. "Take care of your family," I said, reluctant to let him go.

"I will, Dad." Anthony pulled away from me a bit. "How are you feeling?" he asked, his voice low. "You should get checked out, Dad."

I knew he noticed that I still wasn't quite myself. "I'm okay, Anthony," I tried to reassure him. "I have a cold, that's all. Don't worry about me."

Jon came next. "You're leaving in the morning?" I asked him.

"Yes, Dad," he said, eyeing me with a familiar concern.

Later that night Helen and I spent a quiet hour watching TV and reading.

"Thank you, Chris," she said, putting aside her book and standing up. "I had a lovely time. It was so good to have all the children here today, wasn't it?"

"Yes it was," I smiled, poking the smoldering ash that remained in the fireplace. Fires still kept us warm, not to discredit electric or gas heaters.

"I'm going to go to bed," she said, kissing my cheek.

"I'll be up shortly," I told her, patting her hand.

I watched the news on TV and then followed Helen upstairs. Halfway up the steps I paused and looked down into the hall. This was my home and I loved it.

• • •

My flulike symptoms grew in intensity in the coming days and Helen had me in to see Dr. Anderson, a heart specialist who had seen me over recent years, but the only thing he determined that I had was bradycardia, or a slow heartbeat. Dr. Anderson suggested I get a pacemaker, but I replied that black coffee with a tad of skim milk had been sufficient to get my heart going each and every morning.

"Well, Chris, you sound a little congested, but otherwise you seem okay. I want you to walk on the treadmill for a while."

The treadmill, which was similar to the one at the health club I had recently joined, was wired to give the doctor all sorts of information about my cardiovascular system. The results of the tests showed nothing wrong, but the doctor prescribed an antibiotic, just in case. I also picked up some cold medicine.

My weakness continued intermittently, however, and I soon came to believe that something was indeed very wrong. I did not speak of it to Helen, preferring instead to continue my daily activities, though at a slower pace. No matter what physical blows life dealt you, a positive attitude only served to brighten your prospects, which in turn improved the condition. There was nothing to be gained by turning morose.

I self-medicated with generous servings of hot honey-lemon tea and various home remedies, but nothing really helped. I tried to remain quiet, watching TV and reading, and I spent a couple of icy evenings thumbing through an interesting book I had ordered on Thrace. It covered the troubled eleven-year period from 1912–1923, beginning with the Balkan Wars and spanning World War I.

Late that evening after Helen had gone to bed, I picked up the first volume of my *Britannica* and turned to a passage about "Achilles: Son of mortal Peleus, king of Myrmidond, and sea nymph, Thetis. Achilles was the bravest, handsomest, and greatest warrior of the Army of Agamemnon in the Trojan War…." Soon my thoughts strayed from my reading.

I closed my eyes for a moment, visualizing my azaleas in bloom, hoping that I would soon see them and the flowers that adorned my island.

Perhaps I fell into a doze, for suddenly I was on the porch of our small home on Imbroz. I could see Papa and hear his voice. "Then Agamemnon got into an argument with his greatest warrior Achilles," he was saying.

"Papa," I responded. "It has been over seventy years. I am not a child. I am an old man now. I'm sorry, Papa." I shut my *Britannica.*

As I walked up the stairs that evening, I felt short of breath. I knew that my time was short. Soon God would call me home, but I felt no regret. I had led the life that Mama and Papa had wished for me, and I suddenly felt their presence very near.

A few moments later as I dressed for bed, I kissed the relic coin Papa had given me so long ago and whispered a familiar prayer: "Thank You, God, for giving me health and strength. Thank you for my family: my wife, our children, and our grandchildren—all the flowers in my life. Amen."

In the darkness, Helen stirred. "Chris, did you say something?"

"No, dear, nothing," I reassured her. "Go back to sleep."

• • •

In mid-March the temperature rose sufficiently to once again reduce the ice to a messy slush. One evening I called Jon.

"Have you talked to MacGilligot?" He had a small seafood restaurant that sold mostly crabs and was our tenant.

"Not yet."

"See if you can get him to give us a rent check. I have to pay the bank this month."

"Okay, Dad. I'll do that tomorrow. How are you feeling?"

"Not bad," I told him, hedging a little. "How about you?"

"I'm fine. I have a Civil War reenactment coming up in a couple of weeks."

"Jon," I said suddenly, "you know how we prepare the turkey at Thanksgiving, the lamb and rice pilaf at Christmas and Easter? I mean, you know how we do it, don't you?"

"Sure, Dad. Why do you ask?"

"I want you to continue the tradition every year with your brother and sister. Do you understand?"

"Of course, but—"

"Just remember," I said firmly, cutting him off. "I want you to stay together as a family."

"Yes, Dad. Of course, I promise."

"And be sure to take care of yourself."

"I will, Dad," Jon said, sounding puzzled. "Is anything wrong?"

"No, no, I'm just giving out some fatherly advice. I want you to try to straighten yourself up."

Everyone knew this was code for getting married. Jon knew I wanted him to marry and have a family—I had made no secret of that.

"Don't worry about me, Dad," he said, and I could hear the smile in his voice. "I'll be fine."

Anthony had put a down payment on the house one block away from ours. "Dad can you come over and help us move in next Sunday?"

"I will come over after church this Sunday.

Later that evening I called Ianthe.

"I'm coming over to plant azaleas tomorrow," I told her. "They're from my garden."

"That will be fine, Daddy. I'm glad you're coming."

"You'll like the azaleas," I told her. "You'll see how beautiful they are when they bloom."

Digging up and replanting two azaleas the next morning was a tougher job than I had expected it to be. I was both tired and relieved when the planting was complete. Although my body was becoming quite frail, my spirits lifted as I worked in the sunshine and saw the early signs of spring all around me. Soon my beautiful friends would bloom.

When I finished planting I went inside to say goodbye to my daughter.

"Thank you, Daddy," she smiled. "I can't wait to see them bloom."

"Take care of yourself," I said as I embraced her. "Take care of little Krislyn, too." I was flattered that Ianthe had named her sweet daughter after me.

"I will, Daddy," she said, hugging me back. "I'll see you soon."

"Perhaps not," I replied as I prepared to leave. "I may not see you for a while."

For an instant Ianthe appeared startled by my words. Then she shook her head and smiled.

"Goodbye, Daddy." She waved, brushing her hand in the air, dismissing such talk.

• • •

The following morning I went about my routine, but had a heavy feeling in my chest and decided not to go to church. My mind was alert, but my body felt worn out.

"Is it my time?" I whispered in a prayer.

The weighty feeling in my chest had plagued me off and on in the past, but this time it had been seven weeks and I simply could not shake it. I went slowly downstairs to my den and sat at my desk. All the pictures of my life were arranged around that room—the pictures of my parents, siblings, wife, children, grandchildren, aunts, uncles, nieces, and nephews all comforted me.

My eyes rested on Uncle Russo and Aunt Cleo. How kind they were to me in my youth and how distant my boyhood seemed now. There was Mama with her warm smile and Papa with his gentle blue eyes and handlebar mustache. I missed them all so much.

For several long minutes I sat there surrounded by the pictures of my life. How quickly it all had passed. Days, weeks, months, years, decades—all gone to eternity, just so many specks in the infinite parade of time. I was filled with so many memories, fleeting moments held captive in my mind.

Later that morning my nephew Peter—Taki and Sultana's son—called to tell me he had found a book about Imbroz printed by Amnesty International. "It's fascinating," he said. "It tells about all the atrocities that were committed there when you were young, Theo Christo."

Oddly, I was not as interested in this as I might have been a few weeks or months earlier, but I listened as he told me what he had read, and then I asked about his family. What had inflamed my passion just a short while earlier seemed almost not to matter.

• • •

That afternoon my old friend Lincoln Vance called and we finally made a date to go out for coffee the next day. "I'll pick you up at nine in the morning," I told him, pleased at the prospect of seeing him again.

As I watched the news that evening, I had the pleasant feeling of having accomplished a great deal. Truthfully, I was relieved to have gotten so many details out of the way in preparation for whatever tomorrow might bring, but there were still a few things left to do. There never seemed to be enough time to finish the work of life.

The next morning over coffee at McDonald's, Lincoln and I chatted about current events and caught up on each other's news.

"How are the kids?" Since Lincoln didn't have children, he was always interested in mine.

"They are fine. Thanks for asking." He then turned to my health.

"How are you feeling?" he asked.

"Well, I have the flu," I told him.

"You have had it now for weeks. It's not anything more serious, is it?"

"Oh, no, just a bad cold."

We chatted like this for an hour or so, and then I drove Lincoln home. As he got out of the car, he hesitated.

"Chris, you know, you're the only Greek I would ever do business with."

"Oh, come on, Lincoln," I laughed.

"It's true." He paused, looking at me seriously. Then, out of the blue, "Are you sure you're okay, Chris?"

"Oh, sure, Lincoln. I'm fine."

"I hope so, Chris," he offered in parting. "I sure hope so."

I lifted my hand in farewell, pulled away from the curb, and headed home thinking I was getting a little tired of people asking me if I was okay.

• • •

Later that day Anthony called and wanted to show me the interior of the house I had found for him the next block over. I liked the house and said so. "You'll have lots of room here," I told him.

"Yes," he agreed, as we looked at the spacious rooms around us. "2,400 square feet, compared to the 1,000 feet I have now."

"When will you close on it?"

"I'm waiting to have my loan approved. I might close in a week or two."

I shook my head regretfully. "I wish I could help you, Anthony," I said.

"Dad, you've spent your whole life helping all of us. We'll be fine, honest."

"I'm very happy to have you, Lee Ann, and the children only a street away. Very happy."

"Yes, and it's a nice house."

"Anthony," I went on, "I want you to promise me something. I want you to promise me that you won't ever put your mother into a nursing home."

Anthony looked at me strangely. "Of course not, Dad," he said. "Are you okay?" he asked.

Was it that apparent? I felt my body failing. I might look a little tired, but I didn't think my physical appearance was alarming anyone. It must have been my need to prepare. I could not seem to contain my anxiety that my children would not be ready, and I think this was showing.

"Sure, I'm fine, thanks, just fine," I said, but I could tell that my son was concerned. As we drove back to my house, I felt the same heaviness in my chest rendering me silent. This time I felt the heaviness in my arms, legs, and chest, as well, and I knew I couldn't blame it on the weather. I wasn't in pain, but I was very tired, and my breathing was increasingly short and shallow. My mind was alert and agile, but my body was winding down like an old clock.

• • •

That evening while in my office back home my eyes rested on the picture of my son Anthony. I realized that after I passed, my older son would be responsible for my bills and obligations. I also realized that he had not inherited any of my organizational skills. Come to think of it, none of my children had. Unfortunately, in that department they took after their mother.

Anthony would need as much help as I could give him if he was to manage my affairs after I was gone, so I got out my will and placed it squarely on the top of my desk. Beside it I placed several other important papers that he would need to attend to, and I wrote specific instructions about each on a series of stickies, stuck to the relevant document:

I took out a $15,000 note, with interest due quarterly, from First Virginia Bank last fall. It is secured with my vehicle. If you need an extension, see Mrs. Seal.... I have a second loan at Home Bank for $25,000 that I borrowed last April in addition to the loan on the stores. Jon can see Mr. Parker and he will extend the term if needed.... My cemetery plot as well as Mother's are bought and paid for. Be careful of the other charges.... The documents are right here.... There are some coins that I have labeled for Ianthe, Jon and for you, Anthony—equally divided. I have collected them over the years.... And Anthony, don't forget your promise to keep your mother in our home.

After I finished, I called Katina in New York. Although Helen kept in touch, Katina and I had not talked except briefly at Taki's funeral. My sister's voice brought forth feelings long gone to time and circumstance.

At first, we inquired politely about each other's families, and then I got straight to the point.

"Katina, I am sorry for getting mad at you about Mama and Papa's house. It was wrong of me. You were alone and you had no choice."

For a moment Katina was silent. "It's been so many years, Chrysostomos," she said. "We are no longer there. What does it matter?"

"Katina, remember that time you and I roamed off to play and came home after sundown? Mama and Papa were so worried and angry."

My sister laughed. "Yes, and Papa spanked you."

"That was the only time he ever did. Poor Mama and Papa. I tried, but they wouldn't come to America."

"You know Papa, Chrysostomos. He was so stubborn. He would never leave our home, Turks or no Turks."

"That is true, Katina. And you gave up everything to care for them."

"Don't think of that. That was so many years ago. I have no regrets. My years with Mama and Papa are my fondest memories. Chrysostomos, they were so proud of you. Hardly a day would go by when Papa didn't mention his son was a success in America."

We laughed.

"Besides," she went on, "thanks to you, Costa, Sultana, and I have so many lovely nieces and nephews. The years have gone, little brother. It doesn't matter now. Our island, Mama and Papa… even the Turks… none of it matters now."

I saw the sense of what she was saying. "I believe you are right," I said. "God bless you, Katina."

"Good night, Chrysostomos. I love you."

• • •

The next day, Anthony called. "Dad, we closed on the house. We are your new neighbor. Lee Ann's boxing up stuff now and we plan to move in on Sunday afternoon."

Anthony's news pleased me. "I will help you," I said. "How about if we meet you at three on Sunday? Are you going to church?"

"I don't think so, Dad. Not this Sunday."

"Well, then, we'll see you at the house at three."

"Okay, Dad, thank you." He paused. "Are you feeling better?"

"Anthony, don't worry about me. Tend to your family."

"Dad…"

"I still have this cold," I admitted finally, "but I'm feeling better, thank you."

"Okay see you Sunday."

"Yes, Sunday, but one thing…"

"Yes?"

"Remember what we talked about a few days ago? About your mother?"

"Yes, no nursing home."

"That's right. I just want to make sure you remember."

"I'll remember, Dad. Honest. What's this all about?"

"See you Sunday," I said.

The weather was finally warming, and that afternoon I went out and surveyed my garden. Hands folded behind my back I walked the rows of azaleas, stopping occasionally to remove a fallen branch or twig from my plants. I busied myself like this for quite some time, as if preparing a stage for the colorful show my blossoms would perform. They were just about to bloom and I longed to see them.

That evening I was restless and stayed up to watch the late news. Five minutes into the newscast there was a story from New York City. "A tragic accident occurred in Manhattan this evening. Two Greek Orthodox priests have been fatally struck by a car driven by someone on drugs. The deceased priests are Father Demetrius Frangos, secretariat of the Archdiocese, and Father Germanos Stavropoulos, Chancellor of the Archdiocese. Father Frangos was 81 years old and Father Germanos was in his fifties. This is a tragic accident and a huge loss for the Greek Orthodox Church."

This was astounding news. I made my way upstairs and nudged Helen awake. "Father Frangos and Father Germanos are dead," I told her, and gave her the details of the accident.

"Oh, Chris," she said, patting my hand. "How very, very sad."

"It is," I agreed. Then, thinking of Jimmy, I added, "and how hard for the old Archbishop."

• • •

The next morning, Saturday, I was at the health club at precisely eight o'clock. After changing and stretching my legs, I got on the treadmill and began walking. I usually walked thirty to forty minutes, but I was uncertain how I would go today given my prolonged cold. After twenty minutes, sweat was beading on my forehead and running down my neck. I was out of breath and my legs were tired. I tried to go another two minutes before quitting. I gazed down at my feet as they methodically plodded along the treadmill and I almost dozed off. Suddenly, in my mind's eye, I saw an image of Mama.

"Chrysostomos, I have made you shoes... put them on."

"Yes, Mama..." I started to whisper, then suddenly I snapped awake. Such an odd daydream, I thought, stepping off the treadmill.

I changed back into my street clothes and on the way home I stopped at the grocery store to buy some lentils. By the time I got home I was feeling weak and tired. I took out the lentils and began to prepare dinner.

That evening was marked by unusual peacefulness and quiet. As was our habit, after supper Helen and I sat in the family room, read, and watched the news.

"You know, the kids are doing well," I said.

Helen looked up from her book. "They are, aren't they? And you know, I love our grandchildren," she said happily.

Then we began reminiscing, recalling old times when the children were small. It seemed like yesterday, and in our minds it was. Somehow the years had slipped by and now here we were, remembering fondly the things that once were.

"Helen, it wasn't too bad, was it?" I asked. "Our lives and everything."

"Of course, it was good, honey. The children, their families..."

"I mean us."

She stared at me. "Of course, it was. Oh, so many years and memories." She smiled. "I'm tired, dear. I'm going up to bed."

"Let me give you a kiss," I said, "and I'll be up shortly."

I went into my study and opened a volume of the *Britannica* in my lap. There was never enough time to finish, I reflected. I'll read for another half-hour before I go up to bed, I reasoned, trying to get as much out of the fleeting material possessions that I had so enjoyed.

• • •

Sunday morning as I dressed for church, I glanced out the window and there were the first signs of corals, pinks, reds, and violets. My azaleas had begun to bloom. I went outside to survey them in my church suit.

"Look, Helen, my azaleas, they are blooming," I called as I came back inside. The frigid cold had only lifted days before, yet the buds of my beautiful blossoms had emerged quickly from a late-winter drear.

"Yes, Chris, you can look at them some more later. Christina is waiting for us," she called back. Christina Regas had been widowed twenty years before, and we made it a habit to take her to church.

We sat in the center row at church, directly in front of the altar, next to my physician, Tom Mandes, and his wife.

During the service the same fatigue that had plagued me all winter returned—the fatigue that had caused me to tell Anthony to keep his mother out of a nursing home and to chronicle for him all my affairs; the fatigue that had caused me to ask Jon if he knew how to prepare the holiday meals without my assistance; the fatigue I had felt when planting azaleas at Ianthe's house and telling her I may not see her for a while.

During services the Orthodox faith requires parishioners to stand several times. Only the oldest, weakest members of church would sit. That day the fatigue enveloped me, and I sat.

Mrs. Mandes leaned toward me. "Chris, are you all right?"

"Fine, fine, thank you," I responded in what was now becoming a familiar refrain. "I am fine," I assured her and looked straight ahead to discourage further discussion.

• • •

After the service ended we went downstairs for a few brief minutes of "coffee and friendship" as they call it. The congregation was abuzz with news of the tragic deaths of the two Greek Orthodox priests. It was not often that the Church made the evening news, and these were men many of us had met and known personally. Then I collected Helen and Christina and took them to the Key Bridge Marriott for brunch. It was a treat to be there after such a harsh winter, yet that day I had no appetite.

When we returned home I glanced out my kitchen window at my azaleas in first bloom, in a beautiful array of color. During that cold, frigid winter I had often wondered if I would see my beautiful friends again and was so relieved that they arrived in time. I descended the stairs, hardly aware of my weakened state, and called out to Helen.

"I'll be in the yard if you need me," I said as I walked out the door.

"Okay. When are you going to help Anthony and Lee Ann?"

"Not until three," I told her, glancing at the kitchen clock.

I walked out my back door and across the lawn to my little friends. My favorites, the red azaleas, sparkled with the new spring's dew. In just a few days they would be in full bloom.

"You didn't forget me," I said to them. Like a wide-eyed child, I gazed at the glorious buds, a beautiful pageantry of stimulating colors.

Holding a bud, I called out to Helen, "Honey, you see the azaleas?" She didn't respond. I then began picking up fallen branches and straightening up around the bushes, not even bothering to change out of my Sunday clothes. I felt unusually tired, yet I pored over my azaleas intently, my eyes refusing to leave the first buds of spring.

In a distant echo I heard Helen. "Yes, dear," she replied dutifully.

As I entered the kitchen, I saw Helen putting away dishes. "I'm going to the den to rest a bit," I told her. "Wake me a little before three please."

"Okay, Chris," she smiled, and continued her work in the kitchen.

Walking to the window, I opened the blinds to take one final glance at my azaleas and then sat in the corner of the sofa, directly exposed to shafts of warm sunlight. Though recent years had labeled sunlight a danger, and my wife often worried about overexposure, I ignored the risk. Old men often ignore new risks in pursuit of the comfort of old habits.

Yawning, I placed my hands behind my neck with fingers interlaced. As the muted shafts of light burrowed through my closed eyelids, I felt the friendly warmth of the sunlight on my shoulders and arms, lulling me to doze. I fell asleep with the warmth of the sun on my face, and the satisfaction of a life well lived.

Epilogue

Do not stand at my grave and weep
I am not there; I do not sleep.
I am a thousand winds that blow,
I am the diamond glints on snow,
I am the sun on ripened grain,
I am the gentle autumn rain.
When you awaken in the morning's hush
I am the swift uplifting rush
of quiet birds in circled flight.
I am the soft stars that shine at night.
I am not there. I did not die.

—MARY ELIZABETH FRYE, 1932

HE WAS AN OLDER BLACK MAN, muscular and sinewy, who, although 60 years of age, pedaled his decorative twelve-speed bike with the ease of a man half his age. At dawn on the Bay Bridge, which stretches four-and-a-half miles across the Chesapeake Bay, his silhouette was eclipsed by the rising sun. He was biking west from Berlin, Maryland, to Saint Sophia Cathedral in Washington D.C., a one hundred and sixty-mile trip, to attend the funeral of his longtime friend Mr. Christ.

Bernard rarely attended funerals, but this was different. Mr. Christ had given him his job and Bernard had worked for him for nearly forty years. More than an employer, Mr. Christ was like the father Bernard had never had.

Bernard had peddled non-stop all night just to reach the bridge by sunup, and the cathedral was still fifty miles away. Bernard didn't think about the distance. Instead, he thought about the battery in the headlight of his bike, and was relieved it had survived the night.

In the morning's first light, on the suspension bridge three hundred and fifty feet above the Bay, the Maryland state trooper driving alongside Bernard did not know what to make of him. At first he thought he should ticket him for riding a bike across the bridge. Then he wondered if Bernard was a vagrant, or if perhaps he should be taken to the state hospital in Cambridge. Using his spotlight he examined the ornament-riddled bike, from the tassels hanging from the handlebars, to the horn and headlight, to the foxtail on the back. When the light flickered on Bernard's face, he offered the trooper an unthreatening, friendly smile.

Driving parallel to the bike at about twenty miles an hour, the officer picked up his microphone and switched on the speaker.

"There are no bicycles allowed on the bridge," he announced sternly. Then curiosity got the better of the officer.

"What are you doing?" he asked in a milder tone.

"Mr. Christ died, sir," Bernard replied as he pedaled, "and I'm going to his funeral in Washington the only way I know how. And you got to excuse me, sir, 'cause if I don't get going, I'm going to be late."

The trooper, who had no idea who Mr. Christ was, considered the spectacle of Bernard pedaling so intently across the bridge in the grey light of first dawn, and finally shook his head and turned off his spotlight.

"Bike carefully," he finally admonished Bernard, then sped on past.

"Yes, sir," Bernard called after him, never wavering from his focus. He didn't want to be late for Mr. Christ's funeral.

• • •

"Ted, get up, we'll miss the train. You don't want to be late, do you?"

The old man opened his eyes. His receded hairline outlined a worn and wrinkled face, engraved by decades. He was almost 82 years old. He slowly threw back the covers and slid out of bed.

"Of course, I'm coming," Ted Theologos told Anna, his wife.

As he slowly pulled up his trousers, he thought of his good friend. "We must pay our respects to Chrysostomos," he said quietly.

Reaching into the closet for a fresh, white shirt, Ted went on, half to himself, "He was my dear friend. He brought me to the Embassy, and he introduced us to each other."

He sat in silence for a moment, losing himself in memory. Snapping back to the present, Ted glanced at the clock on the bedside table and calculated the time he needed to shower, dress, and drive to the station. The train for Washington left Altoona at six thirty and would arrive at Union Station at nine that morning.

"Honey, are you sure you should go?" Anna asked her husband worriedly as he finished dressing. "You haven't been feeling well, and you know you're not a young man anymore."

Ted sighed heavily at his wife's concern. "I'm an old man but Chris and I go back a long way," his voice was heavy but deliberate. "Like me, he struggled hard to come to America. I haven't seen him for many years, Anna, but Chris and I were close; he was special." Anna knew it was true.

She knew the depth of feeling her husband had for Chrysostomos. Ted looked at his wife. "God has taken one of His finest from us. Anna, bring our coats."

Anna touched her husband's hand. "I know," she said gently.

Ted gave his wife a quick, affectionate smile. "Now hurry, Anna," he said briskly, "or we'll miss the train."

• • •

The man sat in his chair by his bed with the lights out. He had dressed himself and was reaching for his shoes. He had lost his vision years earlier as a young man. Despite his blindness, he was a well-regarded developer who had renovated many shopping centers.

Vincent Allan was Jewish, not Greek, but he had met Chris while a patron at the Apollo Restaurant in 1950 and they had remained good friends.

He heard the bedroom door open and knew his wife, Sue, had entered the room.

"Chris was the hardest working man I ever knew," he mused aloud.

"I know, honey." She paused. "Do you need any help?"

"Not at all," he replied. "Let's get going."

• • •

"Dad, get up," Johnny said, poking his head into his parents' bedroom door. As a seven-year-old neighbor in Ocean City, Johnny would nudge open the sliding screen door to Mr. Christ's townhouse and talk with Mr. Christ. He was the youngest of Dr. and Mrs. Carrol's five kids. The Carrols owned the townhouse next to the Christs for thirty years. Mr. Christ lectured Johnny on life in general, much as he might have his own children when they were his age.

Johnny's father, Dr. Carrol, blinked and rubbed his eyes.

"Come on, Dad, Mom," Johnny urged. "I don't want to be late."

Johnny turned on his crutches to leave. Crippled in a motorcycle accident and now 26, Johnny had strapped on his leg braces and dressed himself carefully.

Even after his motorcycle accident, Mr. Christ had always given him encouragement, and Johnny would never forget that. Apart from his family, Mr. Christ had been a very influential person in Johnny's life.

"Mom, Dad, come on or we'll be late."

• • •

Early that morning, after dressing in a widow's attire, Helen sat alone at the kitchen table she had shared for so many years with Chris. She fingered the mailgram that had been sent by courier from

Archbishop Iakovos, which contained a special prayer he had written upon this occasion.

Rather than reread it, she reflected on the call. It was mid-afternoon when Jimmy called Helen with great regret. Having taken sick, he was unable to attend the funeral. Archbishop Iakovos's voice was effusive and emotional, uncharacteristic of a man in his position. "Chrysostomos was different than most; he was a special man. We mourn our loss together, but the beloved memories will be cherished and will endure," he had said. Jimmy Coucouzes, Breadcrumb's childhood friend, was left with a lifetime of irreplaceable memories.

A moment passed between them.

"Thank you, Your Eminence, so kind of you to call," Helen responded.

The day before he called, Jimmy's secretary had telephoned.

"Mrs. Christ, this is Paulette, the Archbishop's assistant," a voice said on the line. "The Archbishop wanted to attend, but he has not been well and is not able. When he heard your husband had died, he was conducting a prayer service and he collapsed."

The words lingered as she looked tearfully across the small kitchen table at Chris's empty chair.

• • •

It was seven in the morning and Peter Hatzi was up and showering. Usually on a Saturday his wife, Kathy, had to rouse him, but today was different. He had lost his father four months earlier; now his favorite uncle had died at age 76 and Peter, stricken by grief and unable to sleep, was up early. Uncle Chris was always positive and supportive, and ever since childhood Peter had had a special bond with him.

Downstairs, Peter's mother and aunt, who were Uncle Chris's sisters, Sultana and Katina, readied themselves for the drive to the cathedral and their beloved brother's funeral. Possibly more than anyone else, they had been witnesses to—and beneficiaries of—Chris's strength and productive influence.

He had been the patriarch of the family. They especially knew how he had, at a very young age and in a time of terrible need, provided and cared for all of them. Chris had been the strength of their family for more than six decades. He was also the undisputed leader of their small family since Mama and Papa had died. They knew how hard he had worked to come to America and how he had sacrificed to bring them over, as well. His sudden and unexpected death had left his sisters with a terrible void in their lives.

Chris was not only special to his sisters and his nephew Peter, but also to Peter's wife. Kathy, like Chris, was also from Imbroz. Like him, she was an accomplished cook, yet she always marveled at Uncle Chris's talents in the kitchen.

"I can't believe we've lost Uncle Chris," she told her husband sadly. "I will miss him."

Peter swallowed hard, fully realizing how important Uncle Chris had been to his life since childhood. He finished dressing and ushered his wife downstairs where they joined Sultana and Katina.

"Come on, Mama, Thea. We have to get going," he said.

"We're supposed to meet Anthony and Ianthe at Thea Helen's and go on to the cathedral together. We'll stop by Thea Afrodite's on the way. She and the kids will follow us."

• • •

At Thea Helen's house intense grief filled the morning air. Sultana and Katina got out of Peter's car and embraced Helen. Helen and Sultana were in tears, while Katina consoled them and Peter embraced his red-eyed cousins.

Anthony, Chris's older son, wept with sadness just as Chris had sobbed long ago when his Papa had died. Today his best friend had left him. Jon stood quietly next to his brother, equally grief-stricken. Minutes later Ianthe, her eyes red and swollen with tears, arrived with her husband. With Chris's death, she had lost her greatest ally and her strongest source of material, emotional, and spiritual support. Her face was pale with grief.

As the family climbed into their cars, all felt their personal loss in their separate ways. As they resumed their journey to the cathedral, a light drizzle began to fall. Chris was gone, and his loss was felt by everyone he had touched. Even a misty sky began softly weeping.

• • •

Struggling with his cane, Lincoln Vance righted himself and walked the five steps from his car to the door of Harry Jagoda, his business partner.

"Come on, Harry," he rasped, knocking at the door. "Let's get going before we're late."

"Hold on, Lincoln," Harry replied impatiently in a voice as raspy as his. "I'm coming, I'm coming."

Like Chris, Harry and Lincoln were both depression-era children. Even though they were born in different cultures—Harry was Jewish, Lincoln was Greek—they had been partners for thirty years. Their friendship with Chris was rooted in a shared past, a rigorous work ethic, and mutual respect.

"You know, we've met a lot of people over the years," Lincoln said as Harry greeted him at the door, "but Chris was the best, most honest man I have ever known."

"That he was," Harry nodded as he and Lincoln made their way to the car.

Harry had known Chris for forty-five years and his affection for his Greek Christian friend was as great as Lincoln's. Like Chris, Harry and Lincoln were hardworking, self-made men who had overcome adversity in youth to achieve success.

• • •

Two blocks from the Washington National Cathedral on Massachusetts Avenue is Saint Sophia Cathedral. Its cornerstone was dedicated by President Eisenhower in 1956. Named after

Constantinople's historic Hagia Sophia, which is Greek for Holy Wisdom. Although not as large as the original, it is every bit as opulent, with colorful mosaics and icons carved from marble and cast in gold.

When filled to capacity, Saint Sophia held nearly a thousand worshippers. Today, the cathedral overflowed with Chris's friends and family who had come to pay their last respects. Father John, who had buried generals and congressmen, doctors and lawyers, could not remember a time in his thirty-five years at Saint Sophia that the church was any fuller for a funeral—but it had filled for Chrysostomos Chrysostomidies, an immigrant, a common man, who, through perseverance and discipline, led an uncommon life.

Although Chris had been married at Saints Constantine & Helen Cathedral, and was a founding member of Saint Katherine's in Northern Virginia, it was Saint Sophia that brought back memories of his childhood churches, and it was there where he would have his final service.

Father John put on his vestments and came to the cathedral early that morning. He and his wife had eaten with Chris on many an occasion. He had also sought out his judgment often. He trusted Chris, his confidant. For several long minutes he stood at the altar and gazed motionless at the soaring, mosaic-encrusted dome overhead.

A patchwork of people filled the Cathedral to attend the funeral of Chris Christ. Gus Pappas, the dentist whose wife died at a young age of cancer; Mr. and Mrs. Markesas, who were in their eighties; John Simms and his wife, who twenty years earlier had purchased Anthony's Carryout and rented his small store, were all in attendance. All were in states of grief and reflection.

Chris's widow, Helen, and their children arrived at the cathedral, leading the family procession from the suburbs. Father John instinctively moved toward the doors to greet the family he knew so well.

"Father, we have lost Chris," Helen said simply as her eyes filled with tears.

"Yes, I know," was all he could manage to say, and for a long moment he embraced her, consoling Helen as well as himself.

Then he stepped back and allowed her to lead her family down the aisle toward their seats. The two front pews on the right of the center aisle, traditionally reserved for the family, were soon filled with Chris's sisters, Sultana and Katina, his nieces and nephews, as well as his children, grandchildren, and widow.

• • •

When the hearse arrived, Chris's older son, Anthony, turned to his brother and one of his cousins. "Jon, Peter," he said, "come on, let's help Dad."

The three men made their way back up the aisle to the doors of the cathedral and down the steps to the street. There they helped lift the casket up the stairs to the entrance of the cathedral, where it was placed on rollers and moved down the center aisle to the altar, accompanied by Jon and Anthony. At the altar the casket was turned and opened for viewing.

Anthony wanted to see his father's face one last time. Chris's warm expression, his affectionate manner, had always comforted Anthony and placed him at ease, but when the casket was opened the lifeless face of his father was unrecognizable. The intelligent, passionate warmth that had served as a guiding light to his family and friends was gone. So, too, were his rosy cheeks and infectious smile. What Anthony saw was a longer, more somber face. Chrysostomos Chrisostomides was gone, leaving behind in death the face of a stranger.

• • •

As the cathedral filled with mourners, an elderly black man on a bike stopped a couple of miles up Wisconsin Avenue to ask directions of a stranger.

"Excuse me, sir, where is Massachusetts Avenue? I'm looking for Saint Sophia."

It was Bernard, still wearing his goggles. Like the police officer on the Bay Bridge at dawn, the stranger's eyes took in the fancy bike. Finally, his gaze returned to Bernard's face.

"Go straight down Wisconsin Avenue for nine or ten blocks," he said, choosing to overlook the eccentric sight Bernard and his bike presented, "then make a left on Massachusetts Avenue. You'll see Saint Sophia a block and a half farther on the left."

"Thank you, sir," Bernard said with a somber smile while pedaling away. Now he would be on time for Mr. Christ. He knew how Mr. Christ was a stickler on time.

People were still filling the church when Father John finally began the service. One of the last to enter the cathedral, Bernard removed his hat and goggles, lit a candle, and stood in the back of the church. There he quietly mourned Mr. Christ, his employer, mentor, and faithful friend.

After the formal part of the service, Father John, who had performed so many funerals, had to clear his throat. Finally, he began to eulogize his parishioner.

"Chris Christ was a reverent man who endured more than his share of adversity. He was honorable in all his dealings with his fellow man. He was humble before God and those who were less able, and he was honest through and through. He led a Christian life that many aspire to and few attain. He will be missed dearly by everyone who knew him...."

In thirty minutes the service drew to a close. "Everlasting be your memory," the congregation sang melodiously in Greek. "Everlasting be your memory." Then Father John addressed the mourners once again.

"Holy Father," he prayed, "please save a special place for Your loyal servant, Chris Christ, who came to us from so far away, who worked his whole life unselfishly for his family and his Church, both here and in Turkey. He was truly a rare man, an inspiration for many, never speaking an unkind word. Violently uprooted from his family at the age of ten, he not only endured, he triumphed. He endured poverty and deprivation, working rather than complaining, until he rose above his circumstances. Chris Christ was in every respect the best that mankind represents, and we pray for his soul."

Then he added, with a touch of humor Chris would have enjoyed, "I realize many of you do not normally attend services at this cathedral, which is too bad. I wish I could get such a large turnout for my Sunday sermons."

A moment later the family rose, followed by the congregation, for a final viewing of Chris. Helen was the first to approach the coffin.

"I love you, Chris," she whispered.

Beside her, Anthony bent to kiss his father's forehead and then made the sign of the cross and bid farewell. Red-eyed, Ianthe and Jon followed him, and with them came the rest of the family, all sobbing as others followed.

As his mother and siblings were greeted by friends, Anthony watched the mourners slowly making their way past his father's casket. He saw Mr. Vance, leaning heavily on his cane, pause to look at Chris's face. After him came Mr. Jagoda, who tripped on the steps to the altar and had to be steadied by Gus Pappas. Then Johnny Carrol struggled up the altar steps on his crutches, followed by his parents. When the Carrols passed the casket, they were replaced by Vince Allan, guided by his wife Sue, his sightless eyes gazing past the casket and his head bowed in respect for his old friend. Behind him, goggles in hand, was Bernard, patiently waiting his turn.

"Oh, Mr. Christ, what has happened, what have they done to you? Oh, Mr. Christ!" Tears were streaming down his face.

Eyes turned in empathy at the sight of this colorful man lamenting his lost friend. The sight of Bernard touching Chris's lifeless body was heartfelt by all. A familiar gentle smile lit Bernard's face. "I made it, Mr. Christ, and I'm on time. God bless you, Mr. Christ. God bless you and don't worry—I'll help your sons take care of business."

The drear and drizzle of that day supported a mournful, somber wintry mood, yet streaking boldly through the chilled, colored panes of rain-speckled glass, scouting shafts of sunlight promised spring's return.

Glossary

A

Allen, Vincent and Sue: Dear friends of Chris and Helen, and patrons of the Apollo restaurant.

Amele Taburu: Turkish work battalions established by Enver Pasha in Directive 8682, on February 25, 1915; used as extermination camps primarily for Christian males 1918–1922. Ismet Inönü reinstituted them in 1941 under the cloak of World War II; finally disbanded in 1944.

Anatolia: Asia Minor to the Romans; makes up the majority of modern-day Turkey.

Anthony, Nick: Longtime night manager and right-hand man at Anthony's Carryout.

Arhondonis, Bishop Demetrius I (Bartholomew I): Current Ecumenical Patriarch of Eastern Orthodox Church, 1991–Present; babysat by Katina, Chris's sister, on Imbroz.

Assakopoulos, Basil: A retired research engineer who left Constantinople with his family in 1955; member of the Hellenic Society of Constantinopolitans.

Atatürk, Mustafa Kemal: President of Turkey from 1923–38; from Thessaloniki, Salonika, which is referred to as the "Mother of Israel;" "Father of Turkey" and founding member of the Committee of Union and Progress, or CUP, and the Young Turks, and one of the architects of the Christian genocide in Turkey; Chris waited on him at the Pera Palace one evening in November of 1937.

Athenogoras, Bishop: Previous Ecumenical Patriarch of Eastern Orthodox Church, 1948–1972; also from Imbroz.

B

Baydur, Hüseyin Ragip: Turkish Ambassador to the United States from 1945–1948 who brought Chris to the United States as his butler.

Bernard: Longtime loyal employee of Chris at Anthony's Carryout in Ocean City, Maryland.

Breadcrumb: Chris's nickname given to him by his childhood friend Jimmy on Imbroz.

Byzantine Empire: Started by Constantine in 324–337; Constantinople was the capitol city under Theodosius, 379–395, Christianity became the state religion; Byzantium survived for eleven centuries as a powerful economic, cultural and military force in Europe.

C

Carroll, Johnny: Son of Dr. and Mrs. Carroll, townhouse neighbors to Chris and Helen in Ocean City, Maryland.

Chelpon, Father Theodore (Father Ted): Priest at Saint Katherine's Orthodox Church in Falls Church, Virginia.

Chris and Charlie, Uncles: Great maternal uncles of Helen who lived in Norfolk, Virginia.

Christ, Anthony: Oldest son of Chris; husband to Lee Ann, and father to Brian, Katelyn and Ashley; author of *The Immigrant*.

Christ, Chris (Chrisostomides, Chrysostomos, or Christo): Main character of *The Immigrant*.

Christ, Costa (Gus) and Afrodite: Younger brother of Chris and his wife, who also grew up on Imbroz; parents to John, Theope, Mary, and Tommy.

Christ, Helen (Eleni): Wife of Chris; daughter of Anton and Alexandra Anthony, of Cumberland, Maryland; mother of Anthony, Jon, and Ianthe.

Christ, Jon: Younger son of Chris and Helen; owner and operator of Anthony's Liquors.

Chrysostom, Archbishop: Greek Orthodox Archbishop of Smyrna; turned over to a mob by the Turks, and was beheaded in 1922.

Chrisostomides, Dimitris (Theo): Favorite uncle of Chris; older brother of his father Ioanni.

Chrisostomides, Ioanni and Theopiste: Parents of Chris, Sultana, Katina, and Costa who lived their entire lives on Imbroz.

Chrisostomides, Papou and Yiayia: Paternal grandparents of Chris who also lived on Imbroz.

Christi, Agatha: Wrote *Murder on the Orient Express* while staying in room 400 at the Pera Palace.

Coucouzes, Jimmy: Childhood friend of Chris from Imbroz; gave Chris the nickname "Breadcrumb."

D

Daniels, Father Thomas: Orthodox priest who married Chris and Helen.

Delta, M.D., Vasili: Brother of John Delta and member of the Hellenic Society of Constantinopolitans.

Djemal, Ahmed Pasha: One of the "Three Pashas" who ruled the Ottoman Empire; Minister of the Navy; leader of the CUP and crafter of the "butcher battalions;" architect of the Christian genocide with Ismail Enver and Mehmed Talaat; assassinated in 1922.

Demetrius I: Ecumenical Patriarch of Constantinople 1973–1991; previously Metropolitan Bishop of Imbroz.

Dönmeh: Group of Sabbatean crypto-Jews in the Ottoman Empire who converted publicly to Islam but retained their religious beliefs in secret; centered in Salonika, modern day Thessaloniki, Greece. There were about 15,000 in the twentieth century; some took an active part in the Young Turk revolution of 1908.

Dracoulos, Yiaya and Papou: Maternal grandparents of Chris who lived on Samothraki island.

Dracoulos, Theopisti, Great Yiayia: Great grandmother of Chris on his mother's side.

E

Enver, Ismail Pasha: One of the "Three Pashas" who ruled the Ottoman Empire; the Minister of War; leader of the CUP and crafter of the "butcher battalions;" architect of the Christian genocide with Ahmed Djemal and Mehmed Tallat; died leading a revolt near modern-day Tajikistan in 1922.

Eritime Programmi: Turkish program implemented 1961–1964 to eliminate Greek education, and to terrorize and drive the remaining Christians from Imbroz. During this time the Turkish government appropriated ninety percent of all cultivatable land, and moved thousands of convicts to the island where they roamed freely.

Economous, Dr. Surgical internist and fishing buddy of Chris.

G

Gherardi, Blaise: Owner of Place Vendôme, 1950–1956, also Rive Gauche, 1956–1973, in Washington D.C.; hired Chris as waiter and helped Chris become a United States citizen.

H

Hatzi (Hatzikiriakidis), Sultana and Taki (Jim): Younger sister of Chris and her husband; Taki was co-owner of the Apollo restaurant; parents of Peter, Theopi, and Urania.

Holland, Charlie and Mrytle: Property owner in Maryland and his wife from whom Chris rented Taste-Freez, which he later purchased to open Anthony's Carryout.

I

Iakovos, Bishop (Jimmy Coucouzes): Childhood friend of Chris from Imbroz; Greek Orthodox Archbishop of the Americas 1959–1996.

Inönü, Ismet: First became Turkish Prime Minister in 1923, and President in 1938; negotiated the Lausanne Agreement in 1923 that ceded Imbroz island to Turkey; reinstituted the work battalions from 1941–44, and a capital tax on the Christian minority in Turkey 1942–44.

Istanbul: Formerly Constantinople until 1923 when the Ottoman Empire collapsed; largest city in Turkey; Greek for "in the city."

Istanbul pogrommi: Events of organized mob attacks directed at Christian minorities in Turkey that occurred September 6–7, 1955; businesses were burned down and shuttered, Christians were raped and murdered. In 1955 there were over 100,000 Christians in Constantinople and, in 1978, only 7,000 remained.

J

Jagoda, Harry: Successful developer who, with Lincoln Vance, built Chris's home in Falls Church, Virginia.

K

Kahele, Memet: Captain of wait staff at Pera Palace who first hired Chris as a busboy and waiter.

Koine Greek: Alexandrian dialect, Hellenistic, or Biblical Greek, as opposed to Classical Greek; dates back to 400 B.C. The tapestry, a Chrisostomidis family heirloom, was written in Koine Greek.

Koutris, Captain: Captain of the small boat who ferried Chris to Samothraki Island to work at his Uncle Russo's store, and later to board a steamship to Constantinople.

L

Laloussis, Father: Priest at Saint Sophia Cathedral in Washington, D.C., in the 1950s.

M

Mandes, Tom, M.D.: Trusted doctor of Chris who treated him for many things, including a bad case of gout.

Maxime: Rive Gauche chef who taught Chris and his two boys his tomato sauce recipe for pizza at Anthony's Carryout.

Melas, Elias and Ann: Fellow employees at Turkish Embassy with Chris who introduced him to his wife.

Michael, Archbishop: Archbishop of the Americas who preceded Archbishop Iakovos 1949–1958.

N

Nazim, Dr. Selanikli: Chief ideologist of the Young Turk movement.

Nureddin Pasha: Turkish military commander of the First Army under Mustafa Kemal Atatürk; responsible for the genocide of Christians in Smyrna September 10, 1922.

O

O'Brien, Hawk: Captain Reed's brother-in-law and rescuer of Chris's stranded fishing expedition.

Olgalik: Cook at Pera Palace and Park Hotel and later at the Turkish Embassy in Washington, D.C.; an old friend of Chris; former Colonel in the White Russian Army who fled to Constantinople.

Ottoman Empire: State and caliphate that controlled much of Southeast Europe, Western Asia, and North Africa between the 14th and 20th centuries, 1300–1922; started when Osman I founded in 1300; grew into an Empire after sultan Mehmed II conquered Constantinople in 1453 and ended in 1922; the official religion was Muslim and governance was the policy of "Turkification;" expanded through Greece, the Balkans, and Western Europe; peaked around 1560, stagnated until 1827, then declined until 1922.

P

Pappas, Mike: Neighbor and fishing buddy of Chris.

Pananis, Katerina (Katina) and Nikos: Older sister of Chris and her husband, who lived in Brooklyn, New York, after their marriage.

Pasha: Ottoman Turkish term for General.

R

Raki: Armenian Christian owner of a grocery store in Constantinople; Chris's first employer in the city.

Regas, Theologos (Ted) and Ann: Longtime friends of Chris and Helen. Ted was a fellow employee of Chris.

Reed, Captain: Neighbor and boat captain who rescued Chris at sea.

Rendel, George: British diplomat and patron of Pera Palace wrote on the Christian genocide; caught in "Rendel bombing" at Pera Palace hotel in March 1941 when Chris was a waiter.

Russo, Uncle: Uncle of Chris; married his mother's sister.

S

Simms, John: Leased Anthony's Carryout from Chris starting in 1974. He has successfully operated the carryout with his family ever since.

T

Talaat, Mehmed Pasha: One of the "Three Pashas" who ruled the Ottoman Empire; the Prime Minister and Minister of the Interior; leader of the CUP and crafter of the "butcher battalions;" architect of the Christian genocide with Ismail Enver and Ahmed Djemal; assassinated by an Armenian in 1921.

U

Uzanoglu, Vasili: Professor, research engineer, member of the Hellenic Society of Constantinopolitans.

V

Vasil, Nicholas and Anastasia: Survivors of Smyrna massacre with three children Nicholas, Philip, and Thomas; met Chris and his family on Imbroz after they evacuated in 1922.

Vasil, Thomas: Son of Nicholas and Anastasia Vasil; survivor of the Smyrna massacre; met Chris as a child on Imbroz; ran into Chris later on at church and at Constantinopolitan Club in Washington, D.C.

W

William, Mark: Longtime attorney of Chris from whom he often sought sound legal advice.

Y

Yeatras, Ianthe and Steve: Chris and Helen's daughter and her husband; parents of Krislyn and Jonathan.

Yeonas, Paul: Successful Northern Virginia homebuilder and first mate of Chris.

Young Turks: Group of liberal intellectuals and revolutionaries in the early twentieth century who favored the replacement of the Ottoman Empire's absolute monarchy with a constitutional government; overthrew Sultan Abdul Hamid II in 1908; two splinter groups of Young Turks continued until 1913 when the Committee of Union and Progress, or CUP, took control. Originally supported by Christians, the Young Turks turned against the Christian minorities in 1913, imposed gun control, and started Christian genocide in earnest.

Z

Zagu, Ahmet: King Zog of Albania 1922–1939. The last Ottoman King, he abdicated his throne for payment in gold from Italy's Prime Minister Benito Mussolini. Chris assisted him at Pera Palace in 1939.

Bibliography

The historical details in this book are largely from two U.S. diplomats: George Horton in Blight of Asia *and Henry Morgenthau in* Ambassador Morgenthau's Story.

Citizen's Association of Constantinople-Imbros-Tenedos-Eastern Thrace of Thrace. *The Struggle for Justice: 1923–1933: 70 Years of Turkish Provocation and Violations of the Treaty of Lausanne: A Chronicle of Human Rights Violations.* Komotini, 1997.

Horton, George.

Blight of Asia: On Systematic Extermination of Christian Populations in Asia. Bobbs-Merrill Company, 1926.

"Report on Turkey." Journalists Union, Athens, 1985.

Kaplan, Robert D. *Balkan Ghosts.* Saint Martin's Press, 1993.

Kayali, Hasan. *Arabs and Young Turks.* University of California Press, 1997.

Molho, Rena."The Jewish Community of Thessalonica and Its Incorporation into the Greek State." Journal of Hellenic Diaspora, 1988.

Morgenthau, Henry. *Ambassador Morgenthau's Story.* Doubleday, Page & Company, 1919.

Morris, Benny and Ze'evi, Dror. *The Thirty-Year Genocide: Turkey's Destruction of Its Christian Minorities, 1894–1924.* Harvard University Press, 2019.

Ramsaur, Jr., Ernest Edmondson. *The Young Turks: Prelude to the Revolution of 1908.* Princeton University Press, 1957.

Tavoukdjian, Serpouhi. *Exiled: Story of an Armenian Girl.* Herald Publishing, 1933.

Made in the USA
Coppell, TX
01 June 2020

26739468R00215